A-Level Year 1 & AS

Biology

Exam Board: Edexcel A (Salters-Nuffield)

Revising for Biology exams is stressful, that's for sure — even just getting your notes sorted out can leave you needing a lie down. But help is at hand...

This brilliant CGP book explains **everything you'll need to learn** (and nothing you won't), all in a straightforward style that's easy to get your head around. We've also included **exam questions** to test how ready you are for the real thing.

There's even a free Online Edition you can read on your computer or tablet!

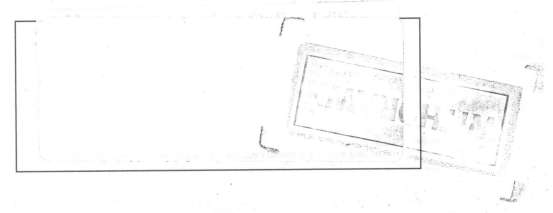

A-Level revision? It has to be CGP!

Published by CGP

From original material by Richard Parsons.

Editors:
Katherine Faudemer, Rachel Kordan, Christopher McGarry, Sarah Pattison, Claire Plowman,
Rachael Rogers, Camilla Simson, Hayley Thompson.

Contributors:
Sophie Anderson, Jessica Egan, Paddy Gannon, Liz Master, Adrian Schmit.

ISBN: 978 1 78294 284 9

With thanks to Lauren Burns and Charlotte Burrows for the proofreading.
With thanks to Laura Jakubowski for the copyright research.

Cover image © duncan1890/iStockphoto.com

Top graph on page 16 from 'Alcohol, tobacco & breast cancer – collaborative reanalysis of individual data from 53 epidemiological studies, including 58 515 women with breast cancer and 95 067 women without the disease.' Reprinted by permission from Macmillan Publishers Ltd on behalf of Cancer Research UK: British Journal of Cancer © Nov 2002

Data used to construct the bottom graph on page 16 reproduced with kind permission from Oxford University Press. P. Reynolds, et al. Active Smoking, Household Passive Smoking, and Breast Cancer: Evidence From the California Teachers Study. JNCI 2004; 96(1):29-37

Data used to construct the graph on page 19 from Townsend N, Williams J, Bhatnagar P, Wickramasinghe K, Rayner M (2014). Cardiovascular disease statistics, 2014. British Heart Foundation: London. © British Heart Foundation, December 2014

Data used to construct the graph on page 26 from P.M. Ridker, et al. Comparison of C-reactive protein and low density lipoprotein cholesterol levels in the prediction of first cardiovascular events. NEJM 2002; 347: 1557-65.

With thanks to Science Photo Library for permission to reproduce the images on pages 62, 67, 91 and 93.

Every effort has been made to locate copyright holders and obtain permission to reproduce sources. For those sources where it has been difficult to trace the originator of the work, we would be grateful for information. If any copyright holder would like us to make an amendment to the acknowledgements, please notify us and we will gladly update the book at the next reprint. Thank you.

Clipart from Corel®
Printed by Elanders Ltd, Newcastle upon Tyne.

Contents

The Scientific Process

These pages are all about the scientific process — how we develop and test scientific ideas. It's what scientists do all day, every day (well, except at coffee time — never come between a scientist and their coffee).

Scientists Come Up with **Theories** — Then **Test Them...**

Science tries to explain **how** and **why** things happen — it **answers questions**. It's all about seeking and gaining **knowledge** about the world around us. Scientists do this by **asking** questions and **suggesting** answers and then **testing** them, to see if they're correct — this is the **scientific process**.

1) **Ask** a question — make an **observation** and ask **why or how** it happens. E.g. why is trypsin (an enzyme) found in the small intestine but not in the stomach?
2) **Suggest** an answer, or part of an answer, by forming a **theory** (a possible **explanation** of the observations) e.g. pH affects the activity of enzymes. (Scientists also sometimes form a **model** too — a **simplified picture** of what's physically going on.)
3) Make a **prediction** or **hypothesis** — a **specific testable statement**, based on the theory, about what will happen in a test situation. E.g. trypsin will be active at pH 8 (the pH of the small intestine) but inactive at pH 2 (the pH of the stomach).
4) Carry out a **test** — to provide **evidence** that will support the prediction (or help to disprove it). E.g. measure the rate of reaction of trypsin at various pH levels.

The evidence supported Quentin's Theory of Flammable Burps.

A theory is only scientific if it can be tested.

...Then They **Tell** Everyone About Their **Results...**

The results are **published** — scientists need to let others know about their work. Scientists publish their results in **scientific journals**. These are just like normal magazines, only they contain **scientific reports** (called papers) instead of the latest celebrity gossip.

1) Scientific reports are similar to the **lab write-ups** you do in school. And just as a lab write-up is **reviewed** (marked) by your teacher, reports in scientific journals undergo **peer review** before they're published.
2) The report is sent out to **peers** — other scientists that are experts in the **same area**. They examine the data and results, and if they think that the conclusion is reasonable it's **published**. This makes sure that work published in scientific journals is of a **good standard**.
3) But peer review **can't guarantee** the science is **correct** — other scientists still need to **reproduce** it.
4) Sometimes **mistakes** are made and bad work is published. Peer review **isn't perfect** but it's probably the best way for scientists to self-regulate their work and to publish **quality reports**.

...Then **Other Scientists** Will **Test** the Theory Too

Other scientists read the published theories and results, and try to **test the theory** themselves. This involves:

- Repeating the **exact same experiments**.
- Using the theory to make **new predictions** and then testing them with **new experiments**.

If the **Evidence** Supports a Theory, It's **Accepted — for Now**

1) If all the experiments in all the world provide good evidence to back it up, the theory is thought of as **scientific 'fact'** (for now).
2) But it will never become **totally indisputable** fact. Scientific **breakthroughs or advances** could provide new ways to question and test the theory, which could lead to **new evidence** that **conflicts** with the current evidence. Then the testing starts all over again...

And this, my friend, is the **tentative nature of scientific knowledge** — it's always **changing** and **evolving**.

The Scientific Process

So scientists need evidence to back up their theories. They get it by carrying out experiments, and when that's not possible they carry out studies. But why bother with science at all? We want to know as much as possible so we can use it to try and improve our lives (and because we're nosy).

Evidence Comes from **Lab Experiments**...

1) Results from **controlled experiments** in **laboratories** are **great**.
2) A lab is the easiest place to **control variables** so that they're all **kept constant** (except for the one you're investigating).
3) This means you can draw meaningful **conclusions**.

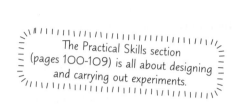

The Practical Skills section (pages 100-109) is all about designing and carrying out experiments.

...and **Well-Designed Studies**

1) There are things you **can't** investigate in a lab, e.g. whether stress causes heart attacks. You have to do a study instead.
2) You still need to try and make the study as controlled as possible to make it **valid**. But in reality it's **very hard** to control **all the variables** that **might** be having an effect.
3) You can do things to help, e.g. have **matched groups — choose two groups** of people (those who have quite stressful jobs and those who don't) who are **as similar as possible** (same mix of ages, same mix of diets etc.). But you can't easily rule out every possibility.

Samantha thought her study was very well designed — especially the fitted bookshelf.

Society **Makes Decisions** Based on **Scientific Evidence**

1) Lots of scientific work eventually leads to **important discoveries** or breakthroughs that could **benefit humankind**.
2) These results are **used by society** (that's you, me and everyone else) to **make decisions** — about the way we live, what we eat, what we drive, etc.
3) All sections of society use scientific evidence to make decisions, e.g. politicians use it to devise policies and individuals use science to make decisions about their own lives.

Other factors can **influence** decisions about science or the way science is used:

Economic factors

- Society has to consider the **cost** of implementing changes based on scientific conclusions — e.g. the **NHS** can't afford the most expensive drugs without **sacrificing** something else.
- Scientific research is **expensive** so companies won't always develop new ideas — e.g. developing new drugs is costly, so pharmaceutical companies often only invest in drugs that are likely to make them **money**.

Social factors

- **Decisions** affect **people's lives** — E.g. scientists may suggest **banning smoking** and **alcohol** to prevent health problems, but shouldn't **we** be able to **choose** whether **we** want to smoke and drink or not?

Environmental factors

- Scientists believe **unexplored regions** like remote parts of rainforests might contain **untapped drug** resources. But some people think we shouldn't **exploit** these regions because any interesting finds may lead to **deforestation** and **reduced biodiversity** in these areas.

So there you have it — that's how science works...

Hopefully these pages have given you a nice intro to how the world of science is run, e.g. what scientists do to provide you with 'facts'. You need to understand this, as you're expected to know all about the scientific process for the exams.

Water and Transport

Your body needs all sorts of different molecules to stay alive. It also needs to be able to transport these molecules around the body. That's where good old water comes in — read on...

Water is Vital to Living Organisms

Water makes up about 80% of a cell's contents. It has some important **functions**, inside and outside cells:

As her legs slowly dissolved, Jenny cursed her holiday.

1) Water is a **solvent**, which means some substances **dissolve** in it. Most biological reactions take place **in solution**, so water's pretty essential.

2) Water **transports** substances. Substances can be transported **more easily** if they're **dissolved** in a solvent. So the fact that water's a **liquid** and a **solvent** means it can easily transport all sorts of materials, like glucose and oxygen, around plants and animals.

Water Molecules have a Simple Structure

Examiners like asking you to relate **structure** to **properties** and **function**, so make sure you know the structure of water.

1) A molecule of water (H_2O) is **one atom of oxygen (O)** joined to **two atoms of hydrogen (H_2)** by **shared electrons**.
2) Because the **shared negative** hydrogen electrons are **pulled towards** the oxygen atom, the other side of each hydrogen atom is left with a **slight positive charge**.
3) The **unshared** negative electrons on the oxygen atom give it a **slight negative charge**.
4) This makes water a **dipolar** molecule — it has a **partial negative** (δ–) charge on one side and a **partial positive** (δ+) charge on the other.

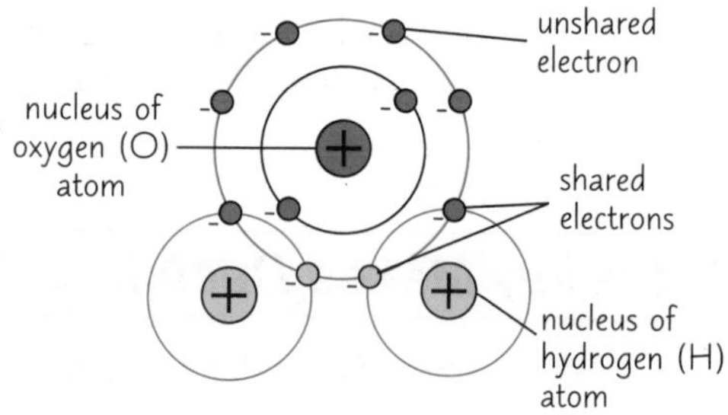

'δ' is the Latin letter 'delta'. So you read 'δ–' as 'delta negative.'

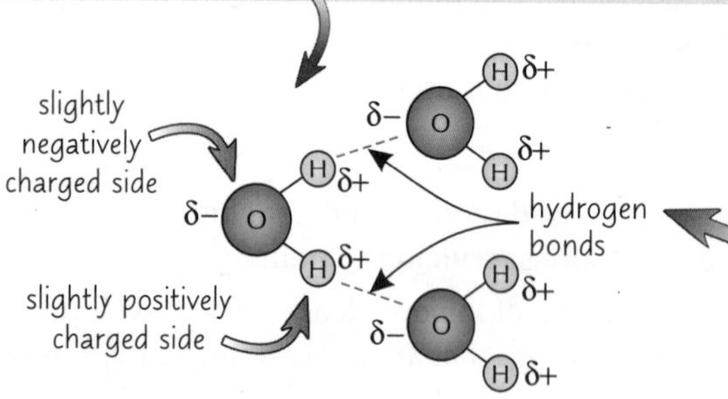

5) The slightly negatively-charged **oxygen atoms attract** the slightly positively-charged **hydrogen atoms** of other water molecules.
6) This attraction is called **hydrogen bonding** and it gives water some of its useful properties.

Water's Dipole Nature Makes it Good at Transporting Substances

Having a slight **negative charge** on one side and a slight **positive charge** on the other makes water **cohesive** and a **good solvent**. These properties make water good at **transporting substances**.

Water is Very Cohesive

1) Cohesion is the **attraction** between molecules of the same type (e.g. two water molecules). Water molecules are **very cohesive** (they tend to stick together) because they're **dipolar**.
2) This helps water to **flow**, making it great for **transporting substances**.

Water and Transport

Water is a Good Solvent

1) A lot of important substances in biological reactions are **ionic** (like **salt**, for example). This means they're made from **one positively-charged** atom or molecule and **one negatively-charged** atom or molecule (e.g. salt is made from a positive sodium ion and a negative chloride ion).
2) Because water is dipolar, the **slightly positive end** of a water molecule will be attracted to the **negative ion**, and the **slightly negative end** of a water molecule will be attracted to the **positive ion**.
3) This means the ions will get **totally surrounded** by water molecules — in other words, they'll **dissolve**.

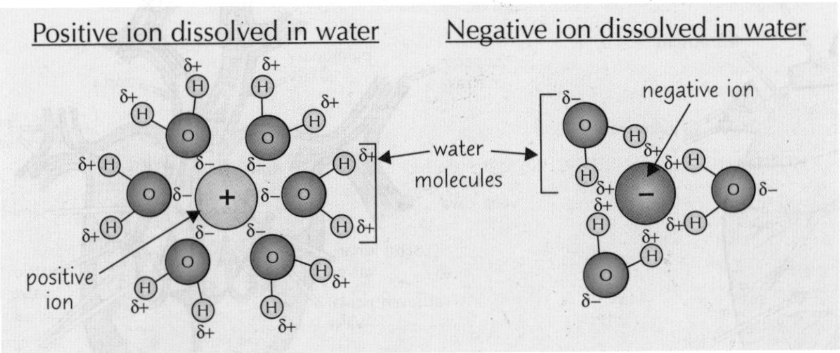

The dipolar nature of bears sometimes results in unexpected hydrogen bonding.

4) Water's **dipole nature** makes it useful as a **solvent** in living organisms. E.g. in **humans**, important **ions** can dissolve in the water in **blood** and then be transported around the body.

Multicellular Organisms Need Mass Transport Systems

1) All cells **need energy** — most cells get energy via **aerobic respiration**. The raw materials for this are **glucose** and **oxygen**, so the body has to make sure it can deliver enough of these to all its cells.
2) In single-celled organisms, these materials can **diffuse directly** into the cell across the cell membrane. The diffusion rate is quick because of the **short distance** the substances have to travel (see page 28).
3) In **multicellular** organisms (like us), diffusion across the outer membrane would be **too slow** because of the **large distance** the substances would have to travel to reach **all** the cells — think of how far it is from your skin to your heart cells.
4) So, multicellular organisms have **mass transport systems**:

   1) The **mass transport systems** are used to **carry raw materials** from specialised **exchange organs** (e.g. the lungs and the digestive system) to the body cells, and to **remove metabolic waste** (e.g. carbon dioxide).
   2) In mammals, the mass transport system is the **circulatory system**, where the heart is used to pump **blood** around the body.
   3) Individual cells in tissues and organs get **nutrients** and **oxygen** from the blood and dispose of **metabolic waste** into the blood.

Richard had a different idea of mass transport to his biology teacher.

Practice Questions

Q1 Briefly describe what is meant by a dipolar molecule.

Q2 Why do multicellular organisms need mass transport systems?

Exam Question

Q1 Explain how the structure of water enables it to transport substances. [3 marks]

Pssssssssssssssssssssssssssssssssssssss — need the loo yet?

Water is pretty darn useful really. It looks so, well, dull — but in fact it's scientifically amazing, and essential for all kinds of jobs — like transporting things around the body. You need to learn its structure so that you can relate its solvent properties to its function as a transport molecule. Right, I'm off — when you gotta go, you gotta go.

The Heart and Blood Vessels

As I'm sure you know already, your heart is the 'pump' that gets oxygenated blood to your cells. It's very important, so unsurprisingly, you need to know how it works. You'll find that these pages definitely get to the heart of it... groan...

The **Heart** Consists of **Two Muscular Pumps**

The diagrams below show the **internal** and **external structure** of the heart. The **right side** of the heart pumps **deoxygenated blood** to the **lungs** and the **left side** pumps **oxygenated blood** to the **rest of the body**. Note — the **left and right sides** are **reversed** on the diagram, cos it's the left and right of the person that the heart belongs to.

External Structure

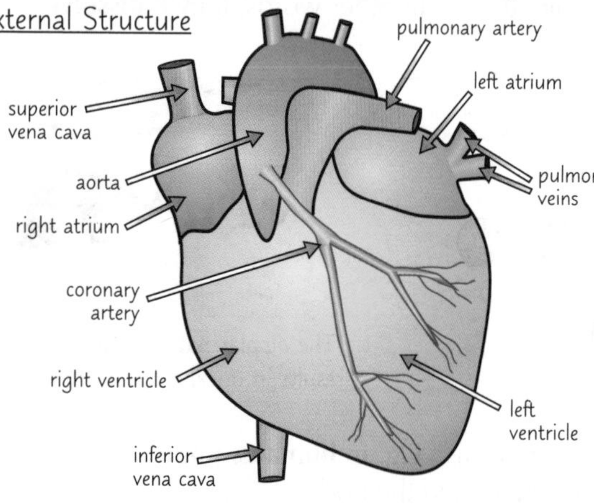

Internal Structure

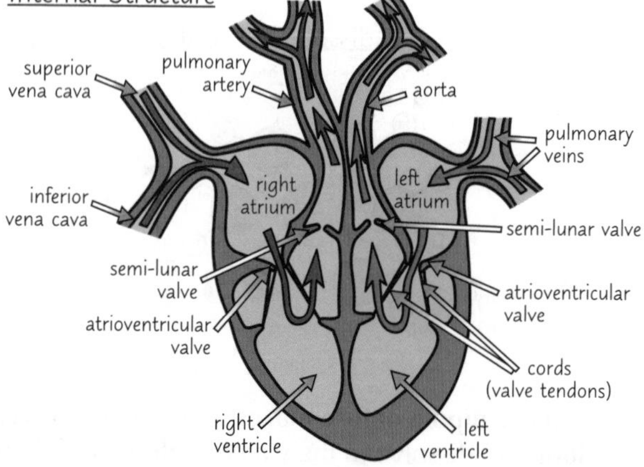

Heart Dissection Shows How the **Heart's Structure** Relates to its **Function**

You may get to carry out a heart dissection or you may get to watch one being carried out.

External examination: If you look at the outside of the heart you will see the **four main vessels** attached to it. The feel of the vessels can be used to help identify each one — arteries are thick and rubbery, whereas veins are much thinner (see next page).

You will also be able to see the right and left **atria**, the right and left **ventricles** and the **coronary arteries**.

Internal examination: The ventricles can be cut open using a scalpel so you can see inside each one. You should be able to see that the wall of the left ventricle is **thicker** than the wall of the right ventricle.

The **atria** can also be cut open. If you look at the atria walls, you should notice that they are **thinner** than the ventricle walls.

You can also look at the structures of the **atrioventricular valves** and **semi-lunar valves**.

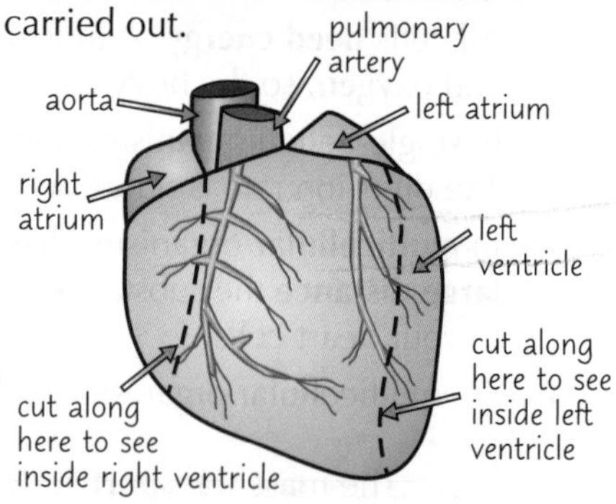

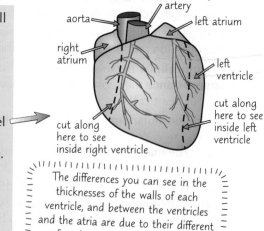

The differences you can see in the thicknesses of the walls of each ventricle, and between the ventricles and the atria are due to their different functions. See below for more.

When using a scalpel, you need to take precautions to avoid injuring yourself or others, e.g. by cutting in a direction away from yourself. Make sure you wash your hands and disinfect work surfaces once you're finished.

You Need to **Know What** the **Different Parts** of the **Heart Do**

Each bit of the heart is adapted to do its job effectively.

1) The **left ventricle** of the heart has **thicker**, more muscular walls than the **right ventricle**, because it needs to contract powerfully to pump blood all the way round the body. The right side only needs to get blood to the lungs, which are nearby.
2) The **ventricles** have **thicker walls** than the **atria**, because they have to push blood out of the heart whereas the atria just need to push blood a short distance into the ventricles.
3) The **atrioventricular (AV) valves** link the atria to the ventricles and **stop blood flowing back** into the atria when the ventricles contract. **Cords** attach the atrioventricular valves to the ventricles to stop them being forced up into the atria when the ventricles contract.
4) The **semi-lunar (SL) valves** link the ventricles to the pulmonary artery and aorta, and **stop blood flowing back** into the heart after the ventricles contract.

The Heart and Blood Vessels

Valves** Help the **Blood** to Flow in **One Direction

The **valves** only **open one way** — whether they're open or closed depends on the relative **pressure** of the heart chambers. If there's higher pressure **behind** a valve, it's forced **open**, but if pressure is higher **in front** of the valve it's forced **shut**. This means blood only flows in **one direction** through the heart.

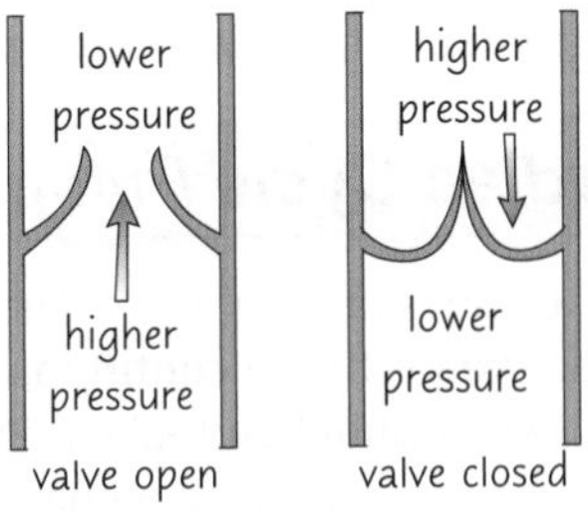

*Substances are Transported Around the Body in **Blood Vessels***

The heart pumps the blood around the body through the blood vessels. You need to know about **three** types of blood vessel — **arteries**, **veins** and **capillaries**. Read on...

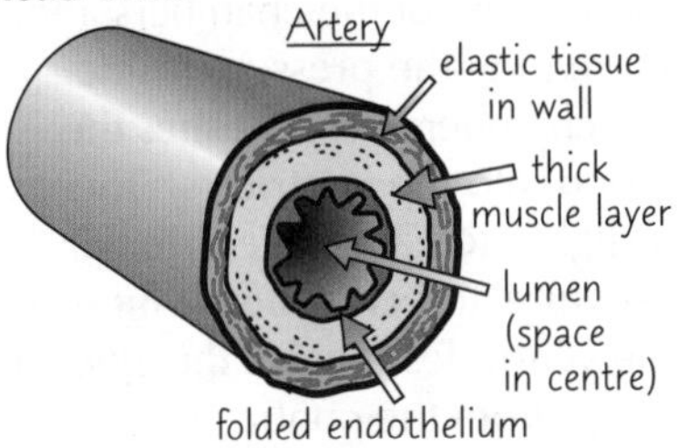

1) **Arteries** carry blood from the heart **to the rest of the body**. They're thick-walled, **muscular** and have **elastic tissue** in the walls to cope with the **high pressure** caused by the heartbeat. The inner lining (**endothelium**) is **folded**, allowing the artery to **expand** — this also helps it to cope with high pressure.

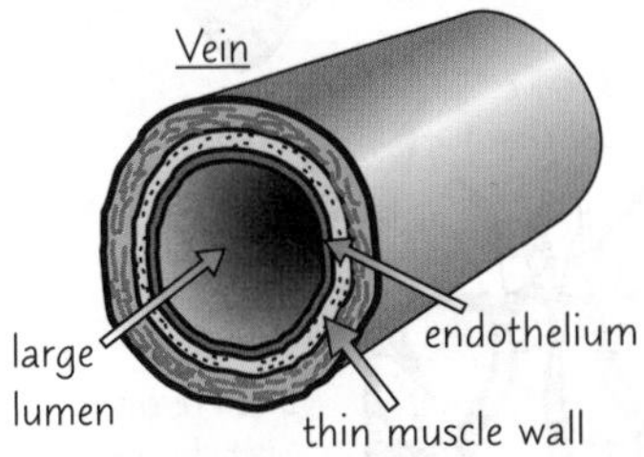

2) **Veins take** blood **back to the heart**. They're **wider** than equivalent arteries, with very little elastic or muscle tissue as the blood is under **lower pressure**. Veins contain **valves** to stop the blood flowing backwards. Blood flow through the veins is helped by contraction of the **body muscles** surrounding them.

3) **Capillaries** are the **smallest** of the blood vessels. They are where **metabolic exchange** occurs — substances are **exchanged** between cells and the capillaries. There are networks of capillaries in tissue (called **capillary beds**), which **increase** the **surface area** for exchange. Capillary walls are only **one cell thick**, which speeds up **diffusion** of substances (e.g. glucose and oxygen) into and out of cells.

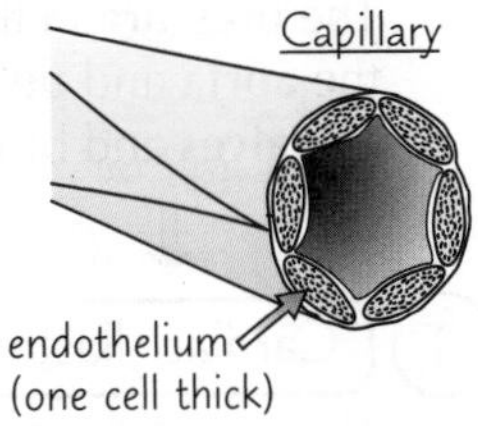

Practice Questions

Q1 Why is the left ventricle wall more muscular than the right ventricle wall?

Q2 Describe the structure of an artery.

Exam Questions

Q1 The diagram on the right shows the internal structure of the heart.
What is the structure labelled **X**?

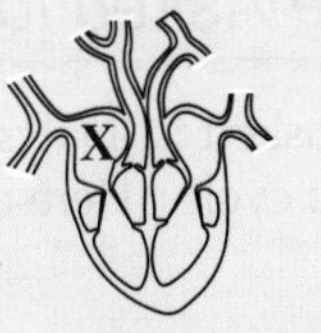

A Aorta **B** Left ventricle **C** Right atrium **D** Vena cava [1 mark]

Q2 Explain how valves in the heart stop blood going back the wrong way. [3 marks]

Q3 Explain how the structure of capillaries enables them to carry out metabolic exchange efficiently. [2 marks]

Apparently an adult heart is the size of two fists. Two whole fists! Huge!

You may have noticed that biologists are obsessed with the relationship between structure and function, so whenever you're learning about the structure of something, make sure you know how this relates to its function. And what better place to start than the heart. Oh and don't forget the arteries, veins and capillaries...

Cardiac Cycle

The cardiac cycle is all the changes that happen in the heart during one heart beat. There's lots of contracting and relaxing and opening and closing of valves. You just need to know what is happening when. Easy.

*The **Cardiac Cycle** Pumps Blood Round the Body*

The cardiac cycle is an ongoing sequence of **contraction** (**systole**) and **relaxation** (**diastole**) of the atria and ventricles that keeps blood **continuously** circulating round the body. The **volume** of the atria and ventricles **changes** as they contract and relax. **Pressure** changes also occur, due to the changes in chamber volume (e.g. decreasing the volume of a chamber by contraction will increase the pressure in a chamber). The cardiac cycle can be simplified into three stages:

(1) Ventricular diastole, atrial systole

The **ventricles are relaxed.** The **atria contract**, decreasing the volume of the chambers and **increasing** the **pressure** inside the chambers. This **pushes** the blood into the **ventricles**. There's a slight **increase** in **ventricular pressure** and **chamber volume** as the **ventricles receive the ejected blood** from the contracting atria.

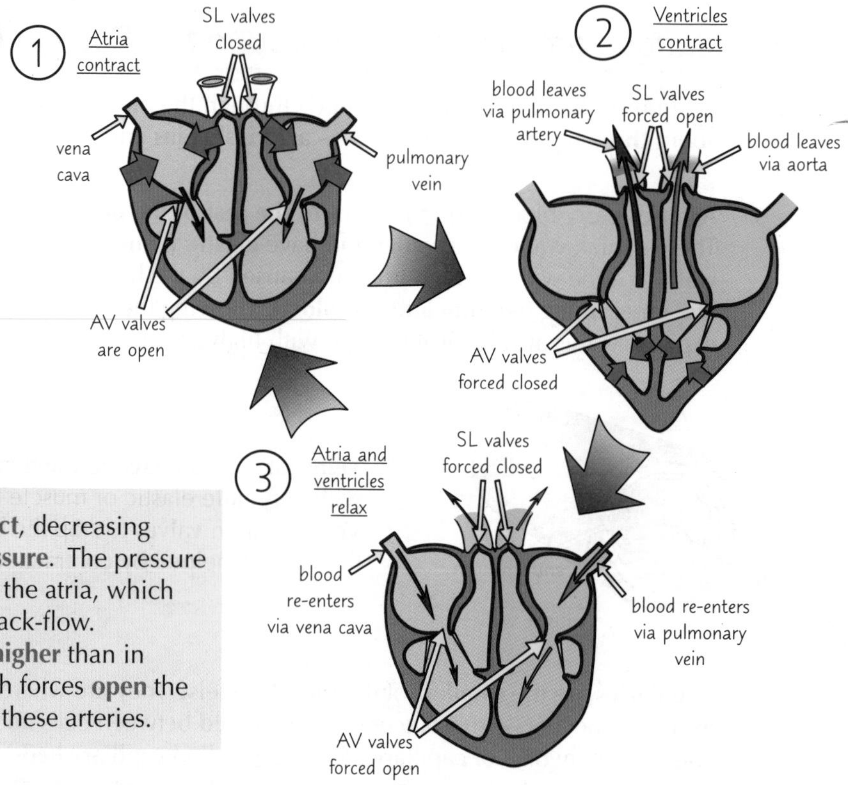

(2) Ventricular systole, atrial diastole

The **atria relax**. The **ventricles contract**, decreasing their volume and **increasing** their **pressure.** The pressure becomes **higher** in the ventricles than the atria, which forces the **AV valves shut** to prevent back-flow. The **pressure** in the **ventricles** is also **higher** than in the **aorta** and **pulmonary artery**, which forces **open** the **SL valves** and blood is forced out into these arteries.

(3) Cardiac diastole

The **ventricles and the atria both relax**. The higher pressure in the pulmonary artery and aorta closes the SL valves to prevent back-flow into the ventricles. Blood returns to the heart and the **atria fill again** due to the higher pressure in the vena cava and pulmonary vein. In turn this starts to **increase** the **pressure** of the atria. As the ventricles continue to **relax**, their **pressure falls below the pressure of the atria** and so the **AV valves open.** This allows blood to flow **passively** (without being pushed by atrial contraction) into the ventricles from the atria. The atria contract, and the whole process begins again.

*You Might be Asked to **Interpret Data** on the **Cardiac Cycle***

You may well be asked to analyse or interpret **data** about the changes in **pressure** and **volume** during the cardiac cycle. Here are some examples of the kind of things you might get:

Example 1

You may have to describe the changes in pressure and volume shown by a **diagram**, like the one on the right. In this diagram the **AV valves** are **open**. So you know that the **pressure** in the **atria** is **higher** than in the **ventricles**. So you also know that the **atria are contracting** because that's what causes the **increase** in **pressure**.

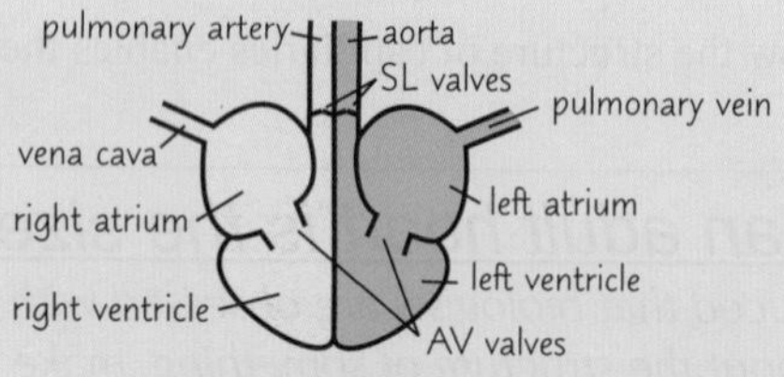

Cardiac Cycle

Example 2

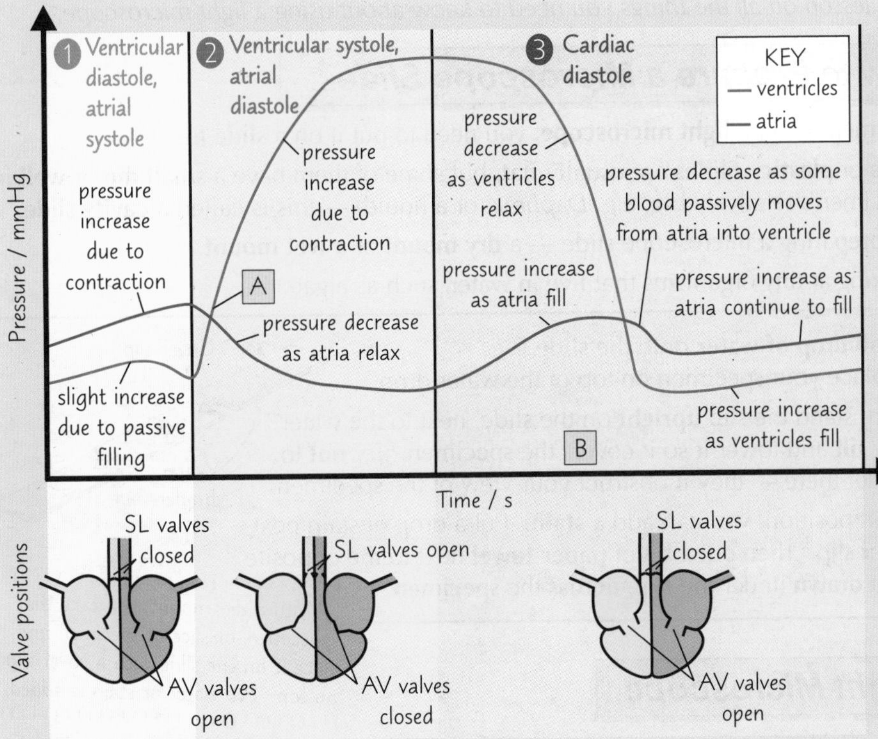

You could be asked **questions** like this:

1) **When does blood start flowing into the aorta?**

At **point A**, the ventricles are **contracting** (and the AV valves are shut), forcing blood into the aorta.

2) Are the **semi-lunar valves** open or closed at **point B**?

Closed. The ventricles are **relaxed** and **refilling**, so the pressure is **higher** in the **pulmonary artery** and **aorta**, forcing the SL valves **closed**.

The left ventricle has a thicker wall than the right ventricle and so it contracts more forcefully. This means the pressure is higher in the left ventricle (and in the aorta compared to the pulmonary artery).

Example 3

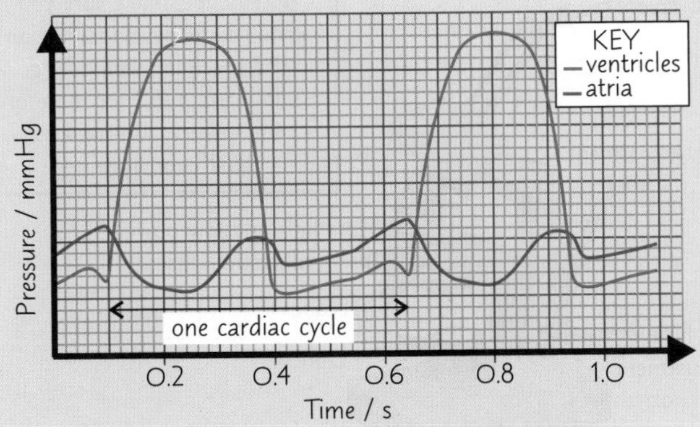

Or you could be asked a **question** like this:

1) **What is the heart rate** of this person in beats per minute?

It takes **0.54 seconds** to complete **one cardiac cycle** (or one heartbeat).
In one minute there will be:
60 ÷ 0.54 = 110 beats (2 s.f.).
So the heart rate is **110 beats per minute**.

Practice Questions

Q1 Which valves open during ventricular systole?

Q2 Describe what happens to the ventricles and atria during cardiac diastole.

Exam Question

Q1 The table to the right shows the blood pressure in two heart chambers at different times during part of the cardiac cycle.

	Blood pressure / kPa	
Time / s	Left atrium	Left ventricle
0.0	0.6	0.5
0.1	1.3	0.8
0.2	0.4	6.9
0.3	0.5	16.5
0.4	0.9	7.0

a) Between what times are the AV valves shut? [1 mark]

b) Between what times do the ventricles start to relax? [1 mark]

c) Calculate the percentage increase in left ventricle blood pressure between 0.0 s and 0.3 s. [3 marks]

The cardiac cycle — a bewilderingly complicated pump-action bicycle...

Two whole pages to learn here, all full of really important stuff. If you understand all the pressure and volume changes then whether you get a diagram, graph or something else in the exam, you'll be able to interpret it, no probs.

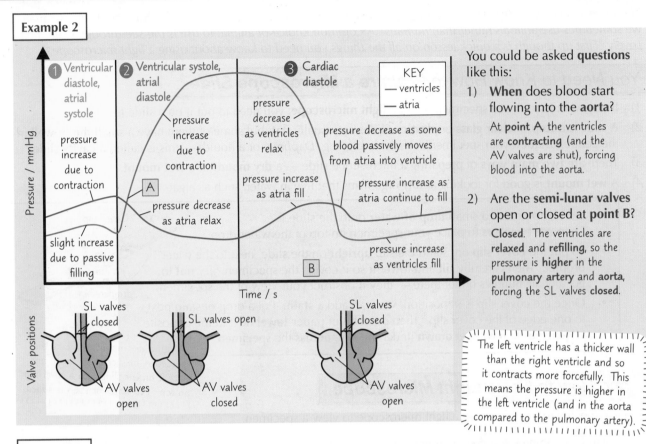

Investigating Heart Rate

There are lots of things that affect heart rate, but when it comes to testing the effect of substances such as caffeine, we sometimes use animals rather than humans. A common choice of animal to use is the see-through water flea. Lovely. First up though is a quick lesson on all the things you need to know about using a light microscope...

You Need to Know How to **Prepare** a **Microscope Slide**...

1) If you want to look at a specimen under a **light microscope**, you need to put it on a **slide** first.
2) A slide is a strip of **clear glass** or **plastic**. Slides are usually **flat**, but some of them have a small **dip** or **well** in the centre (useful if your specimen's relatively big, e.g. *Daphnia*, or a liquid) — this is called a **cavity slide**.
3) There are **two main ways** of preparing a microscope slide — a **dry mount** or a **wet mount**.
4) A **wet mount** is good for looking at tiny organisms that live in water, such as algae.

- Start by pipetting a small **drop of water** onto the slide. Then use **tweezers** to place your specimen on top of the water drop.
- To put the **cover slip** on, stand the slip **upright** on the slide, next to the water droplet. Then carefully **tilt** and lower it so it covers the specimen. Try **not** to get any **air bubbles** under there — they'll obstruct your view of the specimen.
- Once the cover slip is in position, you can add a **stain**. Put a drop of stain next to one edge of the cover slip. Then put a bit of **paper towel** next to the opposite edge. The stain will get **drawn** under the slip, **across** the **specimen**.

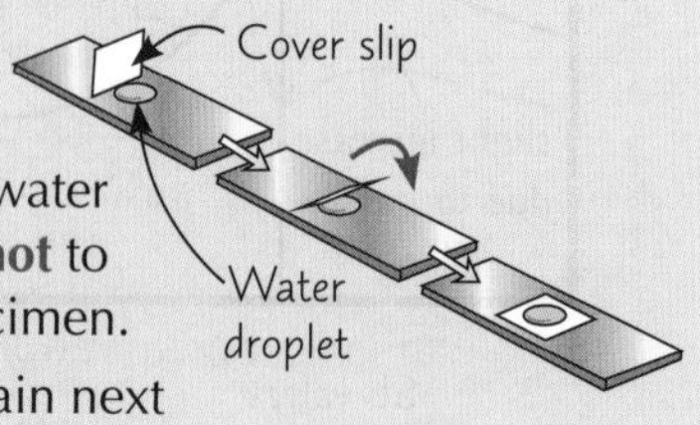

With a dry mount, you take the specimen, or slice of specimen and place it on the slide with a cover slip on top. No water or stain is added.

...and How to Use a **Light Microscope**

You're expected to be able to use a light microscope to view a specimen.

1) Start by clipping the **slide** containing the specimen you want to look at onto the **stage**.
2) Select the **lowest-powered objective lens** (i.e. the one that produces the lowest magnification).
3) Use the **coarse adjustment knob** to move the objective lens down to just above the slide.
4) Look down the **eyepiece** (which contains the **ocular lens**) and adjust the **focus** with the **fine adjustment knob**, until you get a **clear image** of whatever's on the slide.
5) If you need to see the slide with **greater magnification**, swap to a **higher-powered objective lens** and refocus.

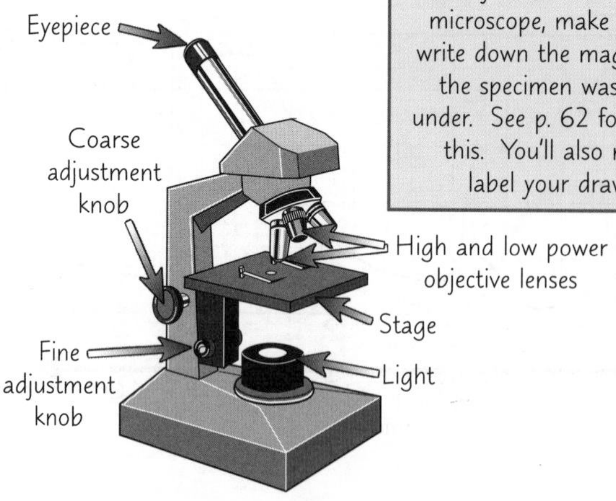

If you're asked to draw what you can see under the microscope, make sure you write down the magnification the specimen was viewed under. See p. 62 for more on this. You'll also need to label your drawing.

You Can **Investigate** the Effect of **Caffeine** on the **Heart Rate** of **Daphnia**

Daphnia are tiny aquatic **invertebrates**. They're **transparent**, so you can see their internal organs. This means you can monitor their **heart rate** (the **number of heartbeats** in a **minute**) by observing them through a **microscope**.

You could use a serial dilution technique to make up your solutions (see p. 101 for more).

1) Make up a **range** of caffeine solutions of **different concentrations** and a **control** solution that has no caffeine in it at all.
2) Transfer **one** *Daphnia* into the dimple on a **cavity slide**.
3) Using a pipette, place a few drops of **caffeine solution** onto the *Daphnia*.
Wait for 5 minutes while the caffeine is absorbed.
4) Place the slide onto the stage of a **light microscope** and adjust the **focus** so you can see the **beating heart** of the *Daphnia*. You can find the heart to the back side of the gut and above the brood pouch.
5) **Count** the number of **heartbeats** in **20 seconds**, timed using a stopwatch, and multiply this by **three** to calculate beats per minute (**heart rate**).

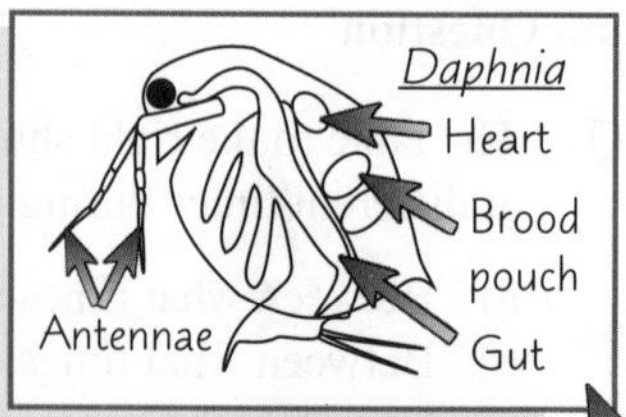

Investigating Heart Rate

6) **Repeat** this 10 times using the **same concentration** of caffeine but a **different** *Daphnia* individual each time.
7) Repeat the experiment using the **other concentrations** of caffeine solution and the **control** solution.
8) **Compare the results** to see how caffeine concentration affects heart rate.

Don't forget to keep all other factors constant (e.g. temperature and volume of caffeine solution).

Heart Rate **Increases** as Caffeine Concentration **Increases**

A good way to see the effect of caffeine concentration on heart rate is to draw a **graph** of the results of the *Daphnia* experiment.

1) Take the **average** of the 10 readings at each concentration and then graph your results — plot average heart rate (beats per minute) against concentration of caffeine.
2) Your results might look something like this.
3) This graph shows a **positive correlation** — as caffeine concentration **increases**, heart rate also **increases**.

See p. 108 for more on correlation.

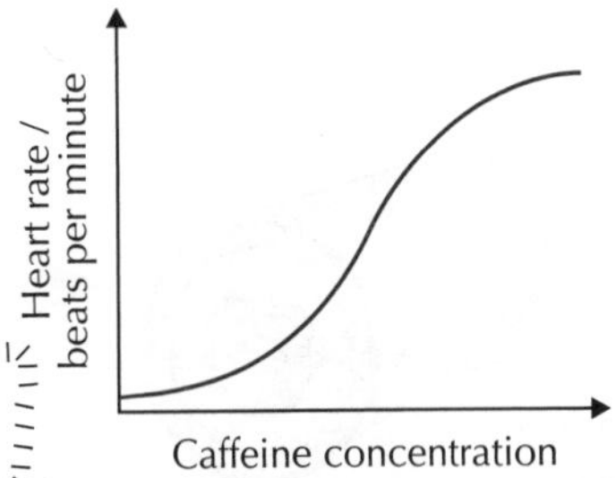

The result of the experiment — hooked on caffeine.

There are Some **Ethical Issues** Involved in Using **Invertebrates**

In the exam, you may have to discuss the **ethical issues** involved with using **invertebrates** in experiments. Here are some points to think about:

1) Experimenting on **animals** allows scientists to study things that would be **unethical** to study using humans. But many people believe that using animals is **also unethical** — they can't give **consent** and they may be subjected to **painful procedures**.
2) Some people believe it's **more acceptable** to perform experiments on **invertebrates** (like *Daphnia*, spiders and insects) than on **vertebrates** (like dogs and monkeys).
3) This is because they're considered to be **simpler organisms** than vertebrates. For example, they have a much **less sophisticated nervous system**, which could mean that they feel less pain (or no pain). Also, invertebrates are more **distantly related** to humans than other vertebrates.
4) But there are still ethical issues to consider when experimenting with invertebrates. For example, some people believe it's unethical to cause **distress** or **suffering** to **any living organism** — e.g. by subjecting them to **extremes of temperature** or depriving them of **food**.

Practice Questions

Q1 Describe how you would prepare a microscope slide to investigate the heart rate of *Daphnia*.

Exam Question

Q1 The graph shows the results of an experiment into the effects of caffeine on *Daphnia* heart rate.

a) Analyse the data to describe the relationship between caffeine concentration and heart rate in *Daphnia*. [1 mark]

b) Give two factors that would need to be kept constant during the experiment. [2 marks]

c) Discuss why some people may feel it's more acceptable to carry out experiments on invertebrates, such as *Daphnia*, than on vertebrates. [3 marks]

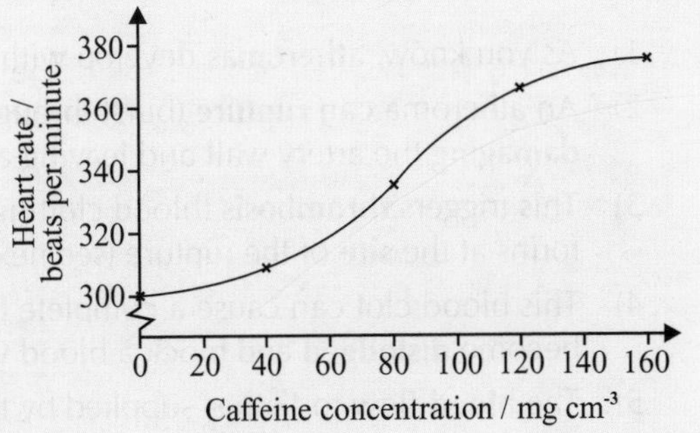

I reckon there are some ethical issues involved with sitting exams...

Breathe deeply, slow your heart rate, and concentrate on investigating the heart rates of Daphnia. *Make sure that you can outline how to set up the experiment and then put your debating hat on because it's time for some ethics.*

Cardiovascular Disease

No, your heart won't break if he/she (delete as appropriate) doesn't return your call... but there are diseases associated with the heart and blood vessels that you have to learn about...

*Most **Cardiovascular Disease** Starts With **Atheroma** Formation*

1) The wall of an **artery** is made up of **several layers** (see page 7).
2) The **endothelium** (inner lining) is usually smooth and unbroken.

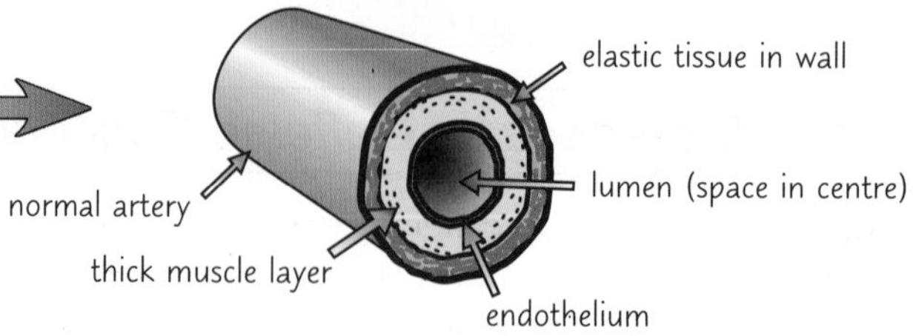

3) If **damage** occurs to the endothelium (e.g. by high blood pressure) there will be an **inflammatory response** — this is where **white blood cells** (mostly macrophages) move into the area.
4) These white blood cells and **lipids** (fats) from the blood, clump together under the endothelium to form **fatty streaks**.

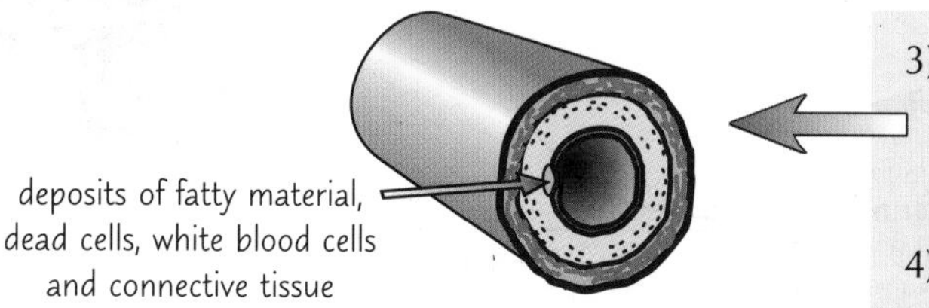

Damage to the endothelium means the endothelium can't function normally — this is called endothelial dysfunction.

5) Over time, **more white blood cells**, **lipids** and **connective tissue** build up and harden to form a **fibrous plaque** called an **atheroma**.
6) This plaque **partially blocks** the lumen of the **artery** and **restricts blood flow**, which causes **blood pressure** to **increase**.

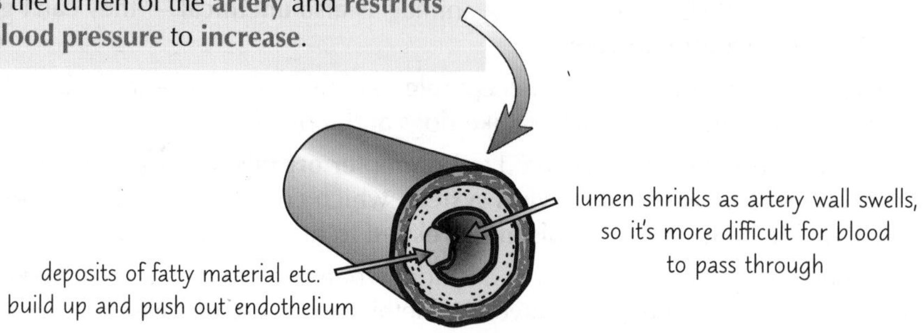

7) The **hardening** of arteries, caused by atheromas, is called **atherosclerosis**.

Atheromas Increase** the **Risk** of **Thrombosis** in **Arteries

1) As you know, **atheromas** develop within the **walls** of **arteries** (see above).
2) An atheroma can **rupture** (burst through) the **endothelium** of an artery, **damaging** the artery wall and leaving a **rough** surface.
3) This triggers **thrombosis** (blood clotting) — a **blood clot** forms at the **site** of the rupture (see next page).
4) This blood clot can cause a complete **blockage** of the artery, or it can become **dislodged** and block a blood vessel elsewhere in the body.
5) The **blood flow** to **tissues** supplied by the blocked blood vessel will be severely **restricted**, so **less oxygen** will reach those tissues, resulting in damage.
6) **Heart attack**, **stroke** and **deep vein thrombosis** are three forms of **cardiovascular disease** that can be caused by blood clots — these are explained in more detail on the next page.

Cardiovascular Disease

You Need to Know How a Blood Clot Forms

Thrombosis is used by the body to **prevent** lots of blood being **lost** when a **blood vessel** is **damaged**.
A **series** of **reactions** occurs that leads to the formation of a **blood clot** (**thrombus**):

1) A **protein** called **thromboplastin** is **released** from the **damaged** blood vessel.
2) Thromboplastin, along with calcium ions from the plasma, triggers the **conversion** of **prothrombin** (a **soluble protein**) into **thrombin** (an **enzyme**).
3) Thrombin then catalyses the **conversion** of **fibrinogen** (a **soluble protein**) to **fibrin** (solid **insoluble fibres**).
4) The fibrin fibres **tangle together** and form a **mesh** in which **platelets** (**small fragments of cells** in the blood) and **red blood cells** get **trapped** — this forms the **blood clot**.

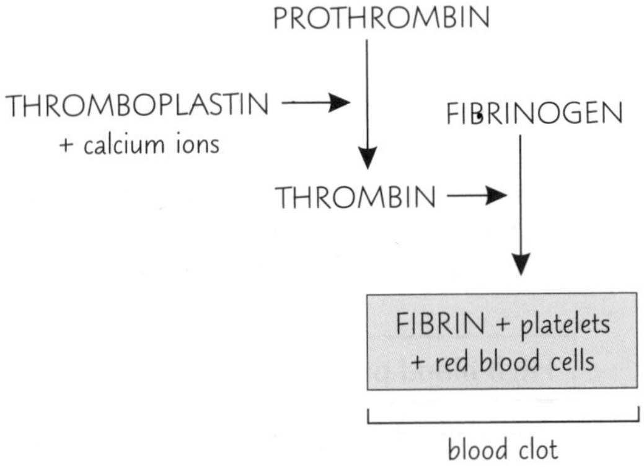

The **cardiovascular diseases** below can result from the formation of blood clots.

Blood Clots can Cause Heart Attacks...

1) The **heart muscle** is supplied with **blood** by the **coronary arteries**.

2) This blood contains the **oxygen** needed by heart muscle cells to carry out **respiration**.

3) If a coronary artery becomes **completely blocked** by a **blood clot** an area of the heart muscle will be totally **cut off** from its blood supply, so it **won't** receive any **oxygen**.

4) This causes a **myocardial infarction** — more commonly known as a **heart attack**.

5) A heart attack can cause **damage** and **death** of the **heart muscle**.

6) **Symptoms** include **pain** in the chest and upper body, **shortness of breath** and **sweating**.

7) If **large areas** of the heart are affected complete **heart failure** can occur, which is often **fatal**.

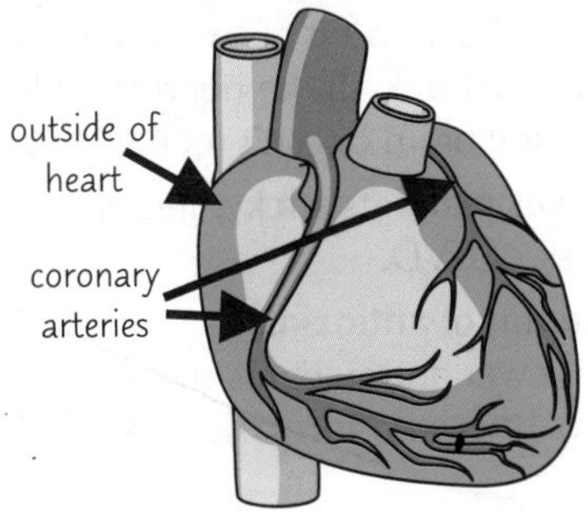

Coronary heart disease (CHD) is when the **coronary arteries** have lots of **atheromas** in them, which restricts blood flow to the heart. The atheromas also increase the risk of **blood clots** forming, leading to an increased risk of heart attack.

...Stroke...

1) A **stroke** is a **rapid loss** of **brain function**, due to a **disruption** in the **blood supply** to the **brain**.
2) This can be caused by a **blood clot** in an **artery** leading to the brain, which **reduces** the amount of blood, and therefore **oxygen**, that can reach the brain.

...and Deep Vein Thrombosis

1) **Deep vein thrombosis** (**DVT**) is the formation of a **blood clot** in a **vein** deep inside the body — it usually happens in **leg veins**.
2) It can be caused by **prolonged inactivity**, e.g. during **long-haul flights**, and the risk **increases** with **age**.

Cardiovascular Disease

Many **Factors** *Can* **Increase** *the* **Risk** *of* **Cardiovascular Disease (CVD)**

Lifestyle Factors:

Diet

A diet **high** in **saturated fat** (see p. 25) increases the risk of CVD. This is because it **increases blood cholesterol level**, which **increases atheroma formation**. Atheromas can lead to the formation of **blood clots**, which can cause a **heart attack**, **stroke** or **DVT**.

A diet **high in salt** also increases the risk of CVD because it increases the risk of **high blood pressure** (see below).

See page 25 for more on cholesterol.

High blood pressure

High blood pressure **increases** the **risk** of **damage** to the **artery walls**, which **increases** the **risk** of **atheroma formation**, which can lead to CVD. **Excessive alcohol consumption**, **stress** and **diet** can **all** increase blood pressure.

Smoking

- **Carbon monoxide** in cigarette smoke combines with **haemoglobin** (the protein that carries oxygen in the blood) and **reduces** the amount of **oxygen** transported in the **blood**. This **reduces** the amount of **oxygen available to tissues**. If the heart muscle doesn't receive enough oxygen it can lead to a **heart attack** and if the brain doesn't receive enough oxygen it can lead to a **stroke**.
- **Nicotine** in cigarette smoke makes **platelets sticky**, increasing the chance of **blood clots forming**, which increases the risk of CVD.
- Smoking also **decreases** the **amount** of **antioxidants** in the blood — these are important for **protecting cells** from damage. Fewer antioxidants means **cell damage** in the **artery walls** is more likely, and this can lead to **atheroma formation**, which increases the risk of CVD.

Inactivity

A **lack** of **exercise** increases the risk of CVD because it **increases blood pressure** (see above).

Factors Beyond *Your* **Control:**

Genetics

Some people inherit particular **alleles** (different versions of genes, see page 50) that make them **more likely** to have **high blood pressure** or **high blood cholesterol**, so they are **more likely** to suffer from CVD (see above).

Age

The risk of developing CVD **increases with age**. This is partly because **plaque** can **build up** very slowly over time, which can eventually lead to CVD.

Gender

Men are **three times more likely** to suffer from CVD than pre-menopausal women. This may be due to their different levels of **hormones** — for example, the hormone **oestrogen**, which is typically higher in females, increases levels of 'good' cholesterol (HDL) — see p. 25. The relatively low level of this hormone in men can lead to **higher levels** of total **blood cholesterol** and **increase** the **risk** of CVD.

Cardiovascular Disease

Perception of Risk *Can be Different from* ***Actual Risk***

1) **Risk** can be defined as the **chance** of something **unfavourable** happening.
   E.g. if you **smoke** you **increase** your chance of developing CVD.
2) The **statistical chance** of something unfavourable happening is supported by **scientific research**.
   E.g. the actual risk of **dying** from **CVD** is **60%** higher for smokers than for non-smokers.
3) People's **perception** of risk may be very **different** from the actual risk:

- People may **overestimate** the risk — they may believe things to be a **greater risk** than they actually are. E.g. they may have **known someone** who **smoked** and **died** from CVD, and therefore think that if you smoke you **will** die of CVD. Also, there are often **articles** in the **media** about health issues, e.g. articles that highlight the link between smoking and CVD or the link between having a high BMI (see p. 27) and CVD. **Constant exposure** to information like this can make people **constantly worry** that they'll get CVD.

- Some people may **underestimate** the risk — they may believe things to be a **lower risk** than they actually are. This could be due to a **lack of information** making them **unaware** of the **factors** that contribute to diseases like CVD.

Melvin underestimated the risk of letting his mum dress him...

Practice Questions

Q1 Describe how an atheroma forms.

Q2 What is the role of fibrin in the blood clotting process?

Q3 Describe why high blood pressure increases the risk of CVD.

Q4 Give three factors that increase the risk of CVD but can't be controlled.

Q5 Give one reason why a person may underestimate the risk of developing CVD.

Exam Questions

Q1 Explain why people might overestimate the risk of developing CVD. [2 marks]

Q2 On the right is a diagram showing the process of blood clotting.

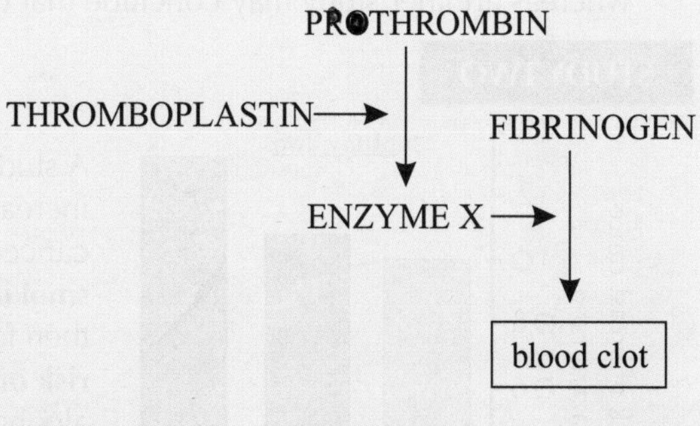

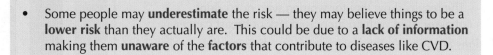

a) Give the name of enzyme X. [1 mark]

b) Name three things which make up a blood clot. [1 mark]

c) What type of ions are involved in the conversion of prothrombin to enzyme X? [1 mark]

d) People with the disorder called hypoprothrombinaemia have a reduced amount of prothrombin in their blood.
Explain the likely effect this will have on their blood clotting mechanism. [2 marks]

Q3 Describe how atheromas can increase the risk that a person will suffer from a heart attack. [4 marks]

Q4* Explain how smoking can increase the risk of developing CVD. [6 marks]

* You will be assessed on the quality of your written response in this question.

Atherosclerosis, thrombosis — more like a spelling test than biology...

I know there's a lot to take in here... but make sure you understand the link between atherosclerosis, thrombosis and CVD — basically an atheroma forms, which can cause thrombosis, which can lead to CVD. Also, practise writing down the flow diagram of all the proteins involved in blood clotting, 'cause you need to know it in detail.

Interpreting Data on Risk Factors

Those pesky examiners may ask you to analyse data on risk factors for other diseases too... do they know no limit?

You May Have to Analyse and Interpret Data About Illness or Mortality

In the **exam** you might have to analyse illness or mortality data (for any disease) to determine if something is a **risk factor**. Watch out for mixing up **correlation** and **causation** in any data you're given — just because results are correlated **doesn't prove** that a change in one causes a change in the other (see page 108).

STUDY ONE

A study was carried out to analyse data, gathered from **53 studies worldwide**, about the **link** between **smoking** and **breast cancer**. The study looked at **22 255** women **with** breast cancer and **40 832** women **without** breast cancer, all of whom reported **drinking no alcohol**. The results below show the **relative risk** of breast cancer for women with **different smoking histories**.

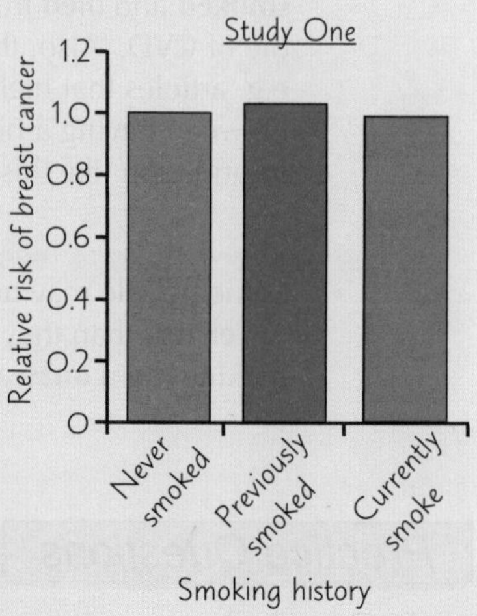

Here are some of the things you might be asked to do:

1) Describe the data — The results show that the **relative risk** of breast cancer for women who don't drink alcohol is **similar regardless of smoking history**.
2) Draw conclusions — The results show that for women who don't drink alcohol, smoking is **not associated** with an **increased risk** of breast cancer.
3) Check any conclusions are valid — This data appears to show **no link** between smoking history and the relative risk of breast cancer in women who don't drink, but you **can't** say that smoking **doesn't affect** breast cancer risk at all. The data **doesn't** take into account women who drink. Smoking and alcohol **together** could **affect the risk** of breast cancer. Also, the study doesn't take into account **other factors** that could affect risk of breast cancer such as the use of **hormone replacement treatment, physical activity**, etc.

You Need to be Able to Recognise Conflicting Evidence

1) The **evidence** from **one study** alone **wouldn't usually be enough** to conclude that a factor is a **health risk**.
2) **Similar studies** would be carried out to investigate the link. If these studies came to the **same conclusion**, the conclusion would become **increasingly accepted**.
3) Sometimes studies come up with **conflicting evidence** though — evidence that leads to a **different conclusion** than other studies. For example, one study may conclude that a factor **isn't a health risk**, whereas another study may conclude that the **same** factor **is a health risk**:

STUDY TWO

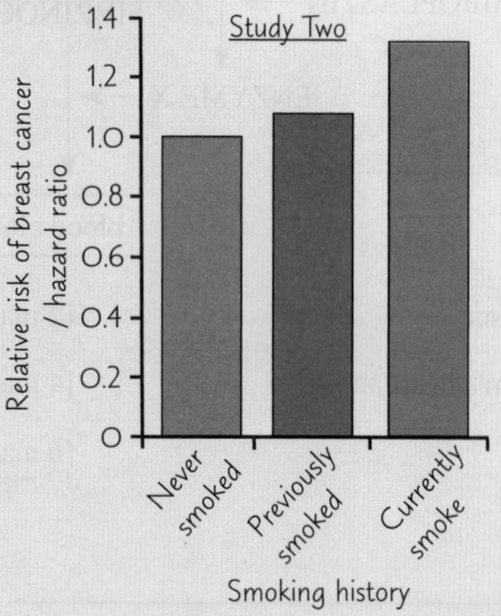

A study was carried out to determine if smoking is linked to an increased risk of breast cancer. **116 544** women without breast cancer in **California** were sent **questionnaires** to establish their **smoking history** and other personal information. The women were then followed for **5 years**. The results on the left show the **relative risk of breast cancer, adjusted** for **other factors** such as age and alcohol consumption, for women with **different smoking histories**.

1) Describe the data — The results show that the **relative risk** of breast cancer for women in California is **higher** for women who **previously smoked** or **still smoke** compared to those who have never smoked.
2) Draw conclusions — The results show that for women in California, smoking **is associated** with an **increased risk** of breast cancer.
3) Comment on the conflicting evidence — This second study shows that smoking **is linked** to an increased risk of breast cancer, which **conflicts** with the evidence from **study one** (see above). Because the two studies have produced conflicting evidence, **more results** would be needed in order to **fully assess** if smoking is an **important health risk** for the development of **breast cancer**.

Interpreting Data on Risk Factors

You May Have to *Evaluate* the *Design* of *Studies*

In the **exam** you could be asked to **evaluate** the **design** of a study they've given you.
Here are some things to look out for:

There's more on reliability and validity in the Practical Skills section — see page 100.

1) **Sample size** — the **greater** the number of people used in a study, the **more reliable** the results.

   Selecting the sample should also be done carefully. The sample should be representative (i.e. it should reflect the variety of characteristics that are found in the population you're interested in studying) so that the results can be generalised to the whole population. A sample that is unrepresentative is biased and can't reliably be generalised to the whole population.
2) **Variables** — the **more variables** (other factors that could affect the results) that have been **controlled** in a study, the **more reliable** the results. This also makes the results more **valid** — by controlling the variables, you're making sure that you're only testing the thing you want to.
3) **Data collection** — the **less bias** involved in collecting the data, the **more reliable** the results.
4) **Controls** — the presence of controls **increases** the validity of the results.
5) **Repetition** by other scientists — if other scientists produce the **same results**, then the results are **more reliable.**

See page 109 for loads more on evaluating data.

EXAMPLE: STUDY ONE

1) **Sample size** — The study had a **large** sample size of **63 087 women** in total, which makes the results more reliable.
2) **Variables** — The study didn't take into account **some variables** that can affect the risk of breast cancer, like **hormone replacement therapy** and **physical activity**. This could have affected the results (decreasing their reliability and validity).
3) **Data collection** — The data was collected from **53 other studies** but we don't know how those other studies were designed.
4) **Controls** — There were a large number of controls, **40 832 women**. This increases the validity of the results.
5) **Repetition by other scientists** — Study two **doesn't agree** with the conclusion of study one.

EXAMPLE: STUDY TWO

1) **Sample size** — This study had a **really large** sample size of **116 544 women**, which makes the results more reliable.
2) **Variables** — This study took into account **other variables** like **hormone replacement therapy, physical activity**, alcohol consumption, etc. This **increases** the **reliability** and **validity** of the results.
3) **Data collection** — The data was collected from **questionnaires**, which can be biased. This **decreases** the **reliability** of the results.
4) **Repetition by other scientists** — Study one **doesn't agree** with the conclusion of study two.

Practice Questions

Q1 What is meant by conflicting evidence?

Q2 Why is it important to look at the data collection method when evaluating study design?

Exam Question

Q1 The results of a study involving 168 000 people in 63 countries have shown a strong correlation between waist measurement and risk of cardiovascular disease. Analysis of the results has shown that waist circumference is independently associated with cardiovascular disease.

a) Give two reasons why the study provides strong evidence for a link between waist measurement and risk of cardiovascular disease. [2 marks]

b) Give two ways that the results of this study could be made more reliable. [2 marks]

Exams — definitely a health risk...

These evaluating evidence questions come up quite a lot. The examiners like to see that you can analyse the data and that you can pick out the good and bad bits of a study. Luckily, I'm giving you plenty of examples of these types of questions. Make sure you look at the section at the back of this book on how to interpret data — then you'll be sorted.

Treatment of CVD

It's not all doom and gloom with CVD — there are some different treatments available.

Drugs Can be Used to **Treat CVD**

Although **prevention** is **better** than **cure**, there are some **treatments** for CVD.
You need to know **how** four of them work and be able to **describe** their **benefits and risks**.

1) Antihypertensives Reduce High Blood Pressure

These drugs include **beta-blockers** (which **reduce** the **strength** of the **heartbeat**) and **vasodilators** (which **widen** the **blood vessels**). They also include **diuretics**, most of which work by **reducing** the amount of **sodium** that's **reabsorbed** by the **blood** in the kidneys. This results in **less water** being reabsorbed (due to **osmosis**), which **reduces blood volume**.

See page 31 for more on osmosis.

All of these drugs **reduce blood pressure**, so there's **less chance** of **damage** occurring to the walls of the arteries. This **reduces** the risk of **atheromas** forming and **blood clots** developing (see p. 12-13).

BENEFITS:

The **different types** of antihypertensives work in **different ways**, so they can be given in **combination** to reduce blood pressure. Also, blood pressure can be **monitored at home**, so the patient can see if the drugs are **working**.

RISKS:

Palpitations (rapid beating of the heart), **abnormal heart rhythms**, **fainting**, **headaches** and **drowsiness** are all side effects of these drugs caused by the **blood pressure** becoming **too low**. Other side effects include **allergic reactions** and **depression**.

2) Statins Reduce Cholesterol in the Blood

Statins **reduce blood cholesterol** in humans by **reducing** the amount of 'bad' LDL cholesterol (see page 25) **produced** inside the **liver**. A lower blood cholesterol level **reduces atheroma formation**, which reduces the risk of CVD.

BENEFITS:

Statins reduce the risk of **developing CVD**.

RISKS:

Side effects include **muscle** and **joint pain**, **digestive system problems** and an **increased risk of diabetes**. **Nosebleeds**, **headaches** and **nausea** are also common side effects.

3) Anticoagulants Reduce the Formation of Blood Clots

Anticoagulants (e.g. warfarin and heparin) **reduce blood clotting**. This means blood clots are **less likely** to form at sites of **damage** in artery walls. So there's **less chance** of a **blood vessel** becoming **blocked** by a blood clot (see p. 12-13), reducing the risk of CVD.

BENEFITS:

Anticoagulants can be used to treat people who **already have blood clots** or **CVD** — they **prevent** any existing blood clots from **growing any larger** and prevent any **new** blood clots from **forming**. However, anticoagulants **can't get rid** of **existing** blood clots.

RISKS:

If a person taking these drugs is badly **injured**, the reduction in blood clotting can cause **excessive bleeding**, which can lead to **fainting** (and in serious cases **death**). Other side effects include **allergic reactions**, **osteoporosis** (weakened bones) and **swelling** of the tissues. These drugs can also **damage the fetus** if they're taken during pregnancy.

Treatment of CVD

4) Platelet Inhibitory Drugs Also Reduce the Formation of Blood Clots

Platelet inhibitory drugs (e.g. **aspirin**) are a type of **anticoagulant** (see previous page). They work by **preventing platelets clumping together** to form a blood clot. So, they **reduce** the formation of **blood clots**, reducing the chance of a blood vessel becoming **blocked** by a clot.

These plate inhibitory drugs were doing a good job of preventing the plates from clumping together.

BENEFITS:

As with anticoagulants, these can be used to treat people who **already have blood clots** or **CVD.**

RISKS:

Side effects include **rashes**, **diarrhoea, nausea, liver function problems** and **excessive bleeding,** especially after a serious injury (see previous page).

Practice Questions

Q1 How do anticoagulants work to reduce the risk of CVD?

Q2 State two benefits of treating CVD with antihypertensives.

Exam Questions

Q1 The graph below shows the numbers of prescriptions used in the prevention and treatment of CVD in England between 2006 and 2013.

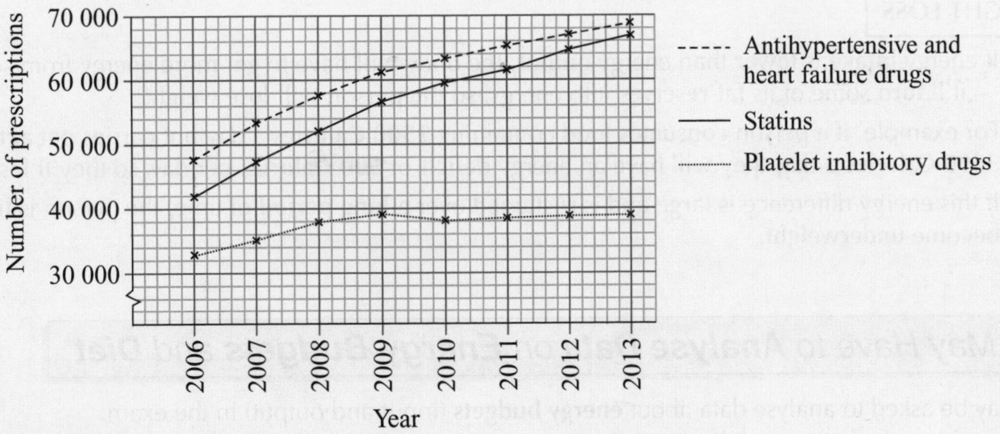

a) Describe the general trend in the number of prescriptions of each treatment of CVD shown by the graph above. [2 marks]

b) State the least commonly prescribed treatment and give one benefit and one risk of that type of treatment. [2 marks]

c) Using values rounded to 2 significant figures, calculate the percentage increase in statin prescriptions between 2006 and 2011. Give your answer as a whole number. [1 mark]

d) Explain how statins reduce the risk of developing CVD. [2 marks]

Q2 A patient who is at risk of developing coronary heart disease (CHD) goes to see his doctor. The patient is obese and suffers from high blood pressure.

a) State one type of drug the doctor could prescribe to treat the patient's high blood pressure and explain how it reduces the risk of CHD. [2 marks]

b) Give one disadvantage of taking this drug. [1 mark]

I'd need several spoonfuls of sugar to help all these medicines go down...

These drugs don't cure the problem — they don't get rid of existing atheromas or blood clots, they just prevent them from getting any worse. Still, it's good to know that there are treatments out there. Now you just need to make sure you know the risks and benefits of each one. May I suggest writing yourself out a handy table...

Diet and Energy

Obesity is a risk factor for cardiovascular disease (CVD) and other diseases too, so it's important to maintain a healthy weight. Weight is affected by your diet as well as how much energy you use doing things like playing video games and stealing traffic cones...*

Organisms Take In and Use Up Energy

1) Organisms need a **supply** of **energy**, so that they can **grow**, **move**, **reproduce** etc. — in animals this energy is provided in the form of **food**.
2) **Energy budget** is a term used to describe the **amount of energy taken in** by an organism (in food) **and** the amount of energy **used up** by an organism (e.g. by moving).

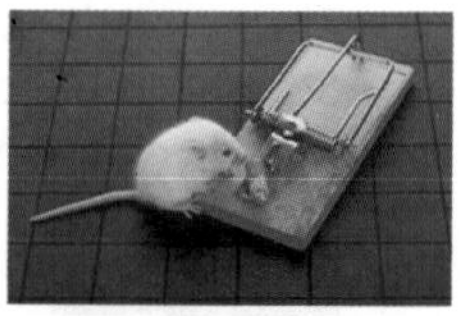

Henri knew the cheese would push him over budget — but what harm could it do?

Energy Imbalance Causes Changes in Weight

Ideally, a person should **take in** the **same amount** of energy as **they use up** — their energy budget should be **balanced**. If there's an **imbalance** in the energy budget, it will **affect** the **person's weight**:

WEIGHT GAIN

1) If energy **intake** is **higher** than energy **output**, the **excess energy** will be turned into **fat reserves** by the body, so the person will **gain weight**.
2) For example, if a person **consumes** food containing **4000 Calories** a day and carries out **activities** that burn **3000 Calories** a day, there'll be an **excess** of **1000 Calories** per day, so they'll put on weight.
3) If the energy difference is **a lot** and it's **sustained** over a **long period** of time, the person could become **obese**.

WEIGHT LOSS

1) If energy **intake** is **lower** than energy **output**, the body will have to **get** more energy from somewhere — it'll **turn** some of its **fat reserves** into energy, so the person will **lose weight**.
2) For example, if a person **consumes** food containing **2500 Calories** a day but carries out **activities** that burn **3000 Calories** a day, they will have an energy **deficit** of **500 Calories** per day, so they'll lose weight.
3) If this energy difference is **large** and is **sustained** over a **long period** of time, the person is likely to become **underweight**.

You May Have to Analyse Data on Energy Budgets and Diet

You may be asked to analyse data about **energy budgets** (input and output) in the exam. Here's an idea of what you might get:

1) The **recommended daily intake** of **Calories** is **2000** for **women** and **2500** for **men**.
2) **Different activities** use up **different amounts of Calories**, as shown in the table.
3) You can use this information to **calculate** people's **energy budgets** — you'll need to use this formula: **energy input – energy output = energy budget**

- Ranjit takes in the recommended daily intake of Calories a day (**2500**). He swims for **one hour** and does **one hour** of **gardening** each day. He also **cooks** for **an hour** each day. His **bodily functions** (e.g. breathing) use up **1500** Calories per day. So his energy budget is:
  Energy input – energy output = energy budget
  2500 – (1500 + 513 + 328 + 159) = **0**
  Ranjit's energy budget is **balanced** — he takes in as much as he uses up.
- Christina takes in **2000** Calories a day. She **walks the dog** for **an hour** every **morning** and every **night**. Her **bodily functions** use up **1200** Calories per day. So her energy budget is:
  Energy input – energy output = energy budget
  2000 – (1200 + 224 + 224) = **352 Calories**
  Christina has an **excess** of **352 Calories** per day.

Activity	Number of Calories used per hour
Cooking	159
Dog walking	224
Gardening	328
Swimming	513

You need to multiply these figures by the number of hours the activity lasts.

* CGP does not condone the stealing of traffic cones.

Diet and Energy

You Can Measure the Amount of Vitamin C in Your Food

1) You need to be able to carry out an **experiment** to find out **how much vitamin C** is in a **food sample**.
2) This can be done using a chemical called **DCPIP** — a **blue** dye that turns **colourless** in the presence of vitamin C.

Here's how you do it:

You could make up the different concentrations using a serial dilution technique — see page 101.

First you need to make a **calibration curve**. To do this you need to:

1) Make up several **vitamin C solutions** of **different, known concentrations.** Ideally, you need about **six** different solutions.
2) Use a measuring cylinder to measure out a **set volume** of **DCPIP** (at a **set concentration**) into a test tube.
3) **Add** one of the **vitamin C solutions** to the DCPIP, **drop by drop**, using a pipette.
4) Gently **shake** the test tube for a **set length of time**, timed using a stopwatch, after each drop of vitamin C solution is added.
5) When the solution turns **colourless**, **record** the **volume** (no. of drops) of vitamin C solution that has been added.
6) **Repeat** the experiment **twice more**, with the **same** solution, and take an **average** of the three readings.
7) Make sure you keep **all** the other **variables** constant during the experiment, e.g. temperature.
8) **Repeat** the above procedure with **each solution.**
9) Use the results to draw a **curve of best fit**, showing volume of vitamin C solution against its concentration — this is the **calibration curve.**

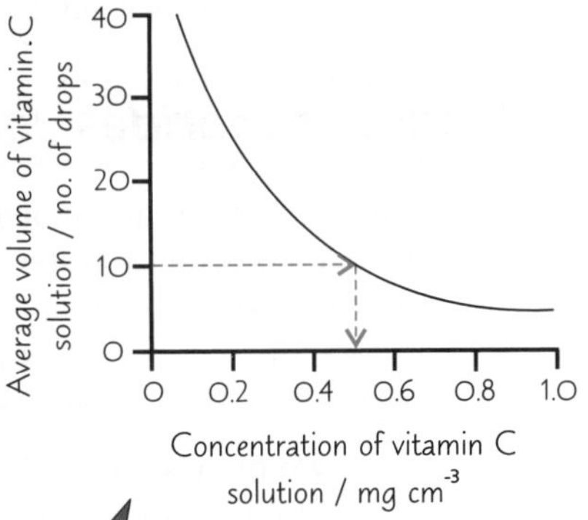

Then you can test the **unknown solution** in the same way as the known concentrations and use the calibration curve to find its concentration. E.g. 10 drops of an **unknown solution** is needed to turn DCPIP colourless. Reading **across** the calibration curve from a volume of **10 drops** shows that the concentration of vitamin C in the unknown solution is **0.5 mg cm^{-3}**.

Practice Questions

Q1 What is an energy budget?

Q2 Explain how an energy imbalance causes weight gain.

Exam Questions

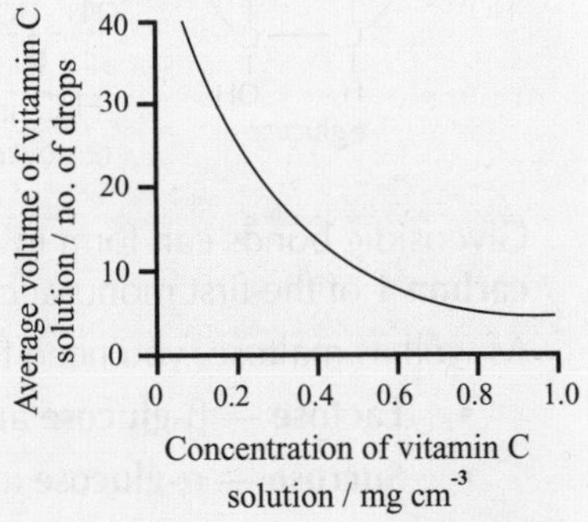

Q1 The graph on the right shows a calibration curve for vitamin C concentration.

a) 25 drops of a food sample of unknown vitamin C concentration were needed to turn DCPIP colourless.
Use the calibration curve to work out the concentration of the solution. [1 mark]

b) State three variables that should be kept constant when making a calibration curve to test an unknown solution for vitamin C concentration. [3 marks]

Q2 A woman takes in 2000 Calories a day in food. She needs 1200 Calories each day to maintain her basic bodily functions. She also swims for two hours and does two hours of gardening each day.

a) i) Use the table on page 20 to calculate her energy budget. [1 mark]

ii) Explain what short-term effect this energy budget will have on her weight. [1 mark]

b) If the woman sustained this energy budget over a long period of time, what effect would it have on her weight? [1 mark]

Eat beans to increase the amount of Calories used for bodily functions...

If you've done an hour's revision you've used up around 120 Calories (which is 90 more than you'd use just sat on your bum watching telly)... well done you — go and have a biscuit to celebrate (and even up your energy balance).

Carbohydrates

Carbohydrates are the main energy supply in living organisms. Unfortunately they look a little bit boring, but don't let that put you off. Time to learn your monosaccharides from your polysaccharides. Let the good times roll...

Carbohydrates are Made from **Monosaccharides**

1) Most carbohydrates are **large**, complex molecules (polymers) composed of **long chains** of **monosaccharides** (monomers — small basic molecular units). For example, starch is a large carbohydrate composed of long chains of glucose.
2) **Single** monosaccharides are also called carbohydrates though.
3) **Glucose** is a monosaccharide with **six carbon** atoms in each molecule.
4) There are **two types** of glucose — **alpha (α)** and **beta (β)** — but you only need to learn about alpha-glucose for this section.

α-glucose

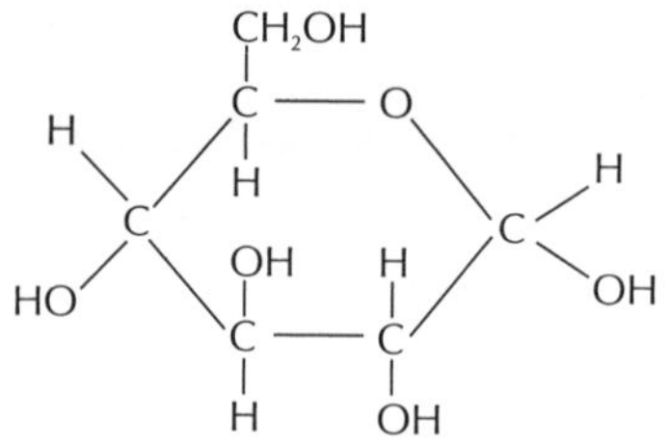

5) Glucose's **structure** is related to its **function** as the main **energy source** in animals and plants. Its structure makes it **soluble** so it can be **easily transported**, and its chemical bonds contain **lots of energy**.

Monosaccharides Join Together to Form **Disaccharides** and **Polysaccharides**

1) Monosaccharides are **joined together** by **glycosidic bonds** in a **condensation reaction** (a reaction where a molecule of **water** is **released**). A **hydrogen** atom on one monosaccharide bonds to a **hydroxyl** (OH) group on the other, releasing a molecule of water.
2) The **reverse** of this is a **hydrolysis reaction** — a molecule of water reacts with the glycosidic bond, **breaking it apart**.

'Mono' = 1, 'di' = 2, 'poly' = many and 'saccharide' = sugar.

3) When **two monosaccharides** join together, they form a **disaccharide**. Disaccharides are also **soluble** (though not as soluble as monosaccharides) and their chemical bonds store **more energy** than monosaccharides.

Two **α-glucose** molecules are joined together by a **glycosidic bond** to form **maltose**:

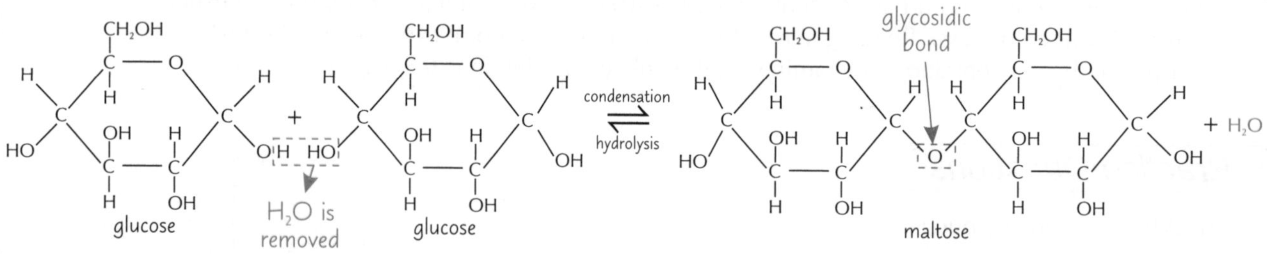

Glycosidic bonds can form in **different places** in different molecules. E.g. in **maltose**, the bonds form between the **carbon 1** of the first monosaccharide and the **carbon 4** of the second, so it's called a **1-4 glycosidic bond**.

As well as maltose, you need to know how two other disaccharides are formed:

- **Lactose** — **β-glucose** and **galactose** with a **1-4** glycosidic bond.
- **Sucrose** — **α-glucose** and **fructose** with a **1-2** glycosidic bond.

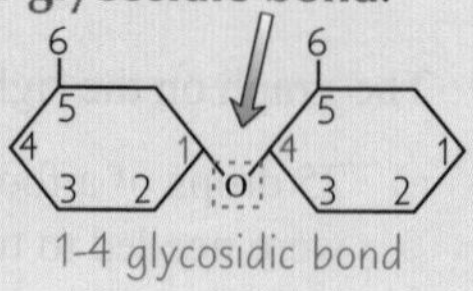

1-4 glycosidic bond

4) A **polysaccharide** is formed when **more than two monosaccharides** join together:

Lots of **α-glucose** molecules are joined together by **1-4 glycosidic bonds** to form **amylose**:

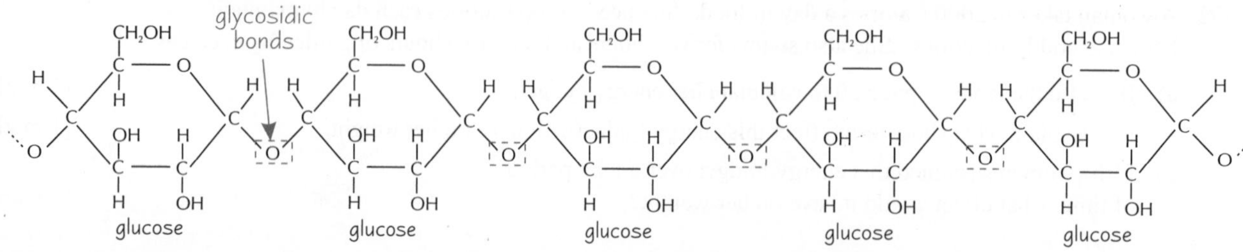

As well as amylose, you need to know how two other polysaccharides are formed:

- **Amylopectin** — **α-glucose** with **1-4 and 1-6** glycosidic bonds, with lots of **side branches** (see next page).
- **Glycogen** — **α-glucose** with **1-4 and 1-6** glycosidic bonds and **even more** side branches than amylopectin.

Carbohydrates

You Need to Learn About **Two Polysaccharides**

You need to know about the relationship between the **structure** and **function** of two polysaccharides:

1 **Starch** — the main **energy storage material** in **plants**

1) Cells get **energy** from **glucose**. Plants **store** excess glucose as **starch** (when a plant **needs more glucose** for energy it **breaks down** starch to release the glucose).
2) Starch is a mixture of **two** polysaccharides of **alpha-glucose** — **amylose** and **amylopectin**:
   - **Amylose** — a long, **unbranched chain** of glucose joined together with **1-4 glycosidic bonds**. The angles of the glycosidic bonds give it a **coiled structure**, almost like a cylinder. This makes it **compact**, so it's really **good for storage** because you can **fit more in** to a small space.
   - **Amylopectin** — a long, **branched chain** of glucose that contains **1-4 and 1-6 glycosidic bonds**. Its **side branches** allow the **enzymes** that break down the molecule to get at the **glycosidic bonds easily**. This means that the glucose can be **released quickly**.
3) Starch is also **insoluble** in water, so it **doesn't** cause water to enter cells by **osmosis** (see p. 31), which would make them swell. This makes it good for **storage**.

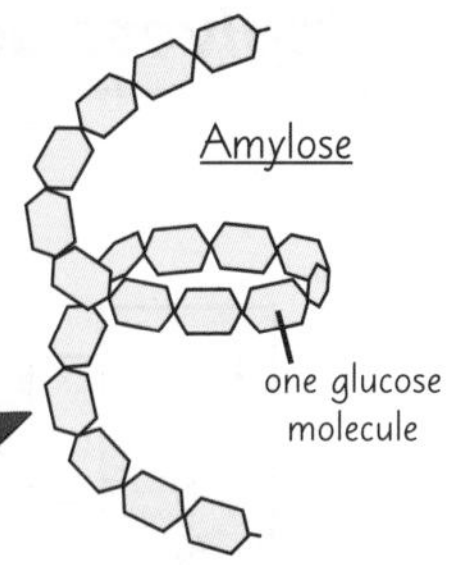

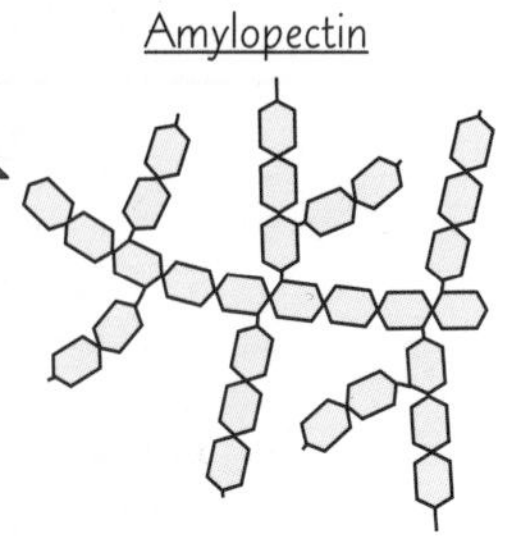

2 **Glycogen** — the main **energy storage material** in **animals**

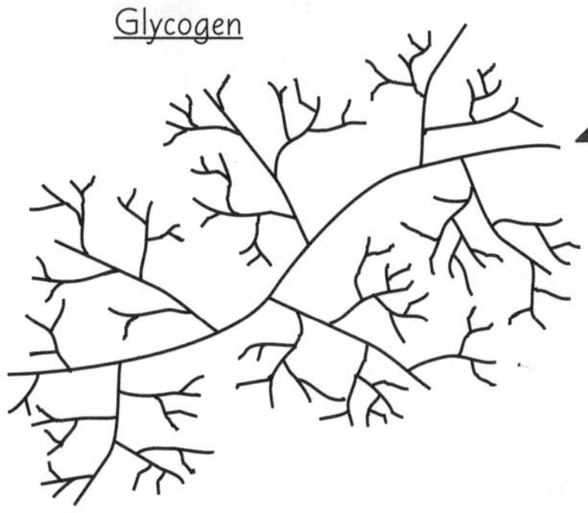

1) Animal cells get **energy** from **glucose** too. But animals **store** excess glucose as **glycogen** — another polysaccharide of **alpha-glucose**.
2) Its structure is very similar to amylopectin (it has **1-4 and 1-6 glycosidic bonds**), except that it has **loads more side branches** coming off it. Loads of branches means that stored glucose can be **released quickly**, which is **important for energy release** in animals.
3) It's also a very **compact** molecule, so it's good for storage.
4) Like starch, glycogen's also **insoluble** in water, so it doesn't cause cells to swell by osmosis.
5) It's a **large molecule**, so it can store **lots of energy**.

Practice Questions

Q1 What type of bonds hold monosaccharide molecules together in a polysaccharide?

Q2 Name the two monosaccharides that join together to form lactose.

Q3 What is the function of glycogen?

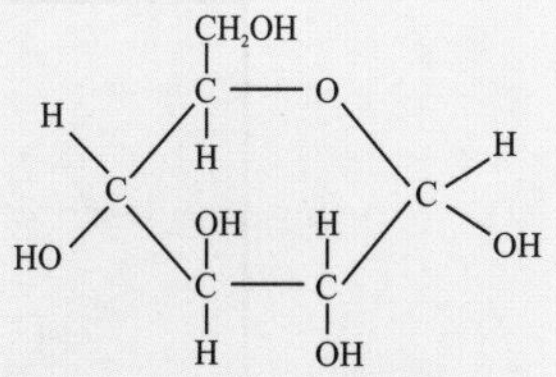

Exam Questions

Q1 The diagram above shows an α-glucose molecule. Two of these molecules can be joined together to form maltose.

a) Draw a diagram to show the products of this reaction. [2 marks]

b) Explain how maltose molecules are broken down. [1 mark]

Q2 Starch is made of two polysaccharides of alpha-glucose — amylose and amylopectin. Explain how the structure of starch relates to its function as an energy storage material in plants. [3 marks]

*Mmmmm, starch... Tasty, tasty chips and beans... *dribble*. Ahem, sorry.*

Remember that condensation and hydrolysis reactions are the reverse of each other. You need to learn how disaccharides and polysaccharides are formed and broken down by these reactions. And don't forget that starch is composed of two different polysaccharides — amylose and amylopectin (which is really similar to glycogen). Phew.

Lipids and Cardiovascular Disease

Right, that's carbohydrates covered. But there's another important kind of molecule you need to know about, and that's lipids, or 'fatty oily things' to you and me. First up, some fatty acid fun, then on to how a certain type of lipid called cholesterol can affect your cardiovascular health. Doesn't sound too thrilling, I know, but just go with it...

Triglycerides are a Kind of Lipid

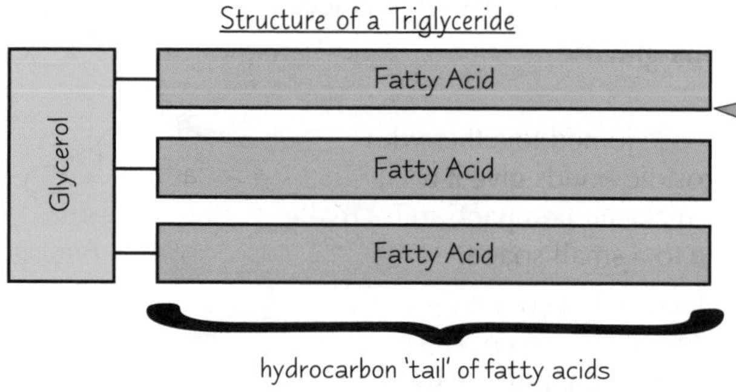

1) There are loads of kinds of **lipid**, but luckily, you only need to know about **triglycerides** (fats).
2) A triglyceride is made of **one** molecule of **glycerol** with **three fatty acids** attached to it.
3) Fatty acid molecules have long tails made of **hydrocarbons** (carbon chains with hydrogen atoms branching off).
4) The tails are **hydrophobic** (water-repelling).
5) These tails make lipids **insoluble** in water.
6) All **fatty acids** consist of the same basic structure, but the **hydrocarbon tail varies**. The tail is shown in the diagram with the letter **R**.

Contrary to popular belief, cows aren't hydrophobic.

Triglycerides are Formed by Condensation Reactions

1) Like carbohydrates, triglycerides are formed by **condensation reactions** and broken up by **hydrolysis reactions**.
2) Three **fatty acids** and a single **glycerol molecule** are joined together by **ester bonds**.
3) A **hydrogen** atom on the glycerol molecule bonds to a **hydroxyl** (OH) group on the fatty acid, **releasing** a molecule of **water**.
4) The **reverse** happens in **hydrolysis** — a molecule of water is added to **each ester bond** to break it apart, and the triglyceride **splits up** into three fatty acids and one glycerol molecule.

Each of the fatty acids in a triglyceride is attached to the glycerol molecule by an ester bond.

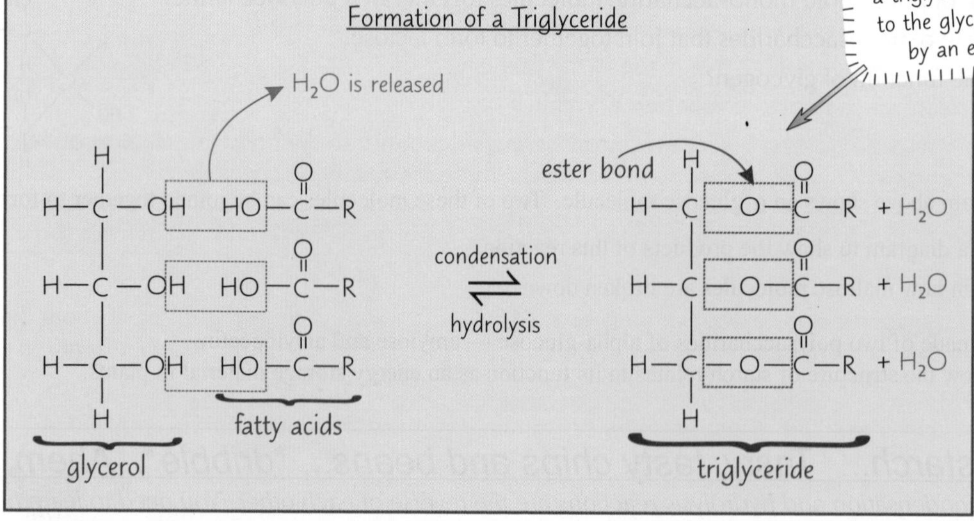

Lipids and Cardiovascular Disease

*Lipids can be **Saturated** or **Unsaturated***

1) There are two types of lipids — **saturated** lipids and **unsaturated** lipids.
2) **Saturated** lipids are mainly found in **animal fats** (e.g. butter) and **unsaturated** lipids are mostly found in **plants** (e.g. olive oil).
3) Unsaturated lipids **melt at lower temperatures** than saturated ones. That's why margarine's easier to spread than butter straight out of the fridge.
4) The difference between these two types of lipids is their **hydrocarbon tails**.

Saturated

Saturated lipids **don't** have any **double bonds** between the **carbon atoms** in their hydrocarbon tails — every carbon is attached to at least two **hydrogen** atoms. The lipid is 'saturated' with hydrogen.

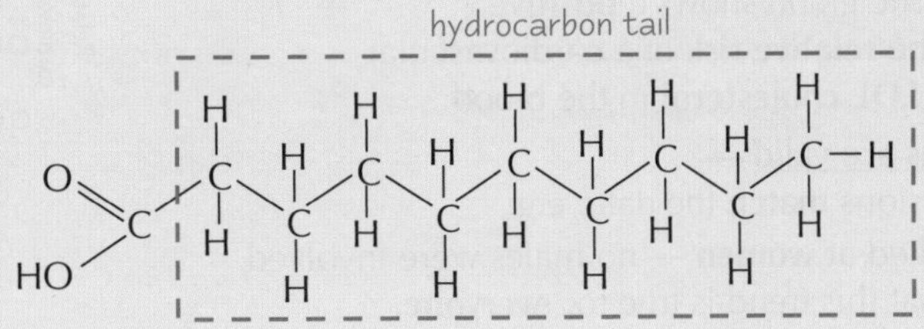

Unsaturated

Unsaturated lipids **do** have **double bonds** between the **carbon atoms** in their hydrocarbon tails. These double bonds cause the chain to kink. If they have **two or more** of them, the lipid is called **polyunsaturated**.

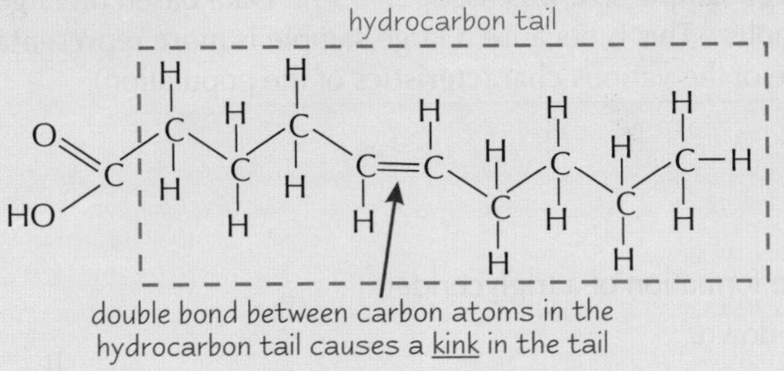

Bruce was pretty sure his tail contained double bonds.

5) A diet high in **saturated fat** increases your risk of developing **CVD** (cardiovascular disease) because it increases your **blood cholesterol level** — see below.

See pages 12-15 for more on CVD.

High Blood Cholesterol Increases the Risk of CVD

1) **Cholesterol** is a type of **lipid** that is made in the body.
2) Some is **needed** for the body to **function normally**.
3) Cholesterol needs to be attached to **protein** to be moved around, so the body forms **lipoproteins** — substances composed of both **protein** and **lipid**. There are **two types** of lipoprotein:

HIGH DENSITY LIPOPROTEINS (HDLs)

1) They are **mainly protein**.
2) They transport **cholesterol** from **body tissues** to the **liver** where it's **recycled** or **excreted**.
3) Their function is to **reduce total blood cholesterol** when the level is **too high**.

LOW DENSITY LIPOPROTEINS (LDLs)

1) They are **mainly lipid**.
2) They transport cholesterol from the **liver** to the **blood**, where it circulates until needed by cells.
3) Their function is to **increase total blood cholesterol** when the level is **too low**.

4) **High total blood cholesterol level** (the level of HDL, LDL and other cholesterol) and **high LDL level** have both been linked to an **increased risk** of **CVD**.
5) As you saw on page 14, this is because an **increased cholesterol level** is thought to increase **atheroma formation**.

Lipids and Cardiovascular Disease

You May Have to **Interpret** Data on the **Link** Between **Cholesterol** and **CVD**

Take a look at the following example of the sort of study you might see in your **exam**:

Example: The graph shows the results of a study involving **27 939 American women.** The **LDL cholesterol level** was **measured** for each woman. These women were then **followed** for an average of **8 years** and the **occurrence** of **cardiovascular events** (e.g. heart attack, surgery on coronary arteries) or **death** from cardiovascular diseases was **recorded.** The **relative risk** of a cardiovascular event, **adjusted** for **other factors** that can affect cardiovascular disease, was then calculated.

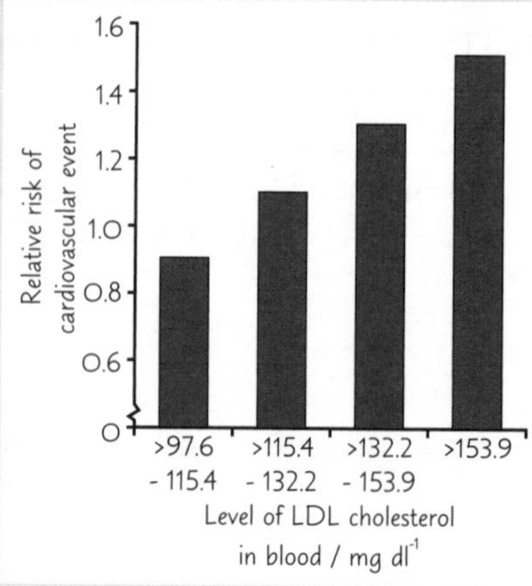

Here are some of the things you might be asked to do:

1) <u>**Describe the data**</u> — The **relative risk** of a cardiovascular event **increases** as the level of **LDL cholesterol** in the blood **increases.**
2) <u>**Draw conclusions**</u> — The graph shows a **positive correlation** between the **relative risk** of a cardiovascular event and the level of **LDL cholesterol** in the blood.
3) <u>**Check any conclusions are valid**</u> — Make sure any conclusions **match** the data, e.g.
   - This data only looked at **women** — no males were involved, so you can't say that this trend is true for **everyone.**
   - You can't say that a high LDL cholesterol level is **correlated with** an increased risk of **heart attacks**, because the data shows **all** first cardiovascular events, including surgery on coronary arteries.
   - Also, you can't conclude that a high LDL cholesterol level **caused** the increased relative risk of a cardiovascular event — there may be other reasons for the trend.
4) <u>**Other things to think about**</u> — A **large sample size** was used (27 939). Data based on large samples is **better** than data based on small samples. This is because a large sample is **more representative** of the whole population (i.e. it shares more of the various **characteristics** of the population).

There's more on correlation and cause on page 108.

Practice Questions

Q1 What sort of reaction occurs during the formation of a triglyceride?

Q2 Describe how triglycerides are broken down.

Q3 What type of lipid is found in olive oil?

Q4 What is a polyunsaturated lipid?

Q5 What is a lipoprotein?

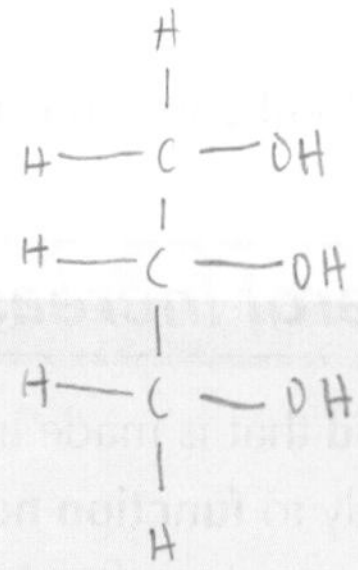

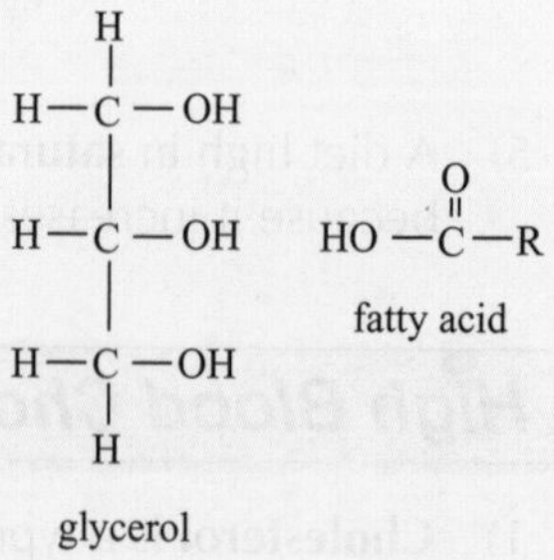

Exam Questions

Q1 Triglycerides are formed from glycerol and fatty acid molecules. These molecules are shown in the diagrams on the right.

a) Draw a diagram to show the structure of a triglyceride. [1 mark]

b) What sort of bonds are formed between these molecules in a triglyceride? [1 mark]

Q2 Explain the difference in structure between a saturated lipid and an unsaturated lipid. [2 marks]

Q3 a) Describe the differences in structure and function between high density lipoproteins and low density lipoproteins. [3 marks]

b) Low density lipoproteins are sometimes referred to as 'bad cholesterol'. Explain why low density lipoproteins are sometimes referred to in this way. [1 mark]

Hydrocarbon tails, unsaturated lipids... Whatever happened to plain old lard?

You don't get far in life without extensive lard knowledge, so learn all the details on these pages good and proper. Once you've got your HDLs sorted from your LDLs, make sure you know what to look for in data about the effect of cholesterol. You'll need to check if the conclusions are valid by going over the methods used with a fine-toothed comb.

Reducing Risk Factors of CVD

As you saw on the last couple of pages, and back on page 14, there are lots of potential risk factors for developing cardiovascular disease (CVD). Chin up though — there are some changes you can make to your lifestyle to reduce your risk of developing CVD...

Lifestyle Advice to Reduce the Risk of CVD is Based on Scientific Research

There've been loads of **scientific studies** carried out to **identify risk factors** (see page 14) for CVD. The **results** from these scientific studies are published in **scientific journals**. **Government organisations** (like the **NHS**) and the **media** report the findings to the **general public**. People can use this information to **make choices** about their **lifestyle**, so they can **reduce** their chance of developing CVD.

EXAMPLE: DIET

1) Scientific research has linked a **diet high in saturated fat** (see page 25) to an **increased risk** of CVD.
   - This information can be used to **educate people** about the risk of **certain diets** and to encourage them to **reduce** their saturated fat intake.
   - The **Food Standards Agency** encourages **food manufacturers** to label their products to show the amount of **saturated fat** in them, so people can make an **informed choice** about what they eat.
2) Scientific studies have also shown that **obese** people are **more likely** to develop CVD. **Obesity indicators** such as **waist-to-hip ratio** or **BMI (body mass index)** can be used to assess if people are **overweight** or **obese**.

Waist-to-hip ratio is calculated using this formula:

$$\text{Waist-to-hip ratio} = \frac{\text{waist (cm)}}{\text{hips (cm)}}$$

BMI is calculated using this formula:

$$\text{BMI} = \frac{\text{body mass (kg)}}{\text{height}^2\ (\text{m}^2)}$$

A 'normal' BMI for adults is between 18 and 25.

The results of these obesity indicators are compared to 'normal' values in a **published data table**. For example, if a male has a waist-to-hip ratio of more than 1.0, he is carrying too much weight around his abdomen. If someone is overweight or obese, then that person can make **choices** to **reduce** their **weight** and reduce their **risk of CVD** — e.g. they may go on a low-calorie **diet** or **increase** their **activity level**. These obesity indicators can then be used to **monitor** the **effects** any **changes in lifestyle** have on the person's weight.

Example:
Calculate the BMI of a person who weighs 63 kg and is 1.7 m tall.

$$\text{BMI} = \frac{\text{body mass (kg)}}{\text{height}^2\ (\text{m}^2)}$$
$$= 63 \div 1.7^2 = \mathbf{21.8\ kg\ m^{-2}}$$

EXAMPLE: SMOKING

1) Scientific research has linked **smoking** to an **increased risk** of CVD.
2) This research has led to **TV adverts** and **warnings** on **cigarette packets** about the risks of smoking. The NHS encourages people to give up by giving **free advice** and **prescribing nicotine patches**.
3) All of this encourages people to **stop** smoking and so reduce their risk of CVD.

EXAMPLE: EXERCISE

1) Scientific research has linked **inactivity** to an **increased risk** of CVD.
2) This research has led to campaigns that encourage people to **exercise more frequently** to reduce their risk of CVD.

Practice Questions

Q1 Why are obesity indicators useful?

Q2 Give two examples of how people can be encouraged to stop smoking.

Exam Question

$$\text{Waist-to-hip ratio} = \frac{\text{waist (cm)}}{\text{hips (cm)}}$$

$$\text{BMI} = \frac{\text{body mass (kg)}}{\text{height}^2\ (\text{m}^2)}$$

Q1 A person's hip measurement is 95 cm and their waist measurement is 76 cm. They are 1.68 m tall and they have a BMI of 18.9 kg m^{-2}.

a) Use the formula shown above to calculate the person's waist-to-hip ratio. 76/95 [1 mark]

b) Use the BMI formula shown above to calculate the person's body mass. [2 marks]

Revise more to decrease the risk of exam failure...

There you go — some free lifestyle advice for you. In fact, I'd pay attention to all the lifestyle advice on this page. Taking it on board will be good for your health and good for your grades... It doesn't get much better than that.

Gas Exchange

All organisms need to exchange gases with their environment. Gas exchange involves diffusion...

Diffusion is the Passive Movement of Particles

1) Diffusion is the net movement of particles (molecules or ions) from an area of **higher concentration** to an area of **lower concentration.**
2) Molecules will diffuse **both ways**, but the **net movement** will be to the area of **lower concentration.** This continues until particles are **evenly distributed** throughout the liquid or gas.
3) The **concentration gradient** is the path from an area of higher concentration to an area of lower concentration. Particles diffuse **down** a concentration gradient.
4) Diffusion is a **passive process** — **no energy** is needed for it to happen.

Gas Exchange Surfaces are Adapted for Efficient Diffusion

All living organisms **respire** — they **take in oxygen** and **give out carbon dioxide**. These gases **diffuse** across a surface called the **gas exchange surface**.

Most gas exchange surfaces have two things in common:
1) They give gas exchange organs (like the lungs) a **large surface area to volume ratio** — see below.
2) They're **thin** (often just one layer of epithelial cells) — this provides a **short diffusion pathway** across the gas exchange surface.

The organism also maintains a **steep concentration gradient** of gases across the exchange surface.

All these features **increase the rate of diffusion.**

The rate of diffusion also increases with temperature because the molecules have more kinetic energy — they move faster.

Surface Area to Volume Ratios Always Affect Exchange

1) **Large objects** have **smaller surface area to volume ratios** than **small objects**. For example:
2) The **smaller** the surface area to volume ratio (sa:vol) the **slower** the **rate of exchange**. E.g. a substance would **diffuse more slowly** out of the **big cube** than the **small cube**. **Gas exchange organs** need a **large sa:vol** to exchange gases **quickly**.

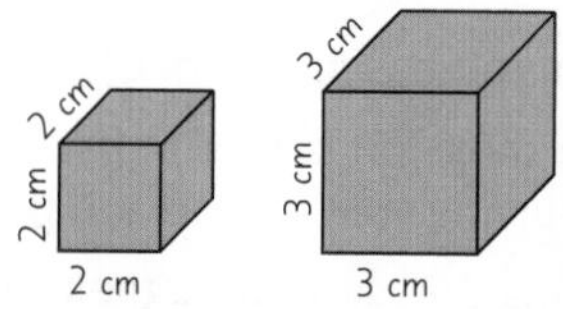

	Small cube	Big cube
Surface area (cm^2)	2 x 2 x 6 = 24	3 x 3 x 6 = 54
Volume (cm^3)	2 x 2 x 2 = 8	3 x 3 x 3 = 27
Surface area to volume ratio	24 : 8 = 3 : 1	54 : 27 = 2 : 1

The Lungs are Adapted for Efficient Gaseous Exchange

In mammals, the gas exchange surface is the **alveolar epithelium** in the **lungs**:

1) **Oxygen** diffuses **out of** the alveoli, across the **alveolar epithelium** (a layer of thin, flat cells) and the **capillary endothelium** (a type of epithelium that forms the capillary wall), and into the **blood.**
2) **Carbon dioxide** diffuses **into** the alveoli from the blood and is **breathed out.**

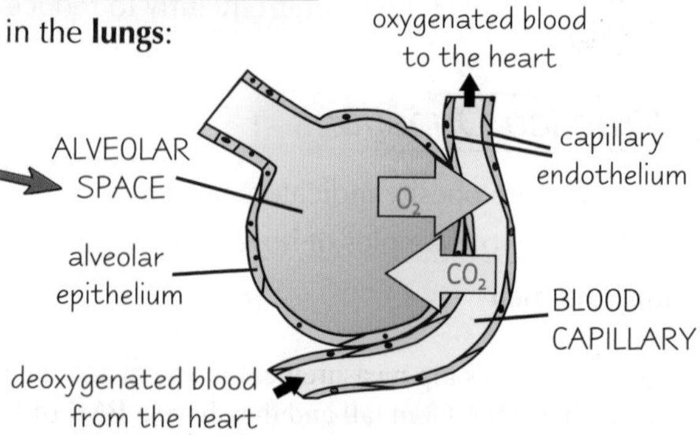

The mammalian lungs have the following features, which all help to **increase** the **rate** of **gas exchange**:

1) Having **lots of alveoli** means there is a **large surface area** for diffusion to occur across.
2) The **alveolar epithelium** and **capillary endothelium** are each only **one cell thick**, giving a **short diffusion pathway.**
3) All the alveoli have a **good blood supply** from capillaries — they constantly **take away oxygen** and **bring more carbon dioxide**, maintaining the **concentration gradient.**
4) **Breathing in and out** refreshes the air in the alveoli, keeping the **concentration gradients** high.

Gas Exchange

Fick's Law Describes the *Rate of Diffusion*

Fick's Law relates the rate of diffusion to the **concentration gradient**, the **surface area** and the **thickness** of the **exchange surface**. It states that:

'∝' means 'is proportional to'.

$$\text{rate of diffusion} \propto \frac{\text{area of diffusion surface} \times \text{difference in concentration}}{\text{thickness of diffusion surface}}$$

The 'proportional to' bit means that the **rate of diffusion** will **double** if:

- the **surface area** or the **difference in concentration** **doubles**, OR
- the **thickness** of the surface **halves**.

You can write Fick's Law as an **equation**, which allows you to **calculate** the **rate of diffusion**. For example:

A fast rate of diffusion — not good in a swimming pool.

$$\text{Rate} = P \times A \times \frac{(C_1 - C_2)}{T}$$

Where: P = permeability constant
A = surface area
$(C_1 - C_2)$ = difference in concentration
T = thickness of the exchange surface

The units need to be the same throughout the equation. E.g. if the thickness is given in μm then the area should be in μm^2.

Example:

A section of alveolar epithelium has a **surface area** of **2.2 μm^2** and is **1.0 μm thick**. The **permeability constant** of the alveolar epithelium for oxygen is **0.012 s^{-1}**. The **concentration** of oxygen on one side of the epithelium (C_1) is **2.3×10^{-16} mol μm^{-3}** and the concentration of oxygen on the other side (C_2) is **9.0×10^{-17} mol μm^{-3}**. To calculate the **rate of diffusion of oxygen** across the alveolar epithelium, you need to put these values into the equation above:

$$\text{Rate of diffusion} = 0.012\ s^{-1} \times 2.2\ \mu m^2 \times \frac{(2.3 \times 10^{-16}\ \text{mol}\ \mu m^{-3} - 9.0 \times 10^{-17}\ \text{mol}\ \mu m^{-3})}{1.0\ \mu m}$$

$$= \mathbf{3.7 \times 10^{-18}\ mol\ \mu m^{-2}\ s^{-1}}$$

There are **different ways** of writing Fick's Law as an equation. **Don't worry** though — no matter what equation you're given in the exam, you'll also be given **all the information you need** to **use it**. Then it's just a case of popping the numbers into their correct places in the equation and running it all through your calculator.

Practice Questions

Q1 Diffusion is a passive process. What does this mean?

Q2 How does a thin gas exchange surface help the rate of diffusion?

Q3 What is Fick's Law?

Q4 According to Fick's Law, what will happen to the rate of diffusion if the surface area of a gas exchange surface is doubled?

Exam Questions

Q1 Efficient gas exchange surfaces have the following characteristics:
- large surface area
- short diffusion pathway
- high concentration gradient

Explain how these characteristics apply to human lungs. [4 marks]

Q2 Emphysema is a lung disease that destroys alveoli. Explain why a patient suffering from emphysema would have a decreased rate of gas exchange in their lungs. [2 marks]

I'll give you my gas, if you give me yours...

So gas exchange in mammals happens across the alveolar epithelium. Remember, like all gas exchange surfaces, it's really thin and has a large surface area (thanks to there being loads of alveoli). Both of these things, along with a high concentration gradient, help to keep up a fast rate of gas exchange — making sure you get plenty of oxygen for revision.

Cell Membranes

The cell membrane is basically the cell boundary. Small molecules, like oxygen and carbon dioxide, are able to cross this boundary by diffusion. Other substances enter and leave the cell in different ways. To understand how substances get across the cell membrane, you have to know its structure. Helpfully, it's all explained below...

Cell Membranes have a 'Fluid Mosaic' Structure

The **structure** of all membranes is basically the same. They're composed of **lipids** (mainly **phospholipids** — a type of lipid with a phosphate group attached to it), **proteins** and **carbohydrates** (usually attached to proteins or lipids).

Cell membranes are also called plasma membranes.

1) In 1972, the **fluid mosaic model** was suggested to describe the **arrangement** of **molecules** in the membrane.
2) In the model, **phospholipid molecules** form a continuous, double layer (**bilayer**) — see below. This bilayer is **'fluid'** because the phospholipids are **constantly moving**.

Phospholipid molecules have a 'head' and a 'tail'.

- The **head** contains the **phosphate group**. It's **hydrophilic** — it **attracts water**.
- The **tail** is made of two **fatty acids**. It's **hydrophobic** — it **repels water**.
- Because of this, the molecules automatically **arrange** themselves into a **bilayer** — the **hydrophilic heads face out** towards the water on either side of the membrane. The **hydrophobic tails** are on the **inside**, making the centre of the bilayer **hydrophobic**. This means that the membrane doesn't allow water-soluble substances (like ions) through it.

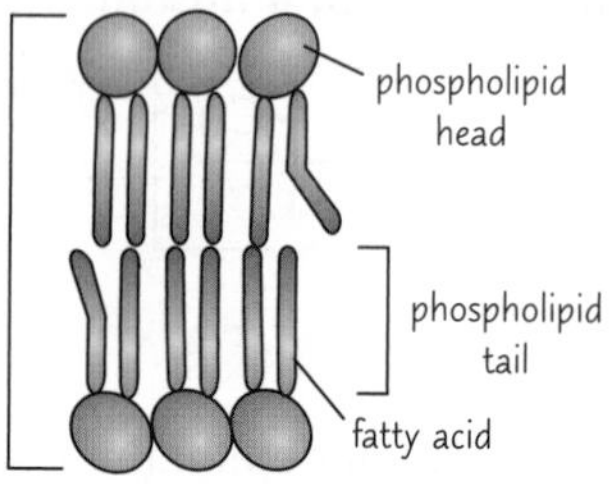

3) **Protein molecules** are scattered through the bilayer, like tiles in a **mosaic**. Because the phospholipid bilayer is fluid, the proteins can **move around** within it.
4) Some **proteins** have a **polysaccharide** (carbohydrate) **chain** attached — these are called **glycoproteins**.
5) Some **lipids** also have a **polysaccharide chain** attached — these are called **glycolipids**.
6) **Cholesterol** (a type of lipid) is also present in the membrane. It fits **in between** the **phospholipids**, forming **bonds** with them. This makes the membrane more **rigid**.

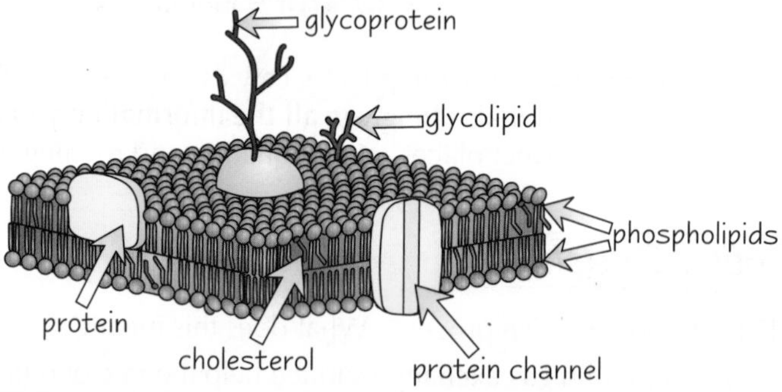

The membrane is **partially permeable** — **small molecules** can move through **gaps** between the **phospholipids**, but **large molecules** and **ions** can only pass through special **membrane proteins** called **channel proteins** and **carrier proteins** (see page 32).

The Fluid Mosaic Model is Based on Scientific Evidence

1) Before the 1970s, most scientists believed cell membranes were composed of a **phospholipid layer** between **two continuous layers of proteins**. This was because **electron microscope** (EM) **images** appeared to show **three layers** in a cell membrane.
2) In time, **improved** EM techniques showed a **bilayer** of phospholipids, and **new methods** for **analysing proteins** showed that they were **randomly distributed** in cell membranes, not in a continuous layer.
3) Scientists also carried out experiments that proved the cell membrane is **fluid** — e.g. they fused a **mouse cell** with a **human cell**, and found that the mouse and human **membrane proteins** completely **intermixed** throughout the cell membrane — the proteins could only **mix** like this if the membrane was fluid.
4) All of this **new evidence** led to the **fluid mosaic model**.

Electron microscopes show more detail than light microscopes — see page 62.

Cell Membranes and Osmosis

You already know that some small molecules can diffuse across cell membranes. Well, water can diffuse across cell membranes too — this is called osmosis.

Osmosis is the Diffusion of Water Molecules

1) Osmosis is the **diffusion** of free **water molecules** across a **partially permeable membrane**, (e.g. a cell membrane) from an area of **higher concentration** of water molecules to an area of **lower concentration** of water molecules.
2) Water molecules will diffuse **both ways** through the membrane, but the **net movement** will be to the side with the **lower concentration** of water molecules.

Partially permeable membranes can be useful at sea.

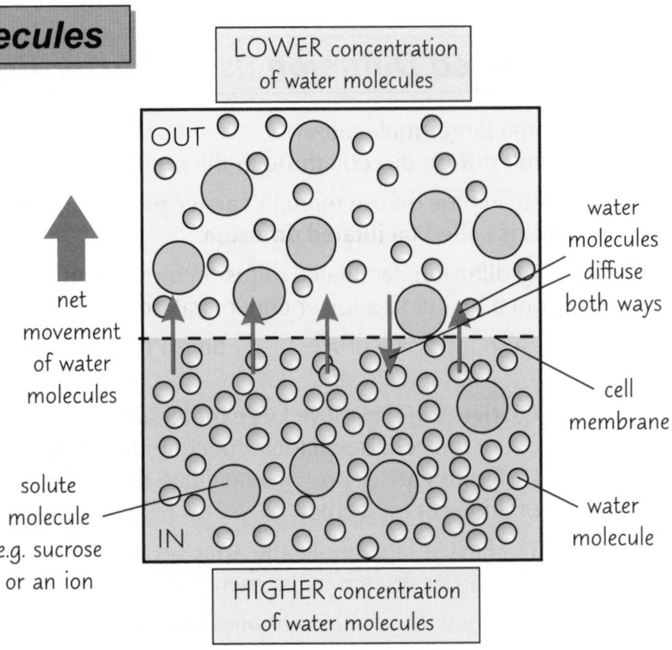

A higher number of solute (e.g. sucrose) molecules means a lower concentration of water molecules and vice versa.

Practice Questions

Q1 How are phospholipids arranged in a cell membrane?

Q2 The membrane of a cell can be described as 'partially permeable'. What does this mean?

Q3 What is osmosis?

Exam Questions

Q1 Which of the following statements about the cell membrane is true?

A The cell membrane is mainly composed of glycolipids.

B The molecules that make up the cell membrane are constantly moving.

C Molecules can only pass through the cell membrane via channel proteins.

D Cholesterol makes the cell membrane less rigid. [1 mark]

Q2 Pieces of potato of equal mass were put into different concentrations of sucrose solution for three days. The difference in mass for each is recorded in the table on the right.

Concentration of sucrose / %	1	2	3	4
Mass difference / g	0.4	0.2	0	– 0.2

a) Explain why the pieces of potato in 1% and 2% sucrose solutions gained mass. [3 marks]

b) Give a reason why the mass of the piece of potato in 3% sucrose solution stayed the same. [1 mark]

c) What would you expect the mass difference for a potato in a 5% solution to be? Explain your answer. [2 marks]

Fluid Mosaic Model — think I saw one being sold at a craft fair...

Scientists are a bit annoying — they keep changing their minds about things like the structure of the cell membrane. But they don't do it on a whim — they need new experimental data that proves something isn't how they thought it was.

Transport Across the Cell Membrane

Like diffusion (and osmosis), facilitated diffusion is a passive transport process.
There's also an active transport process involving energy, which is imaginatively named 'active transport'.
Facilitated diffusion and active transport are actually quite similar — they both involve proteins.

Facilitated Diffusion uses Carrier Proteins and Channel Proteins

1) Some **larger molecules** (e.g. amino acids, glucose), and **charged particles** (e.g. ions) **don't diffuse directly through** the phospholipid bilayer of the cell membrane.
2) Instead they diffuse through **carrier proteins** or **channel proteins** in the cell membrane — this is called **facilitated diffusion**.
3) Like diffusion, facilitated diffusion moves particles **down** a **concentration gradient**, from a higher to a lower concentration.
4) It's also a passive process — it **doesn't** use **energy**.

Andy needed all his concentration for this particular gradient...

Carrier proteins move **large molecules** into or out of the cell, down their concentration gradient. **Different carrier proteins** facilitate the diffusion of **different molecules.**

1) First, a large molecule **attaches** to a carrier protein in the membrane.
2) Then, the protein **changes shape**.
3) This **releases** the molecule on the **opposite side** of the membrane.

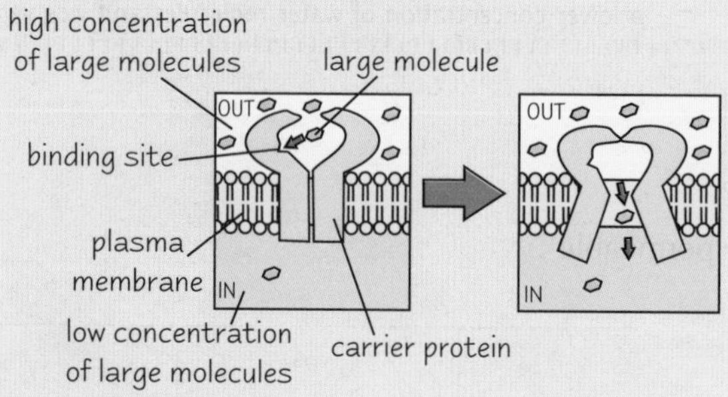

Channel proteins form **pores** in the membrane for **charged particles** to diffuse through (down their concentration gradient). **Different channel proteins** facilitate the diffusion of **different charged particles.**

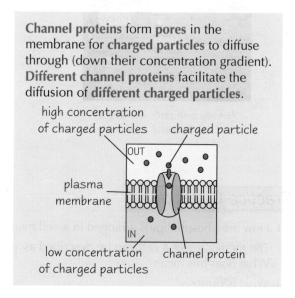

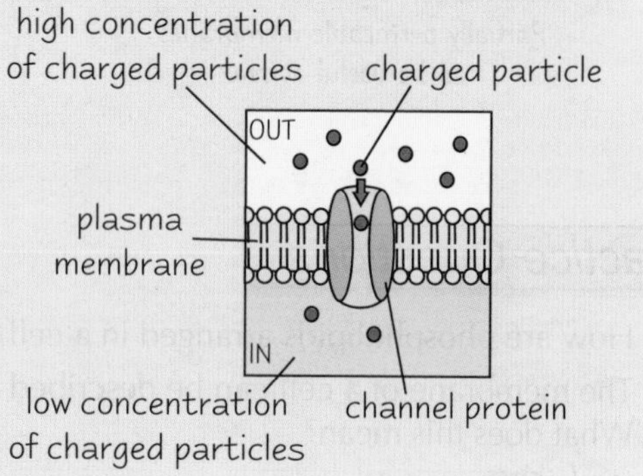

Active Transport Moves Substances Against a Concentration Gradient

Active transport uses **energy** to move **molecules** and **ions** across plasma membranes, **against** a **concentration gradient**. This process involves **carrier proteins**.

Unlike facilitated diffusion, active transport doesn't use channel proteins.

1) The process is pretty similar to facilitated diffusion — a molecule **attaches** to the carrier protein, the protein **changes shape** and this moves the molecule **across** the membrane, **releasing it** on the other side.
2) The only difference is that **energy** is used — this energy comes from **ATP**.
   - ATP is produced by **respiration**.
   - It acts as an **immediate** source of **energy** in the cell.
   - When ATP is **hydrolysed** (broken down) in the cell, energy is **released**. This energy is used to move the molecule against its concentration gradient.

This diagram shows the active transport of **calcium ions** (Ca^{2+}).

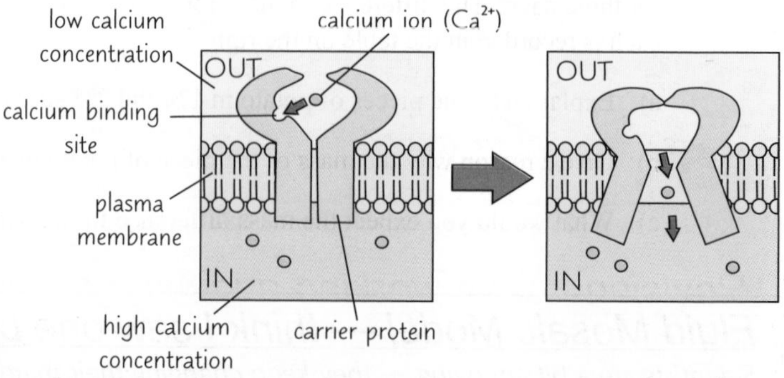

Transport Across the Cell Membrane

Cells can Take in Substances by Endocytosis

1) Some molecules are way too **large** to be taken into a cell by carrier proteins, e.g. proteins, lipids and some carbohydrates.
2) Instead a cell can **surround** a substance with a **section** of its **cell membrane**.
3) The membrane then **pinches off** to form a **vesicle** inside the cell containing the **ingested substance** — this is **endocytosis**.
4) Some cells also take in much **larger objects** by endocytosis — for example, some **white blood cells** (called phagocytes) use endocytosis to take in things like **microorganisms** and **dead cells** so that they can destroy them.
5) Like active transport, (see previous page), this process also uses **ATP** for **energy**.

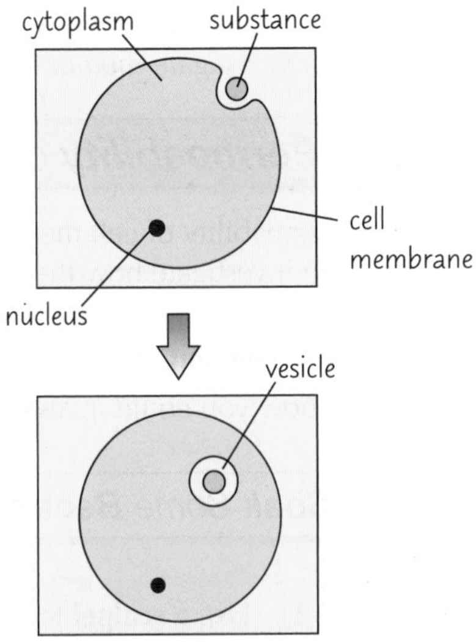

Cells can Secrete Substances by Exocytosis

1) Some substances **produced** by the cell (e.g. **digestive enzymes, hormones, lipids**) need to be **released** from the cell — this is done by **exocytosis**.
2) **Vesicles** containing these substances **pinch off** from the sacs of the **Golgi apparatus** (a structure that processes new proteins and lipids — see p. 59) and **move towards** the cell membrane.
3) The vesicles **fuse** with the **cell membrane** and **release** their contents **outside** the cell.
4) Some substances (like membrane proteins) **aren't** released outside the cell — instead they are **inserted** straight into the cell membrane.
5) Exocytosis uses **ATP** as an **energy source**.

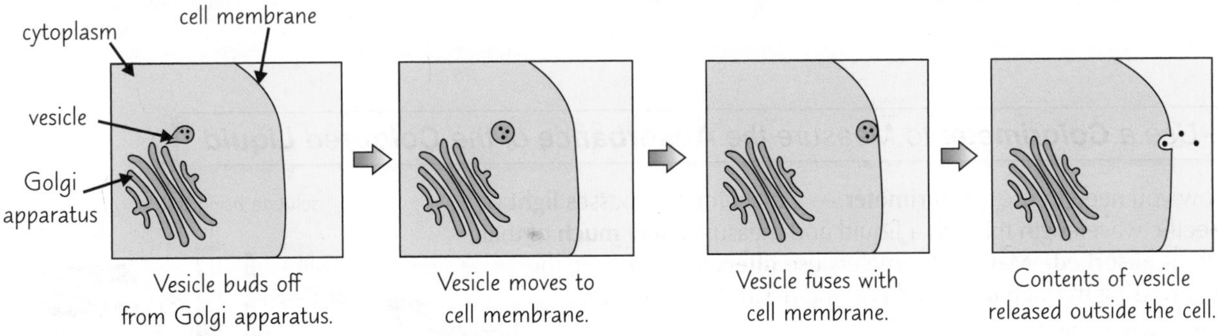

Practice Questions

Q1 When would facilitated diffusion take place rather than simple diffusion?

Q2 What is active transport?

Q3 Which molecule provides the energy for active transport?

Exam Questions

Q1 Describe the role of membrane proteins in facilitated diffusion. [3 marks]

Q2 Explain the difference between endocytosis and exocytosis. [4 marks]

Revision — like working against a concentration gradient...

Wouldn't it be great if you could revise by endocytosis — you could just stick this book on your head and your brain would slowly surround it and take it in... actually when I put it like that it sounds a bit gross. Maybe just stick to the good old 'closing the book and scribbling down the diagrams till you know them off by heart' method.

Investigating Cell Membrane Structure

You might remember from p. 30 that the cell membrane is partially permeable — it allows some molecules through it but not others. But changes in the environment can affect the structure of the membrane, and so how permeable it is. You can investigate membrane permeability using beetroot — a seriously under-appreciated vegetable if you ask me.

*The **Permeability** of the **Cell Membrane** can be **Investigated** in the **Lab***

The permeability of cell membranes is affected by **different conditions**, e.g. **temperature** and **alcohol concentration**. You can investigate how these things affect permeability by doing an experiment using **beetroot**.

Beetroot cells contain a **coloured pigment** that **leaks out** — the **higher** the **permeability** of the membrane, the **more pigment** leaks out of the cell.

Here's how you could investigate how **temperature** affects **beetroot membrane permeability**:

*1) **Soak** Some **Beetroot Cubes** in **Water** at **Different Temperatures***

1) Use a **scalpel** to carefully cut five **equal sized** pieces of beetroot. (Make sure you do your cutting on a **cutting board**.) **Rinse** the pieces to remove any pigment released during cutting.
2) Use a **measuring cylinder** or **pipette** to measure **5 cm³ of water** into five different test tubes.
3) Place the test tubes into **water baths** at **different temperatures**, e.g. 10 °C, 20 °C, 30 °C, 40 °C, 50 °C, for around 5 minutes to allow the water to reach the desired temperature.
4) Place the five pieces of beetroot into the five different **test tubes**, for the **same length of time** (measured using a **stopwatch**).
5) **Remove** the pieces of beetroot from the tubes, leaving just the **coloured liquid**.

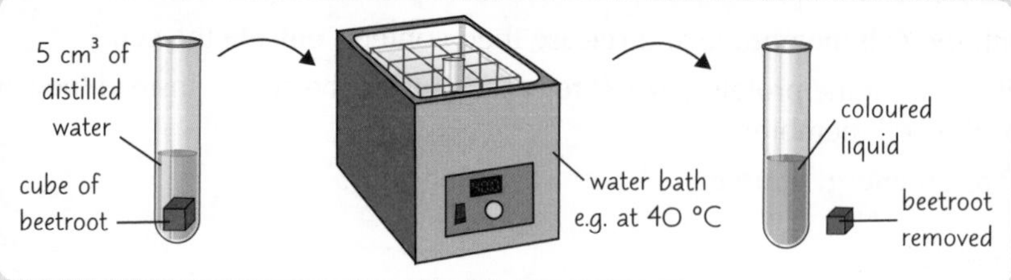

*2) Use a **Colorimeter** to Measure the **Absorbance** of the **Coloured Liquid***

Now you need to use a **colorimeter** — a machine that passes **light** of a specific wavelength through a liquid and measures **how much** of that light is **absorbed**. Many colorimeters use **filters** to make sure the light passing through the liquid is at the desired wavelength. Here's what you do...

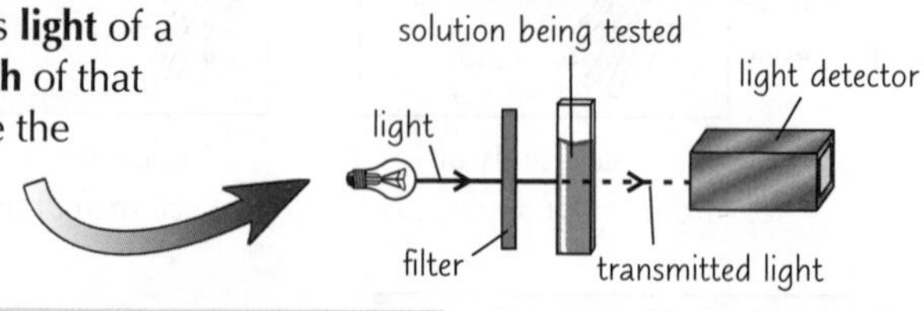

1) Firstly, switch the colorimeter on and allow **five minutes** for it to **stabilise**. Then set up the colorimeter so you're using a **blue filter** (or a wavelength of about **470 nm**) and use pure water to calibrate the machine to **zero**.
2) Next, use a **pipette** to transfer a **sample** of the liquid from the first of your beetroot test tubes to a **clean cuvette** — it should be about **three quarters full**.
3) Put the cuvette in the colorimeter and **record the absorbance** of the **coloured solution**.
4) **Repeat steps 2-3** for the liquids in the remaining four test tubes (using a clean pipette and cuvette each time).
5) You're now ready to analyse your results — the **higher** the **absorbance** reading, the **less light** is passing through the solution. This means **more pigment** has been **released**, so the **higher** the **permeability** of the membrane.

A cuvette is a small container that fits inside a colorimeter.

Depending on the resources you have available, you may be able to connect the colorimeter to a **computer** and use **software** to **collect the data** and **draw a graph** of the results.

Investigating Cell Membrane Structure

Increasing the *Temperature Increases Membrane Permeability*

Experiments like the one on the previous page have shown that membrane permeability **changes** with temperature:

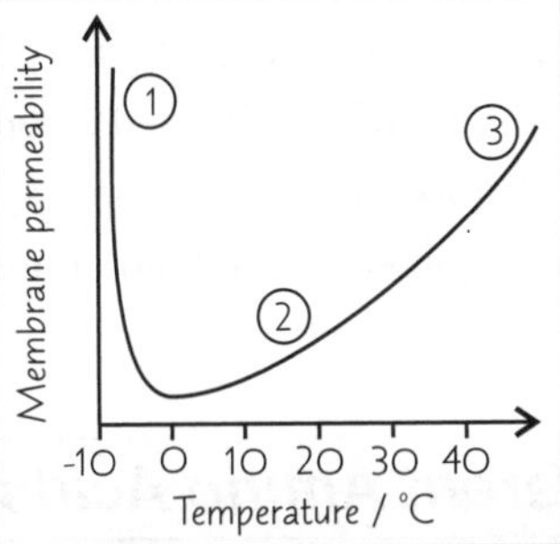

1. **Temperatures below 0 °C** — the phospholipids don't have much energy, so they can't move very much. They're **packed closely together** and the membrane is **rigid**. But **channel proteins** and **carrier proteins** in the membrane **deform, increasing** the **permeability** of the membrane. **Ice crystals** may form and **pierce** the membrane making it **highly permeable** when it thaws.
2. **Temperatures between 0 and 45 °C** — the phospholipids can **move** around and **aren't** packed as tightly together — the membrane is **partially permeable.** As the temperature **increases** the phospholipids **move more** because they have more energy — this **increases** the **permeability** of the membrane.
3. **Temperatures above 45 °C** — the phospholipid bilayer starts to **melt** (break down) and the membrane becomes more **permeable. Water** inside the cell **expands**, putting pressure on the membrane. **Channel proteins** and **carrier proteins deform** so they can't control what enters or leaves the cell — this increases the **permeability** of the membrane.

Increasing the *Alcohol Concentration Increases Membrane Permeability*

1) You can also test the effect of **alcohol concentration** on **membrane permeability.**
2) The graph on the right shows that as alcohol concentration **increases**, the permeability of the cell membrane **increases.**
3) This is because alcohol **dissolves** the **lipids** in the cell membrane, so the membrane **loses** its **structure.**

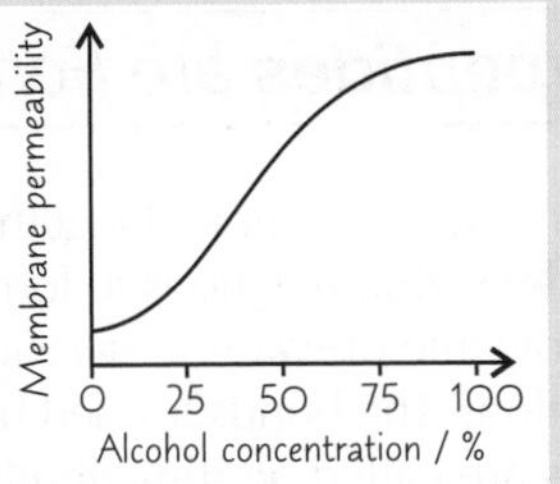

Practice Questions

Q1 What is a colorimeter used for?

Q2 What happens to the permeability of a cell membrane at temperatures below 0 °C?

Q3 What happens to the permeability of a cell membrane as the temperature increases above 0 °C?

Exam Question

Q1 The table on the right shows the results of an investigation into the effect of alcohol concentration on the permeability of beetroot cell membranes.

Alcohol concentration (%)	Absorbance
0	0.14
25	0.22
50	0.49
75	1.03
100	1.28

a) Describe a suitable method that could have been used to obtain these results. [4 marks]

b) What conclusion can be drawn from the results? [2 marks]

c) Give an explanation for the results. [1 mark]

Perm-eability — it's definitely decreased since the 80s...

Ah beetroot. Works nicely in a salad, a chocolate cake (if you're feeling adventurous) and even the odd lab experiment. What more could you ask for from a vegetable..? You need to know a method for investigating membrane permeability in the lab and you need to be able to explain how temperature and alcohol concentration affect cell membranes.

Protein Structure

There are loads of different proteins with loads of different functions. But what are proteins? What do they look like? Well, for your enjoyment, here are the answers to these questions and many, many more...

Proteins are Made from **Long Chains** of **Amino Acids**

1) The **monomers** (see page 22) of proteins are **amino acids**.
2) A **dipeptide** is formed when **two** amino acids join together.
3) A **polypeptide** is formed when **more than two** amino acids join together.
4) **Proteins** are made up of **one or more polypeptides**.

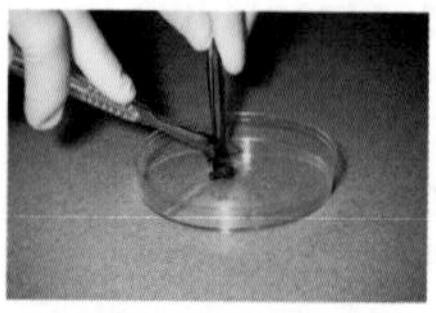

Grant's cries of "die peptide, die" could be heard for miles around. He'd never forgiven it for sleeping with his wife.

Different Amino Acids Have **Different Variable Groups**

Amino acids have the same general structure — a **carboxyl group** (-COOH), an **amine** or **amino group** ($-NH_2$) and a **carbon-containing R group** (also known as a **variable** side group).

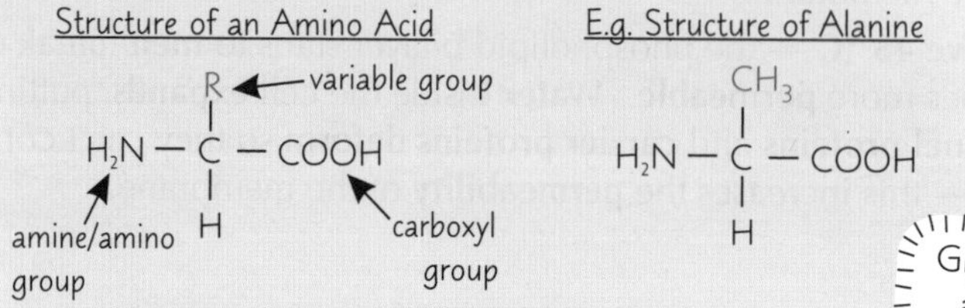

All living things share a bank of only **20 amino acids**. The only **difference** between them is what makes up their carbon-containing **R group**.

Glycine is the only amino acid that doesn't have carbon in its side group. Its R group consists of just one hydrogen atom.

Polypeptides are Formed by **Condensation Reactions**

Amino acids are linked together by **condensation** reactions to form polypeptides. A molecule of **water** is **released** during the reaction. The bonds formed between amino acids are called **peptide bonds**. The reverse reaction happens during digestion.

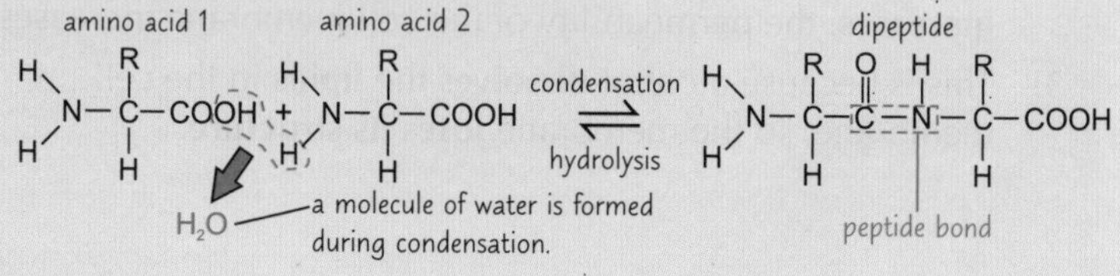

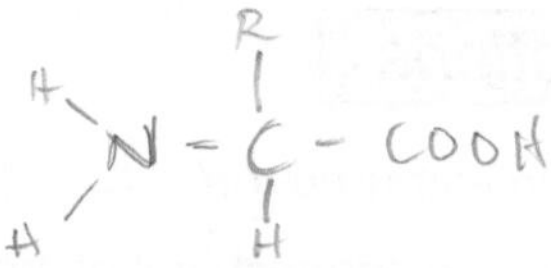

Proteins Have **Four Structural Levels**

Proteins are **big**, **complicated** molecules. They're much easier to explain if you describe their structure in four 'levels'. These levels are a protein's **primary**, **secondary**, **tertiary** and **quaternary** structures.

<u>Primary Structure</u> — this is the **sequence** of **amino acids** in the **polypeptide chain**.

<u>Secondary Structure</u> — the polypeptide chain doesn't remain flat and straight. **Hydrogen bonds** form between the amino acids in the chain. This makes it automatically **coil** into an **alpha** (α) **helix** or **fold** into a **beta** (β) **pleated sheet** — this is the secondary structure.

<u>Tertiary Structure</u> — the coiled or folded chain of amino acids is often **coiled** and **folded further**. More **bonds** form between different parts of the polypeptide chain, including **hydrogen bonds** and **ionic bonds** (see next page). **Disulfide bonds** can also form (see next page). For proteins made from a **single** polypeptide chain, the tertiary structure forms their **final 3D structure**.

<u>Quaternary Structure</u> — some proteins are made of **several different polypeptide chains** held together by **bonds**. The **quaternary structure** is the way these polypeptide chains are assembled together. For proteins made from more than one polypeptide chain (e.g. haemoglobin, insulin, collagen), the quaternary structure is the protein's **final 3D structure**.

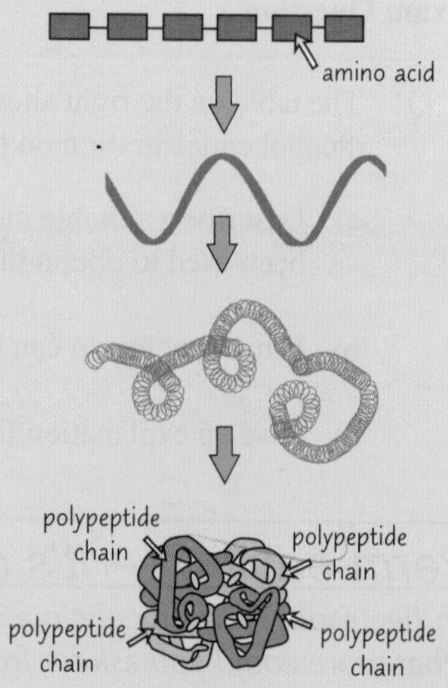

Protein Structure

Different Bonds Hold Different **Structural Levels** Together

The four structural levels of a protein are held together by **different kinds** of **bonds**:

1) **Primary structure** — held together by the **peptide bonds** between amino acids.
2) **Secondary structure** — held together by **hydrogen bonds** (see previous page).
3) **Tertiary structure** — this is affected by a few different kinds of bonds:
   - **Ionic bonds.** These are **attractions** between **negative** and **positive** charges on different parts of the molecule.
   - **Disulfide bonds.** Whenever two molecules of the amino acid **cysteine** come close together, the **sulfur atom** in one cysteine bonds to the sulfur in the other cysteine, forming a disulfide bond.
   - **Hydrophobic** and **hydrophilic interactions.** When **hydrophobic** (water-repelling) groups are close together in the protein, they tend to **clump together**. This means that **hydrophilic** (water-attracting) groups are more likely to be pushed to the **outside**, which affects how the protein **folds up** into its final structure.
   - **Hydrogen bonds.**
4) **Quaternary structure** — this tends to be determined by the **tertiary structure** of the individual polypeptide chains being bonded together. Because of this, it can be influenced by **all the bonds** mentioned above.

Hydrogen bonds are weak bonds between a slightly positively-charged hydrogen atom in one molecule and a slightly negatively-charged atom in another molecule.

A Protein's **Primary Structure** Determines its **3D Structure** and **Properties**

1) The **amino acid sequence** of a protein determines what **bonds** will form and how the protein will **fold up** into its 3D structure. E.g. if there are many cysteines, these will form **disulfide bonds** with each other, so the protein folds up in a certain way.
2) The **3D structure** of a protein determines its **properties**. Its properties relate to its **function** in the body.

Proteins Can Have a **Globular** or **Fibrous 3D Structure**

GLOBULAR

1) Globular proteins are **round, compact** proteins made up of **multiple polypeptide chains**.
2) The chains are **coiled up** so that **hydrophilic** (water-attracting) parts of chains are on the **outside** of the molecule and **hydrophobic** (water-repelling) parts of chains face **inwards**.
3) This makes the proteins **soluble**, so they're **easily transported** in fluids.
4) E.g. **haemoglobin** is a globular protein made of **four** polypeptide chains. It **carries oxygen** around the body in the blood. It's **soluble**, so it can be easily transported in the blood. It also has iron-containing **haem groups** that **bind** to oxygen.

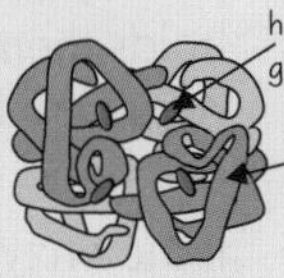

FIBROUS

1) Fibrous proteins are made up of **long, insoluble polypeptide chains** that are **tightly coiled** round each other to form a **rope shape**.
2) The chains are held together by **lots of bonds** (e.g. disulfide and hydrogen bonds), which make the proteins **strong**.
3) Because they're strong, fibrous proteins are often found in **supportive tissue**.
4) E.g. **collagen** is a **strong, fibrous protein** that forms connective tissue in **animals**.

Practice Questions

Q1 Draw the basic structure of an amino acid.

Q2 Name four types of bond that determine the 3D structure of a protein.

Exam Question

Q1 Proteins, such as keratin, are made of polypeptides. Describe how a polypeptide is formed. [3 marks]

The name's Bond — Peptide Bond...

Heating a protein to a high temperature will break up its ionic and hydrogen bonds and hydrophobic/hydrophilic interactions. In turn this will cause a change in the protein's 3D shape, which can lead to it becoming non-functional.

Enzymes

Enzymes crop up loads in biology — they're really useful 'cos they make reactions work quickly. So, whether you feel the need for some speed or not, read on — because you really need to know this basic stuff about enzymes.

Enzymes are Biological Catalysts

Enzymes **speed up chemical reactions** by acting as **biological catalysts.**

A catalyst is a substance that speeds up a chemical reaction without being used up in the reaction itself.

1) Enzymes catalyse **metabolic reactions** — both at a **cellular level** (e.g. **respiration**) and for the **organism** as a **whole** (e.g. **digestion** in mammals).
2) Enzymes can affect **structures** in an organism (e.g. enzymes are involved in the production of **collagen**, see previous page) as well as **functions** (like **respiration**).
3) Enzymes can be **intracellular** (catalyse reactions **inside** cells) or **extracellular** (produced and secreted by cells to catalyse reactions **outside** cells).
4) Enzymes are **proteins** (see pages 36-37).
5) Enzymes have an **active site**, which has a **specific shape**. The active site is the part of the enzyme where the **substrate** molecules (the substance that the enzyme interacts with) **bind to.**
6) Enzymes are **highly specific** due to their tertiary structure (see next page).

Enzymes Lower the Activation Energy of a Reaction

In a chemical reaction, a certain amount of **energy** needs to be supplied to the chemicals before the reaction will **start**. This is called the **activation energy** — it's often provided as **heat**. Enzymes **lower** the amount of activation energy that's needed, often making reactions happen at a **lower temperature** than they could without an enzyme. This **speeds up** the **rate of reaction.**

When a substrate fits into the enzyme's active site it forms an **enzyme-substrate complex** — it's this that lowers the activation energy. Here are two reasons why:

1) If two substrate molecules need to be **joined**, being attached to the enzyme holds them **close together**, **reducing** any **repulsion** between the molecules so they can bond more easily.
2) If the enzyme is catalysing a **breakdown reaction**, fitting into the active site puts a **strain** on bonds in the substrate, so the substrate molecule **breaks up** more easily.

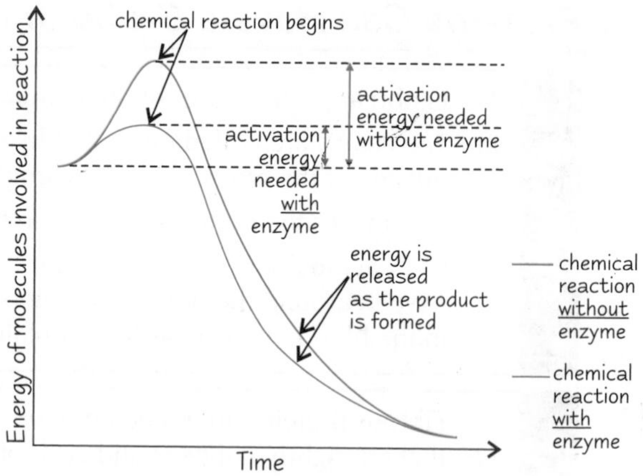

The 'Lock and Key' Model is a Good Start...

Enzymes are a bit picky — they only work with substrates that fit their active site. Early scientists studying the action of enzymes came up with the '**lock and key**' model. This is where the **substrate fits** into the **enzyme** in the same way that a **key fits** into a **lock**.

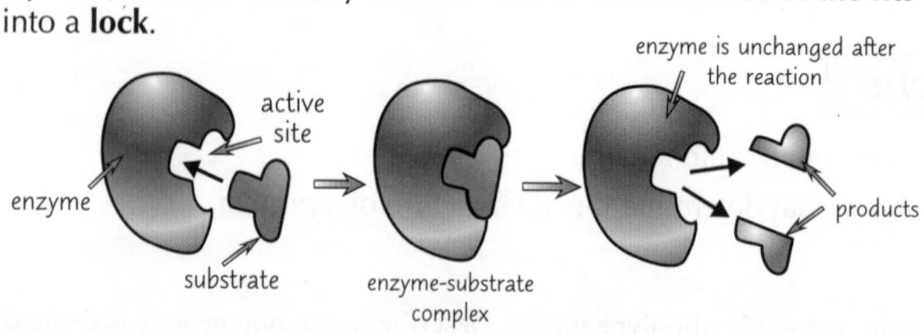

Scientists soon realised that the lock and key model didn't give the full story. The enzyme and substrate do have to fit together in the first place, but new evidence showed that the **enzyme-substrate complex changed shape** slightly to complete the fit. This **locks** the substrate even more tightly to the enzyme. Scientists modified the old lock and key model and came up with the '**induced fit**' model.

Enzymes

...but the 'Induced Fit' Model is a Better Theory

The '**induced fit**' model helps to explain why enzymes are so **specific** and only bond to one particular substrate. The substrate doesn't only have to be the right shape to fit the active site, it has to make the active site **change shape** in the right way as well. This is a prime example of how a widely accepted theory can **change** when **new evidence** comes along. The 'induced fit' model is still widely accepted — for now, anyway.

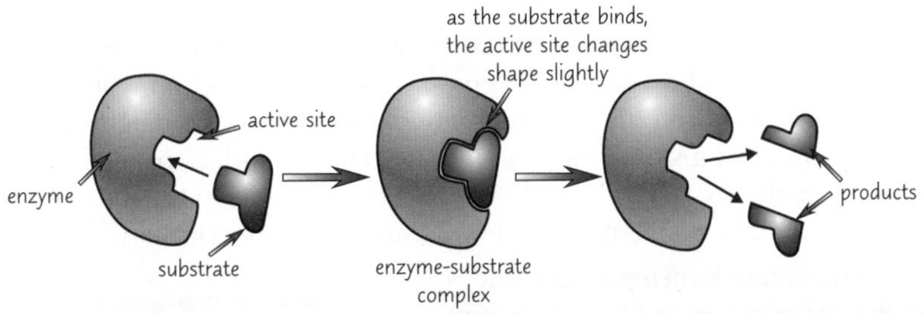

The 'Luminous Tights' model was popular in the 1980s but has since been found to be grossly inappropriate.

Enzyme Properties Relate to Their Tertiary Structure

1) Enzymes are **very specific** — they usually only catalyse **one** reaction, e.g. maltase only breaks down maltose, sucrase only breaks down sucrose.
2) This is because **only one complementary substrate will fit** into the active site.
3) The active site's **shape** is determined by the enzyme's **tertiary structure** (which is determined by the enzyme's **primary structure**).
4) Each **different enzyme** has a **different tertiary structure** and so a **different shaped active site.** If the substrate shape doesn't match the active site, an enzyme-substrate complex **won't** be formed and the reaction won't be catalysed.
5) If the tertiary structure of the enzyme is **altered** in any way, the **shape** of the active site will **change.** This means the **substrate won't fit** into the active site, an enzyme-substrate complex **won't** be formed and the enzyme will no longer be able to carry out its function.
6) The tertiary structure of an enzyme may be **altered** by changes in **pH** or **temperature.**
7) The **primary structure** (amino acid sequence) of a protein is determined by a **gene.** If a mutation occurs in that gene (see page 50), it could change the tertiary structure of the enzyme **produced.**

Enzyme Concentration Affects the Rate of Reaction

1) The **more enzyme molecules** there are in a solution, the **more active sites** are present and therefore the more likely a substrate molecule is to **collide** with an **active site** and form an **enzyme-substrate complex**. So increasing the concentration of the enzyme **increases** the **rate of reaction.**
2) But, if the amount of **substrate** is **limited**, there comes a point when there's more than enough enzyme molecules to deal with all the available substrate, so adding more enzyme has **no further effect. Substrate concentration** has become a **limiting factor.**

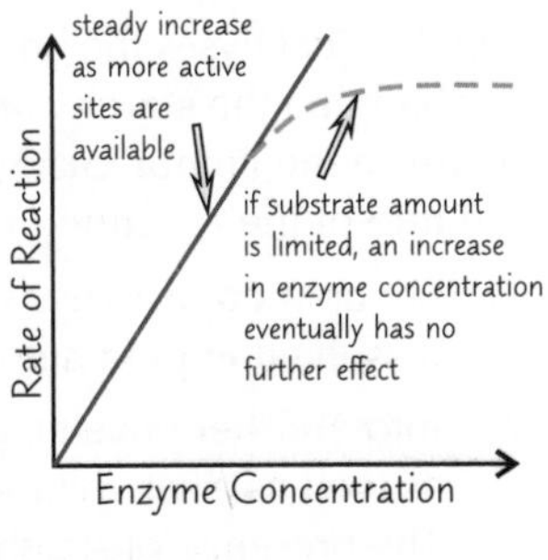

Substrate Concentration Affects the Rate of Reaction Up to a Point

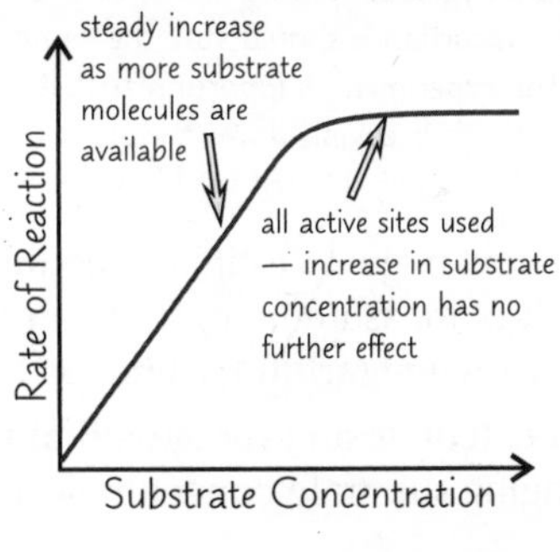

1) The **higher** the substrate concentration, the **faster** the reaction — more substrate molecules means a **collision** between substrate and enzyme is **more likely** and so more active sites will be used. This is only true up until a **'saturation'** point though. After that, there are so many substrate molecules that the enzymes have about as much as they can cope with (all the **active sites are full**), and adding more **makes no difference.**
2) Substrate concentration **decreases** with **time** during a reaction (unless more substrate is added to the reaction mixture), so if no other variables are changed, the **rate of reaction will decrease over time** too. This makes the **initial** rate of reaction (the reaction rate at the **start**) the **highest** rate of reaction.

Enzymes

You can **Measure** the **Rate** of an **Enzyme-Controlled** Reaction

There are **two** ways to measure the **rate** of a reaction. Using these, you can **investigate** the effect of changing the **enzyme** or **substrate concentration** on the **initial rate** of a reaction.

1) You Can Measure **How Fast** the **Product** of the Reaction is **Made**

Catalase catalyses the **breakdown** of **hydrogen peroxide** into **water** and **oxygen**. It's easy to measure the volume of oxygen produced and to work out **how fast** it's given off. Using this reaction, you can **investigate** the effect of **changing** the **enzyme concentration** on the **initial rate** of reaction — the diagram below shows the **apparatus** you'll need. (You'll also need a **stand** and **clamp** to hold the cylinder upside down, as well as a **stopwatch**.) During the experiment, the oxygen released **displaces** the water from the measuring cylinder. You'll need to **decide** on a **range** of **catalase concentrations** to investigate before you start.

1) Add a **set volume** and **concentration** of **hydrogen peroxide** to a boiling tube. To keep the pH constant, add a set amount of a suitable **buffer solution** to the tube. (A buffer solution is able to resist changes in pH when small amounts of acid or alkali are added.)
2) Set up the rest of the **apparatus** as shown in the diagram.
3) Use a pipette to add a **set volume** of one of the **concentrations** of **catalase** to the boiling tube. Then **quickly attach** the **bung** and **delivery tube**.
4) **Record** the volume of oxygen **produced** in the measuring cylinder **every ten seconds** for the **first minute** (60 s) of the reaction. Use a **stopwatch** to measure the time.
5) **Repeat** the experiment twice more, and find the **average volume of oxygen produced** at **each** ten second interval.
6) Plot your data on a **graph** of **volume of oxygen produced** (cm^3) against **time** (seconds) and draw a **tangent** (see next page) to determine the **initial rate** of the reaction.
7) **Repeat** the **whole** experiment at **each** of the other **catalase concentrations** under investigation. You can then **compare** the **initial rate** of the reaction for **each concentration** to determine the **effect** of **changing** the **enzyme concentration** on the initial rate of reaction.

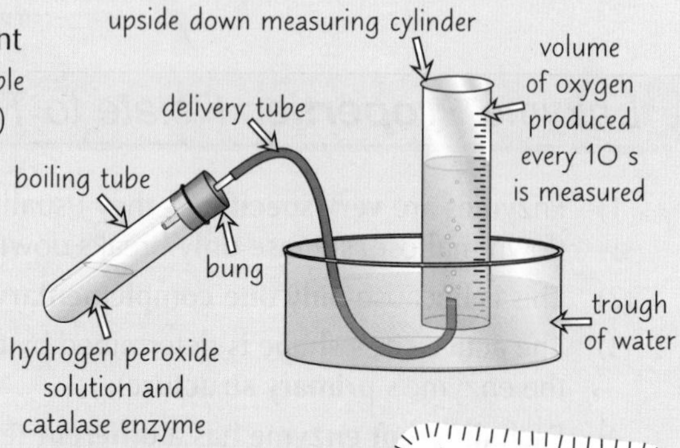

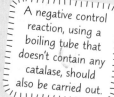

A negative control reaction, using a boiling tube that doesn't contain any catalase, should also be carried out.

2) You Can Measure **How Fast** the **Substrate** is **Removed**

Amylase catalyses the breakdown of **starch** to **maltose**. This experiment shows you how to investigate the **effect** of **changing** the **starch concentration** on the **initial rate** of the **reaction**. It uses a **colorimeter** (see page 34) to measure the **colour change** of a **solution** in response to **enzyme activity**. The **rate** of this **colour change** indicates the **rate** of the **reaction**. You'll need to decide on a **range** of **starch concentrations** to investigate before you start.

1) Set up a **colorimeter** with a **red filter** and **zero** it using a **cuvette** (see page 34) containing **iodine dissolved in potassium iodide solution**. This will have a browny-orange colour.
2) Into **another** cuvette, pipette a set volume of one of the **concentrations** of **starch** that you're investigating, as well as a set volume of **iodine dissolved in potassium iodide solution**, and **mix** the contents together. The presence of starch causes the solution to turn a **dark blue-black colour**. Place the cuvette in the zeroed colorimeter and **record** the **absorbance**.
3) Now **add** a set volume and concentration of **amylase** enzyme to the cuvette and immediately **start** a **stopwatch**.
4) Every **ten seconds** for a set amount of time (e.g. 5 minutes), **record** the **absorbance** shown by the colorimeter.
5) **Repeat steps 1-4** twice more and use the data to calculate an **average absorbance** reading for **each** ten second interval.
6) **Plot** the data on a **graph** of **absorbance against time** and draw a **tangent** (see next page) to estimate the **initial rate** of **reaction**. **Absorbance** is unitless — it **doesn't** have its own proper **unit** of measurement, so it can be described in **arbitrary units**. The unit of the rate will be **arbitrary units per second** (**arbitrary units s^{-1}**).
7) **Repeat** the whole experiment at **each** of the other **starch concentrations** and **calculate** an **average initial rate** for **each**. You can then **compare** these figures to determine the effect of changing substrate concentration.

A negative control experiment should also be carried out for each of the starch concentrations. For this, no amylase should be added to the cuvette. The absorbance should stay the same throughout the experiment, supporting that it is the enzyme that's breaking down the starch.

Enzymes

You Can Use a *Tangent* to *Calculate* the *Initial Rate of Reaction*

The **initial** rate of reaction is the rate right at the **start** of the reaction, close to **time equals zero** ($t = 0$) on the graph. To work out the initial rate of reaction carry out the following steps:

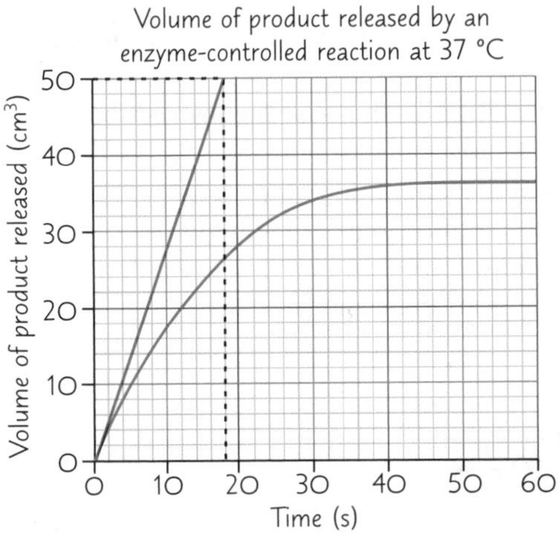

1) **Draw a tangent** to the curve at ***t*** **= 0**, using a ruler. Do this by positioning the ruler so it's an **equal distance** from the curve at **both sides** of where it's touching it. Here you'll have to **estimate** where the curve would **continue** if it carried on **below zero**. Then draw a **line** along the ruler. (For more on drawing tangents see p. 107.)
2) Then calculate the **gradient** of the **tangent** — this is the **initial rate of reaction**. Gradient = change in *y* axis ÷ change in *x* axis On this graph it's: 50 cm^3 ÷ 18 s = **2.8** $\mathbf{cm^3\ s^{-1}}$.

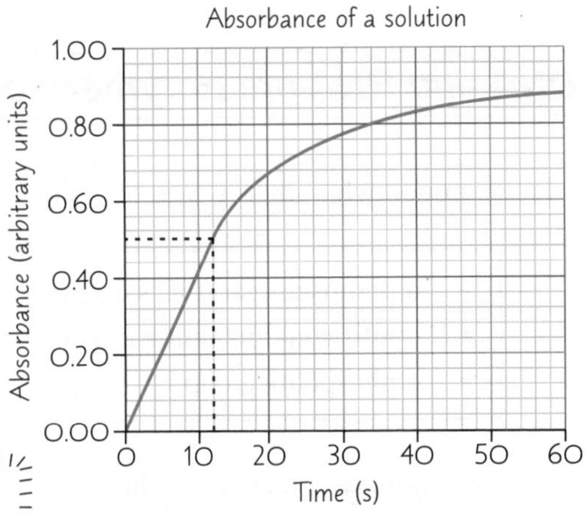

3) In your exam, it's possible that you'll get a graph where there's a **clear straight line** at the **start** of the reaction from ***t*** **= 0**. In this case, you **don't** need to draw a **tangent** — you can just work out the **gradient** of the **straight portion** of the graph.
4) Gradient = 0.50 arbitrary units ÷ 12 s
   = **0.042 arbitrary units** $\mathbf{s^{-1}}$

If you're comparing the initial rate of reaction for two different reactions, you can work out the ratio of the rates to give you a quick and easy comparison.

Practice Questions

Q1 What is an enzyme?

Q2 What is the name given to the amount of energy needed to start a reaction?

Q3 What is an enzyme-substrate complex?

Q4 Why can an enzyme only bind to one substance?

Exam Question

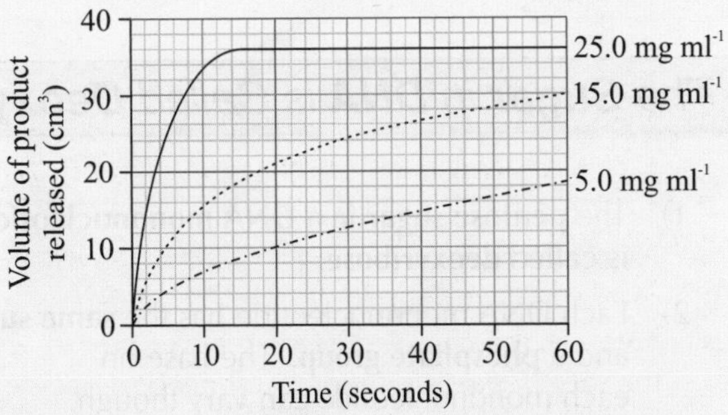

Q1 A student investigated the effect of enzyme concentration on the rate of an enzyme-controlled reaction. The product of the reaction was a gas. A tube was set up containing some substrate solution. A set volume of 5.0 mg ml^{-1} enzyme solution was then added to the tube, and a bung with a hose connected to a gas syringe was put in the top. The amount of gas collected was recorded every 10 seconds for 1 minute. The experiment was then repeated using two different concentrations of enzyme. The volume and concentration of substrate solution was kept the same.

a) Draw a tangent to find the initial rate of reaction when using 25.0 mg ml^{-1} enzyme solution. Show your working. [2 marks]

b) Analyse the graph to explain how the enzyme concentration affects the initial rate of reaction. [2 marks]

c) Give a negative control that should have been included in the investigation. Explain your answer. [2 marks]

d) When the substrate is broken down, the solution changes from blue to colourless. State how this experiment could be adapted to measure the colour change instead of the volume of product released. [2 marks]

But why is the enzyme-substrate complex?

There's plenty to sink your teeth into here, but it's all worth remembering for the exams. Make sure you know all about how enzymes work, and make sure you know how to investigate the initial rate of an enzyme-controlled reaction. If you've got a few spare minutes after that, spend some time arguing with your friends about how to pronounce 'scone'.

DNA and RNA Basics

These two pages are all about nucleic acids — DNA and RNA. These molecules are needed to build proteins, which are required for the cells in living organisms to function. They're right handy little things.

DNA *and* ***RNA*** *Carry* ***Important*** *Information*

DNA and RNA are both types of **nucleic acid**. They're found in **all living cells** and they both carry **information**.

1) **DNA** (deoxyribonucleic acid) is used to store **genetic information** — that's **all the instructions** an organism needs to **grow and develop** from a fertilised egg to a fully grown adult.
2) **RNA** (ribonucleic acid) is similar in structure to DNA. One of its main functions is to **transfer** genetic information from the **DNA** to the **ribosomes**. Ribosomes are the body's '**protein factories**' — they read the RNA to make **polypeptides** (proteins) in a process called **translation** (see page 47). Ribosomes themselves are made from **RNA** and **proteins**.

DNA *and* ***RNA*** *are* ***Polymers*** *of* ***Mononucleotides***

1) A **mononucleotide** is a type of biological molecule. It's made from:

- a **pentose sugar** (that's a sugar with **5** carbon atoms),
- a **nitrogen-containing** organic **base**,
- a **phosphate** group.

'Organic' means that it contains carbon.

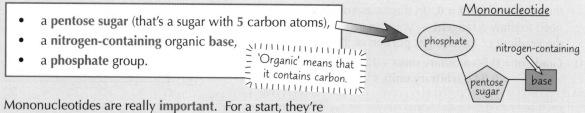

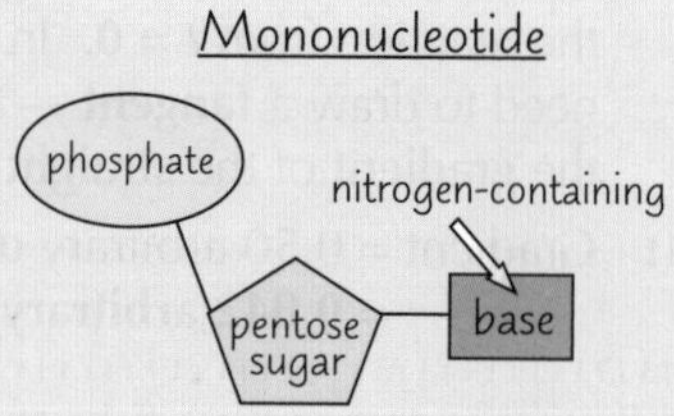

2) Mononucleotides are really **important**. For a start, they're the **monomers** (see page 22) that make up **DNA** and **RNA**.

The ***Sugar*** *in* ***DNA*** *is Called* ***Deoxyribose***

1) The **pentose sugar** in a **DNA mononucleotide** is called **deoxyribose**.
2) Each DNA mononucleotide has the **same sugar** and a **phosphate group**. The **base** on each mononucleotide can **vary** though.
3) There are **four** possible bases — adenine (**A**), thymine (**T**), cytosine (**C**) and guanine (**G**).

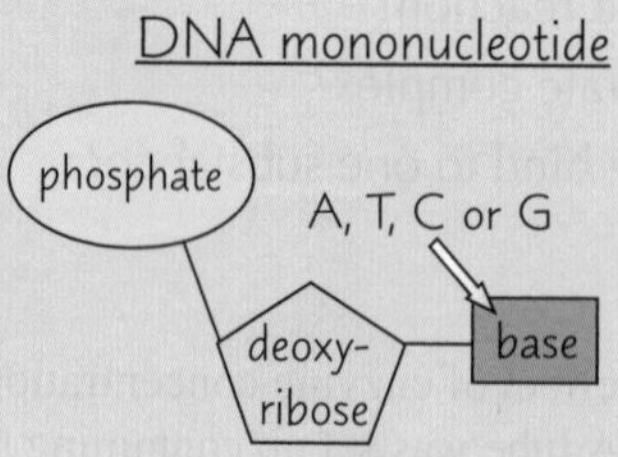

The ***Sugar*** *in* ***RNA*** *is Called* ***Ribose***

1) **RNA** contains mononucleotides with a **ribose sugar** (not deoxyribose).
2) Like DNA, an RNA mononucleotide also has a **phosphate group** and one of **four** different **bases**.
3) In RNA though, **uracil** (**U**) replaces **thymine** as a base.

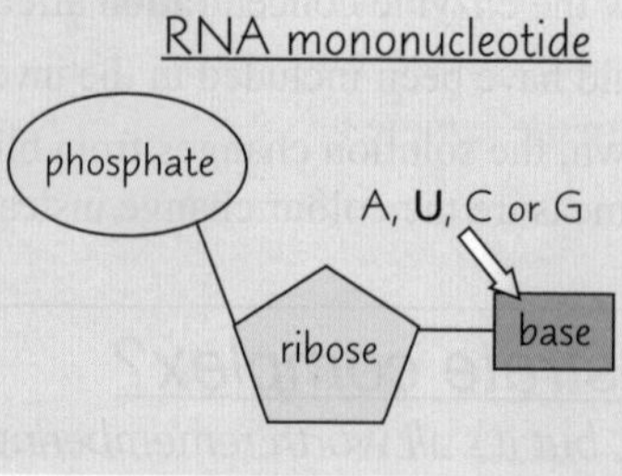

Mary didn't care if it was ribose or deoxyribose, she just wanted her cuppa.

DNA and RNA Basics

Mononucleotides Join Together to Form Polynucleotides

1) A **polynucleotide** is a **polymer** of **mononucleotides.** Both DNA and RNA mononucleotides form polynucleotides.
2) The mononucleotides are joined through **condensation reactions** between the **phosphate** of one mononucleotide and the **sugar** group of another. As in all condensation reactions, **water** is a by-product (see page 22).
3) **DNA** is made of **two polynucleotide strands,** RNA has just **one strand.**

Part of a single polynucleotide strand

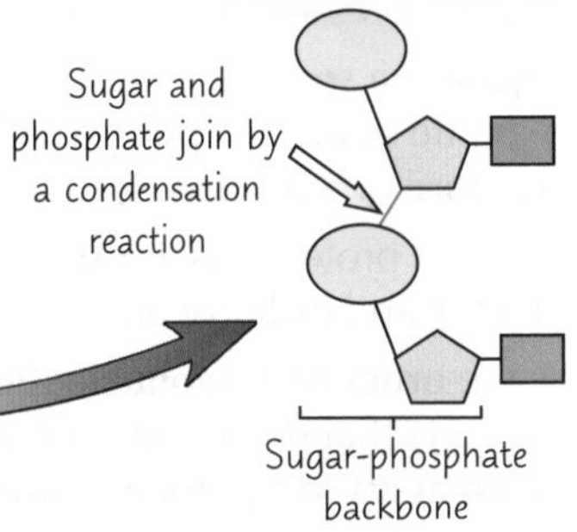

DNA is Made of Two Polynucleotide Chains in a Double-Helix Structure

1) **Two DNA** polynucleotide strands join together by **hydrogen bonding** between the bases.
2) Each base can only join with one particular partner — this is called **complementary base pairing** (or specific base pairing).
3) **Adenine** always pairs with **thymine** (**A - T**) and **cytosine** always pairs with **guanine** (**C - G**). This means that there are always **equal amounts** of adenine and thymine in a DNA molecule and **equal amounts** of cytosine and guanine.
4) **Two** hydrogen bonds form between **A and T**, and **three** hydrogen bonds form between **C and G**.
5) Two **antiparallel** (running in opposite directions) polynucleotide strands **twist** to form the **DNA double-helix**.
6) DNA was first observed in the 1800s, but lots of scientists at the time **doubted** that it could carry the **genetic code** because it has a **relatively simple chemical composition**. Some argued that genetic information must be carried by **proteins** — which are much more **chemically varied.**
7) By 1953, experiments had shown that DNA was the carrier of the genetic code. This was also the year in which the **double-helix structure**, which helps DNA to carry out its function, was determined by **Watson** and **Crick.**

Two joined polynucleotide strands

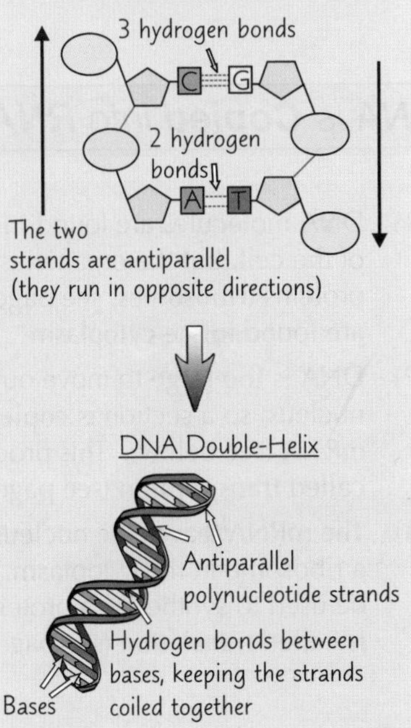

Practice Questions

Q1 Name the bases in RNA.

Q2 Describe the structure of DNA.

Exam Questions

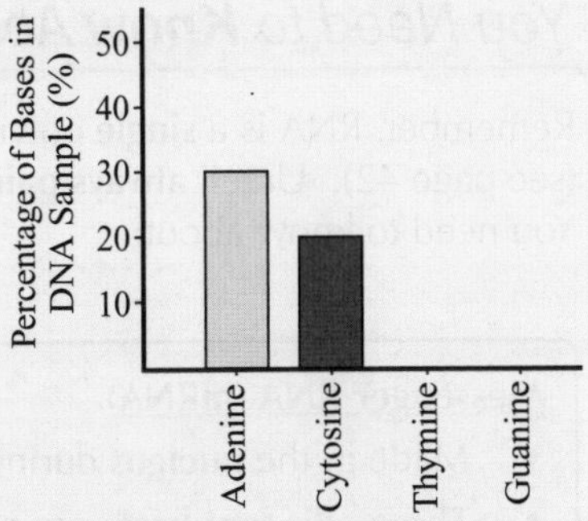

Q1 The bar chart shows the percentage of the bases in a DNA sample that are adenine and cytosine. On the chart, draw bars to show the percentages of thymine and guanine in the sample. [2 marks]

Q2 a) Describe how mononucleotides are joined together in DNA. [2 marks]

b) Describe how two single polynucleotide strands are joined to make a DNA double helix. [3 marks]

Give me a D, give me an N, give me an A! What do you get? — confused...

You need to learn the structures of DNA and RNA as well as the mononucleotides that make them up. Remember that RNA is made up of a single polynucleotide strand, whereas DNA is made up of two strands joined by hydrogen bonds.

The Genetic Code and Protein Synthesis

You need to know how DNA is used to carry information — and how that information gets turned into proteins. Luckily for you, it's all here over the next few pages...

DNA Contains **Genes** Which are **Instructions** for **Making Proteins**

1) A **gene** is a sequence of **mononucleotide bases** on a DNA molecule that codes for the sequence of **amino acids** in a **polypeptide**. The sequence of **amino acids** in a polypeptide forms the **primary structure** of a **protein** (see page 36).
2) Different proteins have a **different number** and **order** of amino acids.
3) It's the **order** of **mononucleotide bases** in a gene that determines the **order of amino acids** in a particular **protein**.
4) Each amino acid is coded for by a sequence of **three bases** (called a **triplet**) in a gene.
5) **Different sequences** of bases code for **different amino acids**. So the **sequence of bases** in a section of DNA is a **template** that's used to make **proteins** during **protein synthesis**.

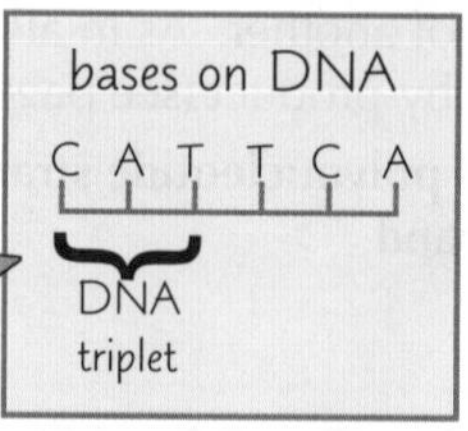

DNA is **Copied** into **RNA** for **Protein Synthesis**

1) DNA molecules are found in the **nucleus** of the cell, but the organelles that make proteins (**ribosomes**, see page 59) are found in the **cytoplasm**.
2) DNA is **too large** to move out of the nucleus, so a section is **copied** into **mRNA** (see below). This process is called **transcription** (see page 46).
3) The mRNA **leaves** the nucleus and joins with a ribosome in the cytoplasm, where it can be used to synthesise a protein. This process is called **translation** (see page 47).

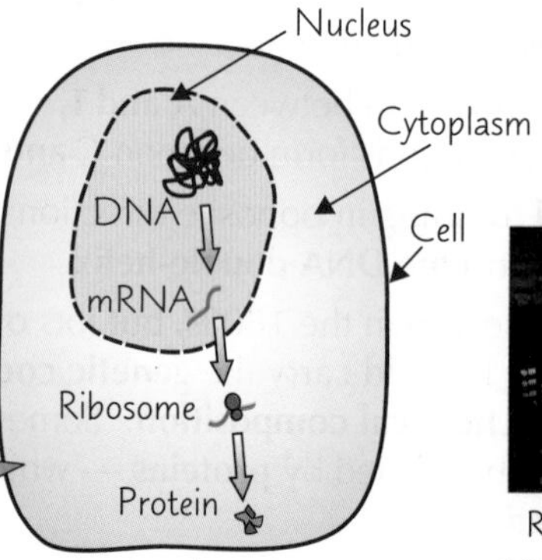

Rita Some knew how to synthesise some great tunes.

You Need to **Know** About **Two Types** of **RNA**

Remember, RNA is a **single** polynucleotide strand and it contains **uracil** (**U**) as a base instead of thymine (see page 42). Uracil **always pairs** with **adenine** during protein synthesis. RNA isn't all the same though. You need to know about:

Messenger RNA (mRNA)

- Made in the **nucleus** during **transcription**.
- **Three adjacent bases** are called a **codon**.
- It **carries the genetic code** from the DNA in the **nucleus** to the **cytoplasm**, where it's used to make a **protein** during **translation**.

Transfer RNA (tRNA)

- Found in the **cytoplasm**.
- It has an **amino acid binding site** at one end and a **sequence of three bases** at the other end called an **anticodon**.
- It **carries** the amino acids that are used to make **proteins** to the **ribosomes** during **translation**.

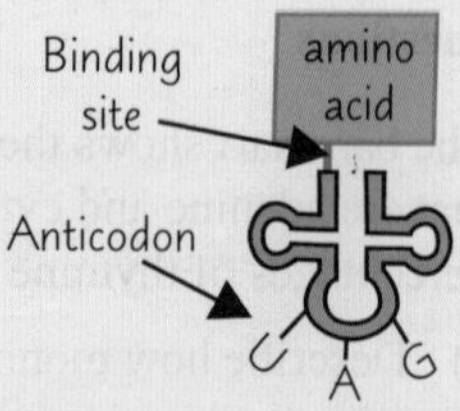

Codons and anticodons are sometimes referred to as triplets.

The Genetic Code and Protein Synthesis

The *Genetic Code* is *Non-Overlapping* and *Degenerate*

1) The genetic code is the **sequence of base triplets (codons)** in **DNA** or **mRNA**, which **codes** for **specific amino acids**.
2) In the genetic code, each base triplet is **read** in sequence, **separate** from the triplet **before** it and **after** it. Base triplets **don't share** their **bases** — the code is **non-overlapping**.

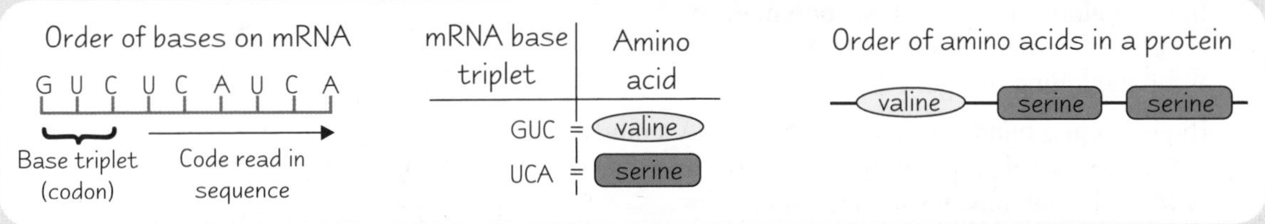

3) The genetic code is also **degenerate** — there are **more** possible combinations of **triplets** than there are amino acids (20 amino acids but 64 possible triplets). This means that some **amino acids** are coded for by **more than one** base triplet, e.g. tyrosine can be coded for by UAU or UAC.
4) Some triplets are used to tell the cell when to **start** and **stop** production of the protein — these are called **start** and **stop codons** (or start and stop signals). They're found at the **beginning** and **end** of the gene. E.g. UAG is a stop codon.

Practice Questions

Q1 What is a gene?

Q2 What is the function of mRNA?

Q3 Why is the genetic code described as degenerate?

Exam Questions

Q1 Which of the following is **not** a correct description of tRNA?

A It has an amino acid binding site.

B It contains the bases adenine, guanine, cytosine and uracil.

C The process by which it is made is called transcription.

D It carries amino acids to the ribosomes during translation. [1 mark]

Q2 A piece of mRNA has the sequence: GUGUGUCGCGCA.

a) How many amino acids does this sequence code for? [1 mark]

b) Using the table on the right, give the amino acid sequence it codes for. [2 marks]

mRNA codon	amino acid
UGU	Cysteine
CGC	Arginine
GGG	Glycine
GUG	Valine
GCA	Alanine
UUG	Leucine
UUU	Phenylalanine

Q3 An artificial mRNA was synthesized to code for a particular protein. Part of the mRNA sequence was: UUGUGUGGGUUUGCAGCA. This produced the following sequence of amino acids: Leucine–Cysteine–Glycine–Phenylalanine–Alanine–Alanine. Use the table above to help you answer the following questions.

a) Explain how the result suggests that the genetic code is based on triplets of mononucleotides in mRNA. [2 marks]

b) Explain how the result suggests that the genetic code is non-overlapping. [2 marks]

Genes contain instructions — wash at 40 °C...

You really need to get your head around how DNA and RNA work together to produce proteins, or the next two pages are going to be a teeeny weeny bit tricky. Don't say I didn't warn you. Turn over too quickly at your own peril...

Transcription and Translation

Time to find out how RNA works its magic to make proteins. It gets a bit complicated but bear with it.

First Stage of Protein Synthesis — Transcription

During transcription an **mRNA copy** of a gene (a section of DNA) is made in the **nucleus**:

1) Transcription starts when **RNA polymerase** (an **enzyme**) **attaches** to the **DNA** double-helix at the **beginning** of a **gene** (start codon).
2) The **hydrogen bonds** between the two DNA strands in the gene **break**, **separating** the strands, and the DNA molecule **unwinds** at that point.
3) One of the strands is then used as a **template** to make an **mRNA copy**.

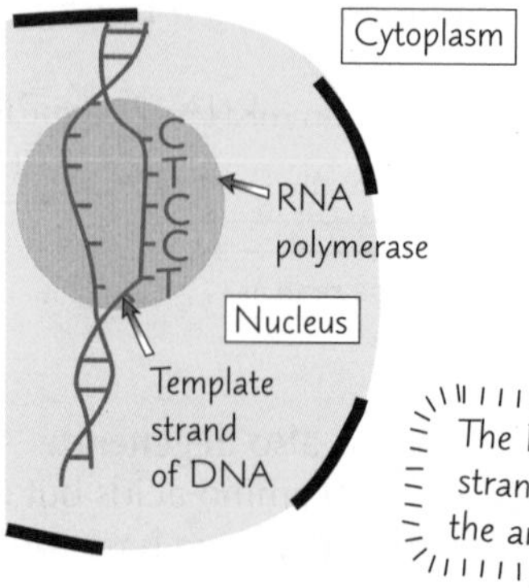

The DNA template strand is also called the antisense strand.

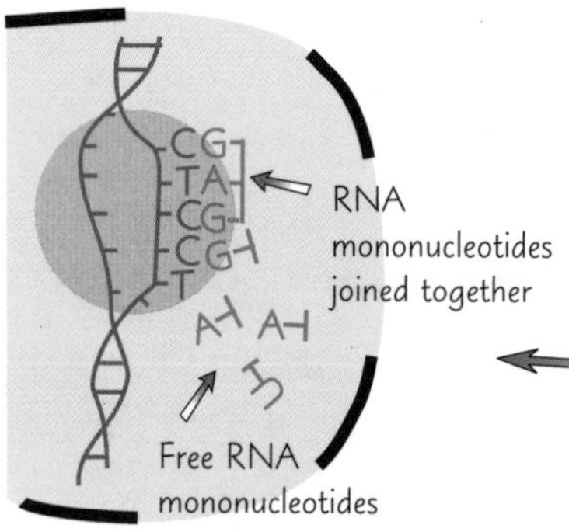

4) The RNA polymerase **lines up** free **RNA mononucleotides** alongside the template strand. **Complementary base pairing** means that the mRNA strand ends up being a **complementary copy** of the DNA template strand (except the base **T** is replaced by **U** in **RNA**).
5) Once the RNA mononucleotides have **paired up** with their **specific bases** on the DNA strand they're **joined together** by **RNA polymerase**, forming an **mRNA** molecule.

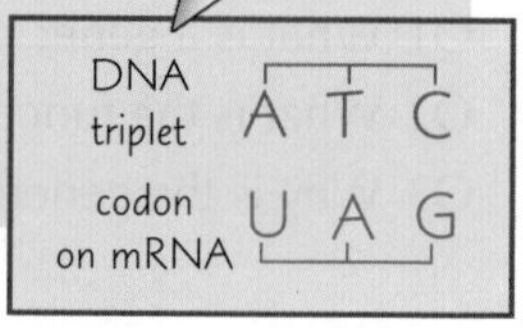

6) The RNA polymerase moves **along** the DNA, separating the strands and **assembling** the mRNA strand.
7) The **hydrogen bonds** between the unwound strands of DNA **re-form** once the RNA polymerase has passed by and the strands **wind back up into a double-helix**.

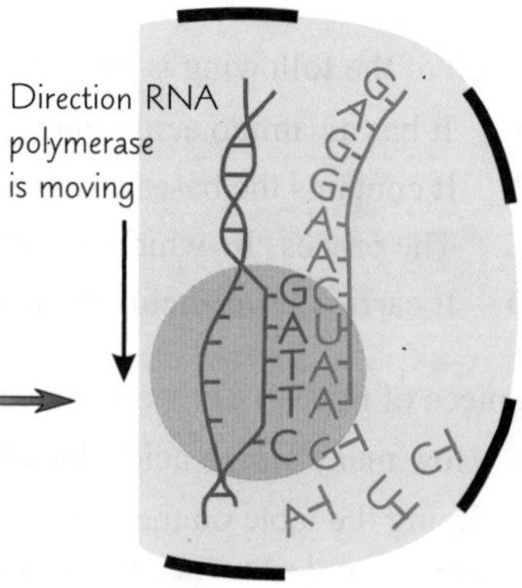

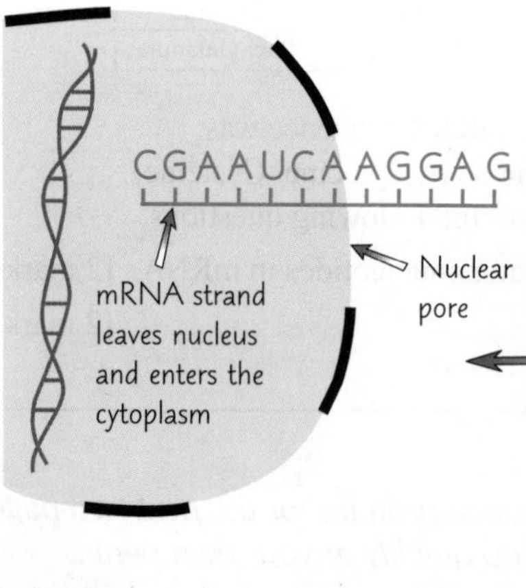

8) When RNA polymerase reaches a **stop codon** (see previous page) it stops making mRNA and **detaches** from the DNA.
9) The **mRNA** moves **out** of the **nucleus** through a **nuclear pore** and attaches to a **ribosome** in the cytoplasm, where the next stage of protein synthesis takes place (see next page).

Transcription and Translation

Second Stage of Protein Synthesis — Translation

Translation occurs at the **ribosomes** in the **cytoplasm**. During **translation**, **amino acids** are **joined together** to make a **polypeptide chain** (protein), following the sequence of **codons** carried by the mRNA.

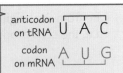

1) The **mRNA attaches** itself to a **ribosome** and **transfer RNA** (**tRNA**) molecules **carry amino acids** to the ribosome.
2) A tRNA molecule, with an **anticodon** that's **complementary** to the **start codon** on the mRNA, attaches itself to the mRNA by **complementary base pairing**.
3) A second tRNA molecule attaches itself to the **next codon** on the mRNA in the **same way**.
4) The two amino acids attached to the tRNA molecules are then **joined** together by a **peptide bond**. The first tRNA molecule **moves away**, leaving its amino acid behind.
5) The ribosome **moves** along to the **next codon**.
6) A third tRNA molecule binds to that codon on the mRNA. Its amino acid **binds** to the first two and the second tRNA molecule **moves away**.
7) This process continues, producing a chain of linked amino acids (a **polypeptide chain**), until there's a **stop codon** on the mRNA molecule.
8) The polypeptide chain **moves away** from the ribosome and translation is complete.

anticodon on tRNA U A C
codon on mRNA A U G

Protein synthesis is also called polypeptide synthesis as it makes a polypeptide.

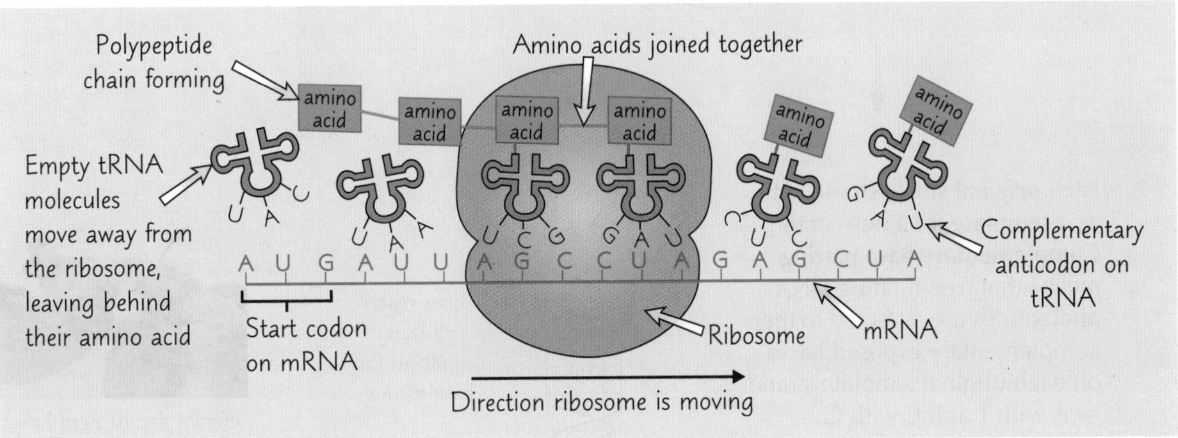

Practice Questions

Q1 What are the two stages of protein synthesis called?

Q2 Where does the first stage of protein synthesis take place?

Q3 When does RNA polymerase stop making mRNA?

Q4 Where does the second stage of protein synthesis take place?

Exam Questions

Q1 A DNA sequence is GCGAAGTCCATG.
   a) Give the complementary mRNA sequence. [1 mark]
   b) Give the sequence of the tRNA anticodons. [1 mark]

Q2 A drug that inhibits cell growth is found to be able to bind to DNA, preventing RNA polymerase from binding. Explain how this drug will affect protein synthesis. [2 marks]

Q3 A polypeptide chain (protein) from a eukaryotic cell is 10 amino acids long. Predict how long the mRNA for this protein would be in mononucleotides. Explain your answer. [2 marks]

I could do with a translation for this page...

So you start off with DNA, lots of cleverness happens and bingo... you've got a protein. Only problem is you need to know the cleverness bit in quite a lot of detail. So scribble it down, recite it to yourself, explain it to your best mate or do whatever else helps you remember the joys of protein synthesis. And then think how clever you are to know it all.

Replication of DNA

DNA has the amazing ability to replicate (copy) itself. These pages cover the facts behind the replication mechanism, as well as some of the history behind its discovery. This stuff is really clever. Honest.

DNA Replicates by **Semi-Conservative** Replication

DNA **copies** itself **before** cell division (see page 66) so that each **new** cell has the **full** amount of **DNA**. The method is called **semi-conservative replication** because **half** of the strands in **each new DNA molecule** are from the **original** DNA molecule. This means that there's **genetic continuity** between generations of cells (i.e. the cells produced by cell division inherit their genes from their parent cells).

1) The enzyme **DNA helicase** **breaks** the **hydrogen bonds** between bases on the two **polynucleotide** DNA strands. This makes the helix **unwind** to form two single strands.

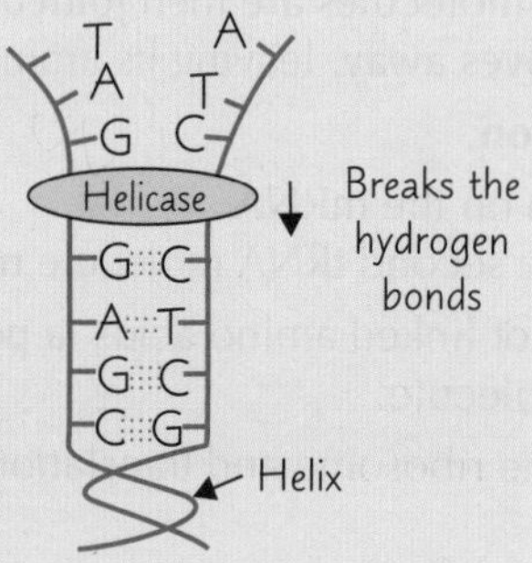
Helicase
Breaks the hydrogen bonds
Helix

See p. 42-43 for more on DNA structure.

2) Each **original** single strand acts as a **template** for a new strand. **Complementary base pairing** means that **free-floating DNA nucleotides** are attracted to their complementary **exposed bases** on each original template strand — A with T and C with G.

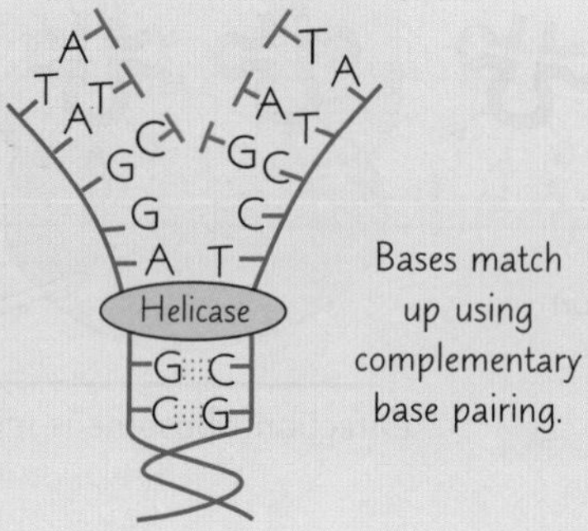
Helicase
Bases match up using complementary base pairing.

Gerald doesn't need helicase to unwind. He just needs a beach full of seals.

3) **Condensation reactions** join the nucleotides of the new strands together — catalysed by the enzyme **DNA polymerase**. Hydrogen bonds **form** between the bases on the original and new strands.

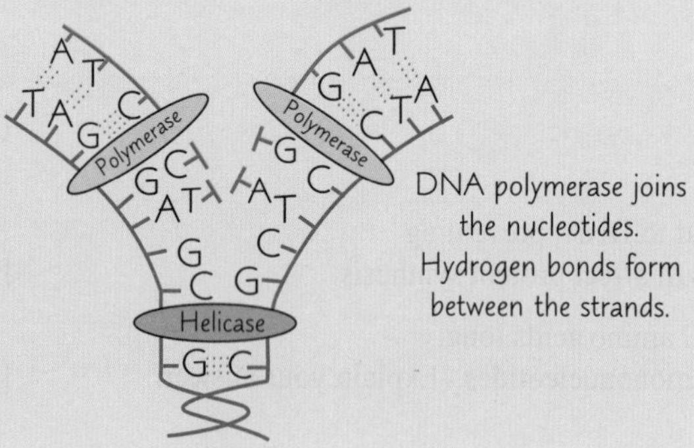
Polymerase
Polymerase
Helicase
DNA polymerase joins the nucleotides. Hydrogen bonds form between the strands.

4) Each new DNA molecule contains **one strand** from the **original** DNA molecule and one **new strand**.

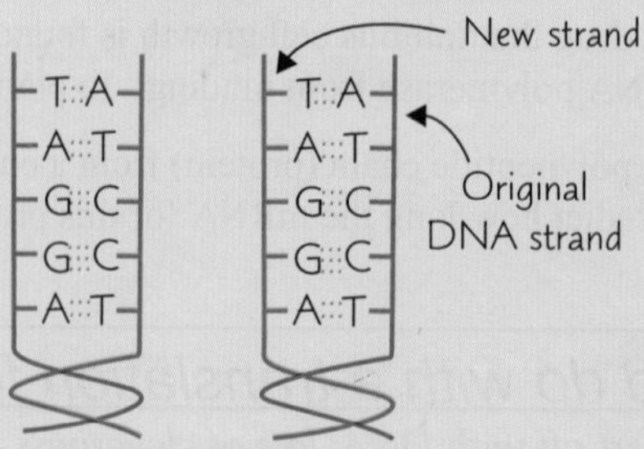
New strand
Original DNA strand

Replication of DNA

Meselson and Stahl Provided Evidence for Semi-Conservative Replication

1) Before **Meselson** and **Stahl's** experiment (see below), people were unsure whether DNA replication was **semi-conservative** or **conservative**. If the method was **conservative**, the original DNA strands would **stay together** and the new DNA molecules would contain **two new strands.**
2) Meselson and Stahl showed that DNA is replicated using the **semi-conservative method**. Their experiment used two **isotopes** of **nitrogen** (DNA contains nitrogen) — **heavy** nitrogen (^{15}N) and **light** nitrogen (^{14}N). Here's how it worked:

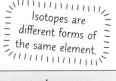

Isotopes are different forms of the same element.

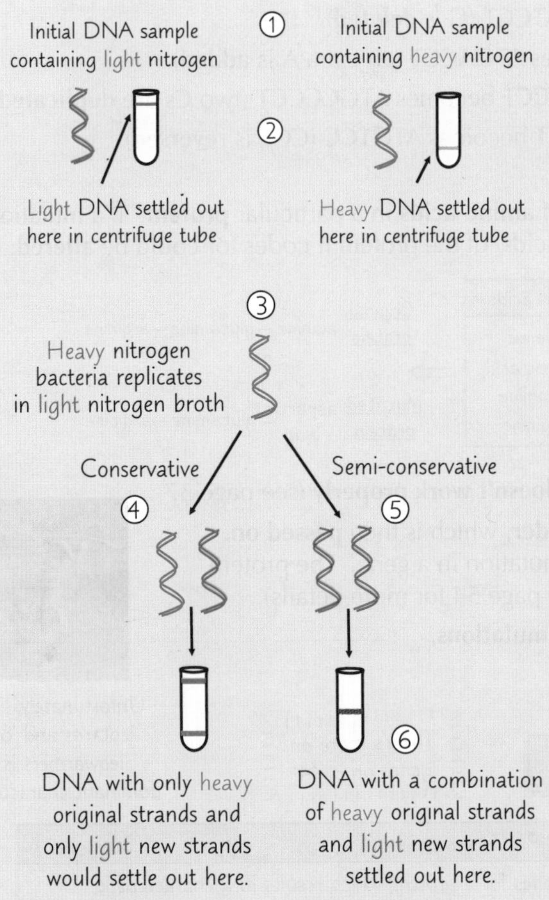

1
Initial DNA sample containing light nitrogen
Initial DNA sample containing heavy nitrogen
2
Light DNA settled out here in centrifuge tube
Heavy DNA settled out here in centrifuge tube
3
Heavy nitrogen bacteria replicates in light nitrogen broth
Conservative
Semi-conservative
4
5
6
DNA with only heavy original strands and only light new strands would settle out here.
DNA with a combination of heavy original strands and light new strands settled out here.

1) Two samples of bacteria were grown — one in a nutrient broth containing **light** nitrogen, and one in a broth with **heavy** nitrogen. As the **bacteria reproduced**, they **took up nitrogen** from the broth to help make nucleotides for new DNA. So the nitrogen gradually became part of the bacteria's DNA.
2) A **sample of DNA** was taken from each batch of bacteria, and spun in a **centrifuge**. The DNA from the **heavy** nitrogen bacteria settled **lower** down the **centrifuge tube** than the DNA from the **light** nitrogen bacteria — because it's **heavier**.
3) Then the bacteria grown in the **heavy** nitrogen broth were **taken out** and put in a broth containing only **light nitrogen**. The bacteria were left for **one round of DNA replication**, and then **another DNA sample** was taken out and spun in the centrifuge.
4) If replication was **conservative**, the original **heavy** DNA, which would still be together, would settle at the bottom and the new **light** DNA would settle at the top.
5) If replication was **semi-conservative**, the new bacterial DNA molecules would contain **one strand** of the **old DNA** containing **heavy** nitrogen and **one strand** of **new DNA** containing **light** nitrogen. So the DNA would settle out **between** where the **light** nitrogen DNA settled out and where the **heavy** nitrogen DNA settled out.
6) As it turned out, the DNA settled out in the **middle**, showing that the DNA molecules contained a **mixture** of **heavy** and **light** nitrogen. The bacterial DNA had **replicated semi-conservatively** in the **light** nitrogen.

Practice Questions

Q1 What is the role of DNA helicase in DNA replication?

Q2 What's the key difference between the conservative and semi-conservative theories of DNA replication?

Exam Question

Q1 a) Describe the process of semi-conservative DNA replication. [5 marks]

b) Describe Meselson and Stahl's experiment to prove the semi-conservative replication of DNA. [4 marks]

c) Explain how the experiment supports semi-conservative replication and refutes competing theories. [2 marks]

DNA DNA Replication Replication is is Semi-Conservative Semi-Conservative

Make sure you can recall the mechanism of DNA replication — you might be asked for it in your exam. You might also be asked to describe Meselson and Stahl's classic experiment, and also to explain how it provided support for the theory of semi-conservative replication of DNA. Don't turn over until you've got these things firmly wedged in your brain.

Genes and Inheritance

Time to learn about genetic disorders — inherited disorders caused by abnormal genes or chromosomes. But first you need to understand how these disorders arise and learn a load of genetic terms — will the fun ever stop...

*Some **Genetic Disorders** are **Caused** by **Mutations***

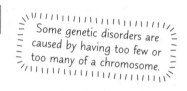

Some genetic disorders are caused by having too few or too many of a chromosome.

1) Mutations are **changes** to the **base sequence** of DNA.
2) They can be caused by **errors** during **DNA replication**.
3) The **type** of errors that can occur include:

Substitution — one base is substituted with another, e.g. ATGCCT becomes ATTCCT (G is **swapped** for T).
Deletion — one base is deleted, e.g. ATGCCT becomes ATCCT (G is **deleted**).
Insertion — an extra base is added, e.g. ATGCCT becomes ATGACCT (an extra A is **added**).
Duplication — one or more bases are repeated, e.g. ATGCCT becomes ATGCCCCT (two Cs are **duplicated**).
Inversion — a sequence of bases is reversed, e.g. ATG**CCT** becomes ATG**TCC** (CCT is **reversed**).

4) The **order** of **DNA bases** in a gene determines the **order of amino acids** in a particular **protein**. If a mutation occurs in a gene, the **primary structure** (the sequence of amino acids) of the protein it codes for could be **altered**:

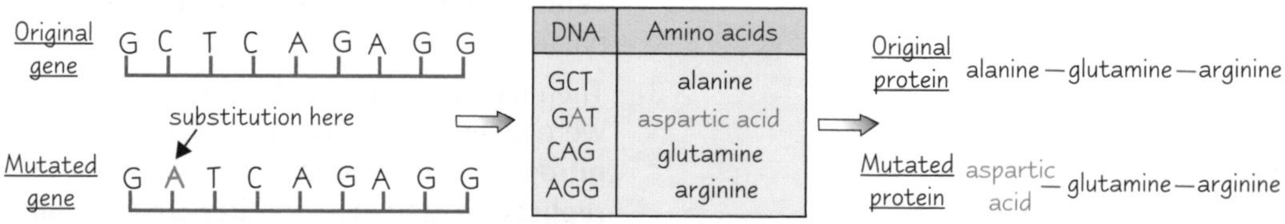

This could **change** the final **3D shape** of the protein so it **doesn't work properly** (see page 37).

5) If a mutation occurs in a **gene** it can cause a **genetic disorder**, which is then **passed on**. E.g. **cystic fibrosis** (**CF**) is a genetic disorder caused by a mutation in a gene. The protein the gene codes for is important for **mucus production** (see page 54 for more details).
6) Some genetic disorders can be caused by lots of **different mutations**, e.g. over 1000 possible mutations are known to cause CF.

Unfortunately, liking leotards and '80s legwarmers is a dominant characteristic.

*You **Need to Know** These **Genetic Terms***

There's more on genes on p. 44.

TERM	DESCRIPTION
Gene	A sequence of bases on a DNA molecule that codes for a protein, which results in a characteristic, e.g. the gene for eye colour.
Allele	A different version of a gene. Most plants and animals, including humans, have two copies of each gene, one from each parent. The two copies can be the same or they can be different. Different versions (alleles) have slightly different base sequences, which code for different versions of the same characteristic, e.g. brown eyes and blue eyes. They're represented using letters, e.g. the allele for brown eyes (B) and the allele for blue eyes (b).
Genotype	The alleles a person has, e.g. BB, Bb or bb for eye colour.
Phenotype	The characteristics displayed by an organism, e.g. brown eyes.
Dominant	An allele whose characteristic appears in the phenotype even when there's only one copy, e.g. the allele for brown eyes (B) is dominant — if a person's genotype is Bb or BB, they'll have brown eyes. Dominant alleles are shown by a capital letter.
Recessive	An allele whose characteristic only appears in the phenotype if two copies are present, e.g. the allele for blue eyes (b) is recessive — if a person's genotype is bb, they'll have blue eyes. Recessive alleles are shown by a lower case letter.
Incomplete Dominance	When the trait from a dominant allele isn't completely shown over the trait produced by the recessive allele, so both alleles influence the phenotype. Some flowers show incomplete dominance, e.g. snapdragons can have alleles for red flowers (RR), white flowers (rr) or pink flowers (Rr).
Homozygote	An organism that carries two copies of the same allele for a certain characteristic, e.g. BB or bb.
Heterozygote	An organism that carries two different alleles for a certain characteristic, e.g. Bb.
Carrier	If a recessive allele can cause disease, a carrier is someone who has one dominant and one recessive allele (heterozygous). They won't have the disease but they carry a copy of the allele for the disease.

Genes and Inheritance

Genetic Diagrams show the Possible Alleles of Offspring

Monohybrid inheritance is the inheritance of a **single characteristic** controlled by **different** alleles. **Genetic diagrams** can be used to predict the **genotypes** and **phenotypes** of the **offspring** produced if two parents are **crossed** (**bred**). You need to be able to **interpret** genetic diagrams for characteristics, so here's an example:

Plant Height

1) The **height** of garden pea plants is controlled by a **single** gene with **two alleles.**
2) The allele for **tall** plants (**T**) is **dominant** over the allele for **dwarf** plants (**t**).
3) The diagrams below show the predicted genotypes and phenotypes of the offspring if **two heterozygous** pea plants (**Tt**) are crossed, and if **two homozygous** pea plants (**TT** and **tt**) are crossed:

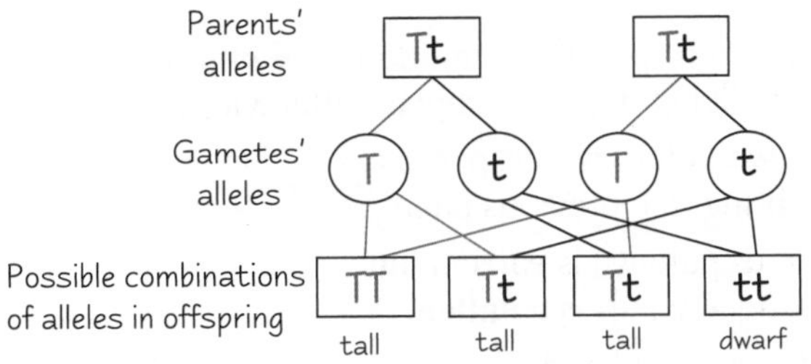

See page 68 for more on gametes.

Predicted genotypes and phenotypes:

- **2 in 4 (50%) chance** of offspring having the **genotype Tt** (**phenotype = tall**).
- 1 in 4 (25%) chance of offspring having the **genotype TT** (**phenotype = tall**).
- 1 in 4 (25%) chance of offspring having the **genotype tt** (**phenotype = dwarf**).

So there's a **75%** (3 in 4) chance of offspring being **tall**, and the **phenotypic ratio** of tall to dwarf plants is **3 : 1**.

The phenotypic ratio is just the ratio of different phenotypes in the offspring.

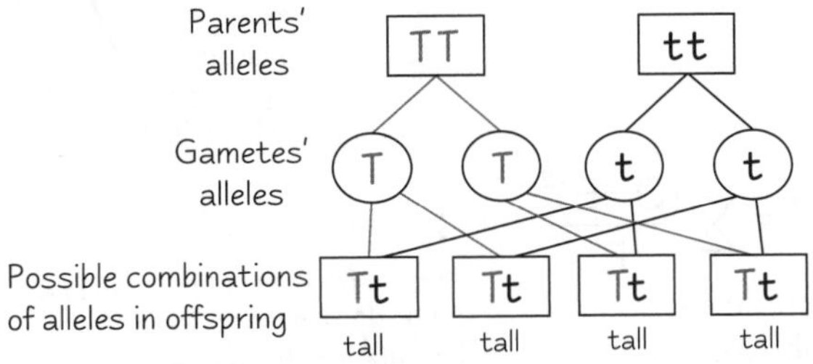

Predicted genotypes and phenotypes:

- 4 in 4 (**100%**) **chance** of offspring having the **genotype Tt** (**phenotype = tall**).
- 0 in 4 (0%) chance of offspring having the **genotype TT** (**phenotype = tall**).
- 0 in 4 (0%) chance of offspring having the **genotype tt** (**phenotype = dwarf**).

Practice Questions

Q1 What are mutations?

Q2 Explain the difference between a dominant and a recessive allele.

Q3 What is incomplete dominance?

Q4 What is monohybrid inheritance?

Exam Question

Q1 A garden pea plant is heterozygous for seed colour.
The allele for yellow colour (Y) is dominant over the allele for green colour (y).

a) Give the genotype and phenotype of the heterozygous plant. [2 marks]

b) Draw a genetic diagram to show the possible genotypes of the offspring produced if the heterozygous plant is crossed with a homozygous plant with green seeds. [3 marks]

c) Give the predicted ratio of green seeds to yellow seeds in the offspring from the genetic cross in part b). [1 mark]

What do you get if you cross a one-legged donkey with a one-eyed donkey?*

There's quite a lot to get to grips with on these two pages — that list of genetic terms just goes on and on and on. You won't get very far in this section without learning them first though, so just grin and bear it. Oh... and learn it of course.

* A winky wonky donkey.

The Chi-Squared Test

Just when you thought it was safe to turn the page... I stick in some maths. Surprise!

The Chi-Squared Test Can Be Used to Check the Results of Genetic Crosses

1) The **chi-squared** (χ^2) **test** is a **statistical test** that's used to see if the **results** of an experiment **support** a **theory**.
2) First, the theory is used to **predict** a **result** — this is called the **expected result**. Then, the experiment is carried out and the **actual result** is recorded — this is called the **observed result**.
3) To see if the results support the theory you have to make a **hypothesis** called the **null hypothesis**.
4) The null hypothesis is always that there's **no significant difference** between the observed and expected results (your experimental result will usually be a bit different from what you expect, but you need to know if the difference is just **due to chance**, or because your **theory is wrong**).
5) The χ^2 **test** is then carried out and the **outcome** either **supports** or **rejects** the **null hypothesis**.
6) You can use the χ^2 test in **genetics** to test theories about the **inheritance** of **characteristics**. For example:

Theory: **Wing length** in fruit flies is controlled by a **single gene** with **two alleles** (**monohybrid inheritance**). The **dominant** allele (N) gives **normal** wings, and the **recessive** allele (n) gives **vestigial** (little) wings.

Expected results: With monohybrid inheritance, if you cross **two heterozygous** parents, you'd expect a **3 : 1 phenotypic ratio** of **normal : vestigial** wings in the offspring (see previous page).

Observed results: The **experiment** (of crossing two heterozygous parents) is **carried out** on fruit flies and the **number of offspring** with normal and vestigial wings is **counted**.

Null hypothesis: There's **no significant difference** between the observed and expected results. (If the χ^2 test shows the observed and expected results are **not significantly different** then we are **unable to reject** the null hypothesis — the data supports the **theory** that wing length is controlled by **monohybrid inheritance**.)

In this kind of statistical test, you can never prove that the null hypothesis is true — you can only 'fail to reject it'. This just means that the evidence doesn't give you a reason to think the null hypothesis is wrong.

First, Work Out the Chi-Squared Value...

Chi-squared (χ^2) is calculated using this formula: where **O** = **observed** result and **E** = **expected** result.

$$\chi^2 = \sum \frac{(O-E)^2}{E}$$

The best way to understand the χ^2 test is to work through an example — here's one for testing the **wing length** of **fruit flies** as explained above:

You don't need to learn the formula for chi-squared — it'll be given to you in the exam.

Heterozygous (Nn) **flies** are **crossed** and **160 offspring** are produced.

1) First, the **number of offspring** (out of a total of 160) **expected** for each phenotype is worked out. E for normal wings: 160 (total) ÷ 4 (ratio total) × 3 (predicted ratio for normal wings) = 120. E for vestigial wings: 160 ÷ 4 × 1 = 40.

Phenotype	Ratio	Expected Result (E)	Observed Result (O)
Normal wings	3	120	
Vestigial wings	1	40	

2) Then the **actual number** of offspring **observed** with each phenotype (out of the 160 offspring) is **recorded**, e.g. 111 with normal wings.

Phenotype	Ratio	Expected Result (E)	Observed Result (O)
Normal wings	3	120	111
Vestigial wings	1	40	49

3) The results are used to work out χ^2, taking it **one step at a time**:

a) First calculate **O – E** (**subtract** the **expected result** from the **observed result**) for each phenotype. E.g. for normal wings: 111 – 120 = –9.

b) Then the resulting numbers are **squared**, e.g. $9^2 = 81$.

c) These figures are divided by the **expected results**, e.g. 81 ÷ 120 = 0.675.

d) Finally, the numbers are **added** together to get χ^2, e.g. 0.675 + 2.025 = **2.7**.

Phenotype	Ratio	Expected Result (E)	Observed Result (O)	O – E	$(O-E)^2$	$\frac{(O-E)^2}{E}$
Normal wings	3	120	111	–9	81	0.675
Vestigial wings	1	40	49	9	81	2.025
					$\sum \frac{(O-E)^2}{E} =$	2.7

Remember, you need to work it out for each phenotype first, then add all the numbers together.

The Chi-Squared Test

...Then Compare it to the Critical Value

1) To find out if there is a **significant difference** between your observed and expected results you need to **compare** your **χ^2 value** to a **critical value.**
2) The critical value is the value of χ^2 that corresponds to a 0.05 (**5%**) level of **probability** that the **difference** between the observed and expected results is **due to chance.**
3) If your χ^2 value is **larger** than or equal to the critical value then there **is a significant difference** between the observed and expected results (something **other than chance** is causing the difference) — and the **null hypothesis** can be **rejected.**
4) If your χ^2 value is **smaller** than the critical value then there **is no significant difference** between the observed and expected results — the null hypothesis **can't be rejected.** E.g. for the example on the previous page the χ^2 value is **2.7**, which is **smaller** than the critical value of **3.84** (see table below) — there's **no significant difference** between the observed and expected results. We've failed to reject the null hypothesis, so the **theory** that wing length in fruit flies is controlled by **monohybrid inheritance** is **supported.**
5) In the exam you might be **given** the **critical value** or asked to **work it out** from a **table:**

Using a χ^2 table:

If you're not given the critical value, you may have to find it yourself from a **χ^2 table** — this shows a range of **probabilities** that correspond to different **critical values** for different **degrees of freedom** (explained below). Biologists normally use a **probability** level of **0.05** (5%), so you only need to look in that column.

- First, the **degrees of freedom** for the experiment are worked out — this is the **number of classes** (number of phenotypes) **minus one.** E.g. 2 – 1 = 1.
- Next, the **critical value** corresponding to a **probability** of **0.05** at **one degree of freedom** is found in the table — here it's **3.84.**
- Then just **compare** your χ^2 value of **2.7** to this critical value, as explained above.

degrees of freedom	no. of classes	Critical values					
1	2	0.46	1.64	2.71	3.84	6.64	10.83
2	3	1.39	3.22	4.61	5.99	9.21	13.82
3	4	2.37	4.64	6.25	7.82	11.34	16.27
4	5	3.36	5.99	7.78	9.49	13.28	18.47
probability that result is due to chance only		0.50 (50%)	0.20 (20%)	0.10 (10%)	0.05 (5%)	0.01 (1%)	0.001 (0.1%)

Practice Questions

Q1 What is a χ^2 test used for?

Q2 How do you tell if the difference between your observed and expected results is due to chance?

Exam Question

Q1 A scientist comes up with the following theory:

> 'Height in plants is controlled by a single gene with two alleles.
> The dominant allele gives tall plants. The recessive allele gives dwarf plants.'

The scientist predicts that if this theory is true, when two heterozygous plants are crossed, a 3 : 1 ratio of tall : dwarf plants will be produced. The scientist then comes up with a null hypothesis and carries out the cross. Of the 52 offspring produced, 9 were dwarf.

a) What should the scientist's null hypothesis be? [1 mark]

b) The formula for calculating chi-squared is: $\chi^2 = \Sigma \frac{(O - E)^2}{E}$

The critical value at one degree of freedom at a probability level of 0.05 is 3.84.
Use the chi-squared test to explain whether the results of the scientist's experiment support his theory. [4 marks]

The expected result of revising these pages — boredom...

...the observed result — boredom (except for the maths geeks among you). Don't worry if you're not brilliant at maths though, you don't have to be to do the chi-squared test — just make sure you know the steps above off by heart.

Cystic Fibrosis

As you enjoyed the genetic diagrams on p. 51 so much, here are some more, only this time they're slightly different.

Genetic Pedigree Diagrams Show How Traits Run in Families

Genetic pedigree diagrams show an **inherited trait** (characteristic) in a group of **related individuals**. You need to be able to **interpret** genetic pedigree diagrams, so here are some examples for cystic fibrosis:

Cystic fibrosis (CF) is an inherited disorder that mainly affects the **respiratory, digestive** and **reproductive systems** (see next page). It's caused by a **recessive** allele (f), so a person will only have the disorder if they're **homozygous** for the allele (ff) — they must inherit one recessive allele **from each parent.** If a person is **heterozygous** (Ff), they **won't** have CF but they'll be a **carrier.**

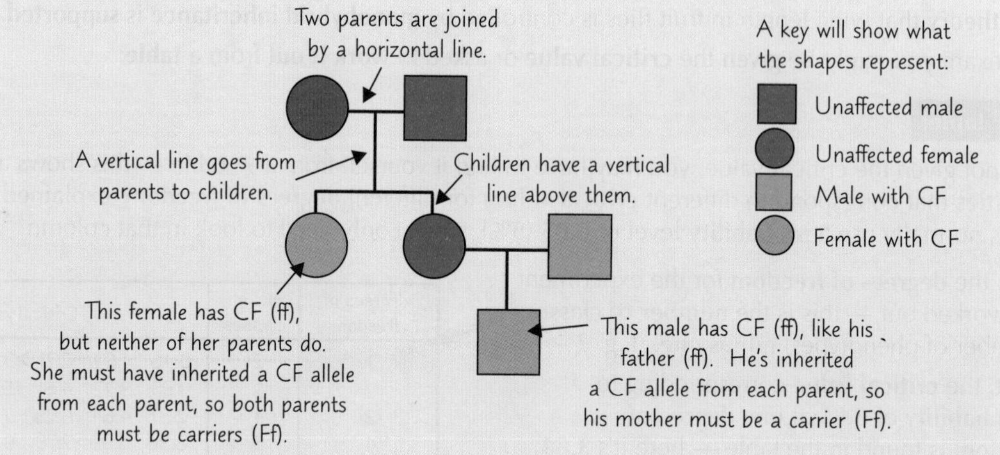

Two parents are joined by a horizontal line.
A key will show what the shapes represent:
Unaffected male
Unaffected female
Male with CF
Female with CF
A vertical line goes from parents to children.
Children have a vertical line above them.
This female has CF (ff), but neither of her parents do. She must have inherited a CF allele from each parent, so both parents must be carriers (Ff).
This male has CF (ff), like his father (ff). He's inherited a CF allele from each parent, so his mother must be a carrier (Ff).

Sometimes carriers are also shown on the key:

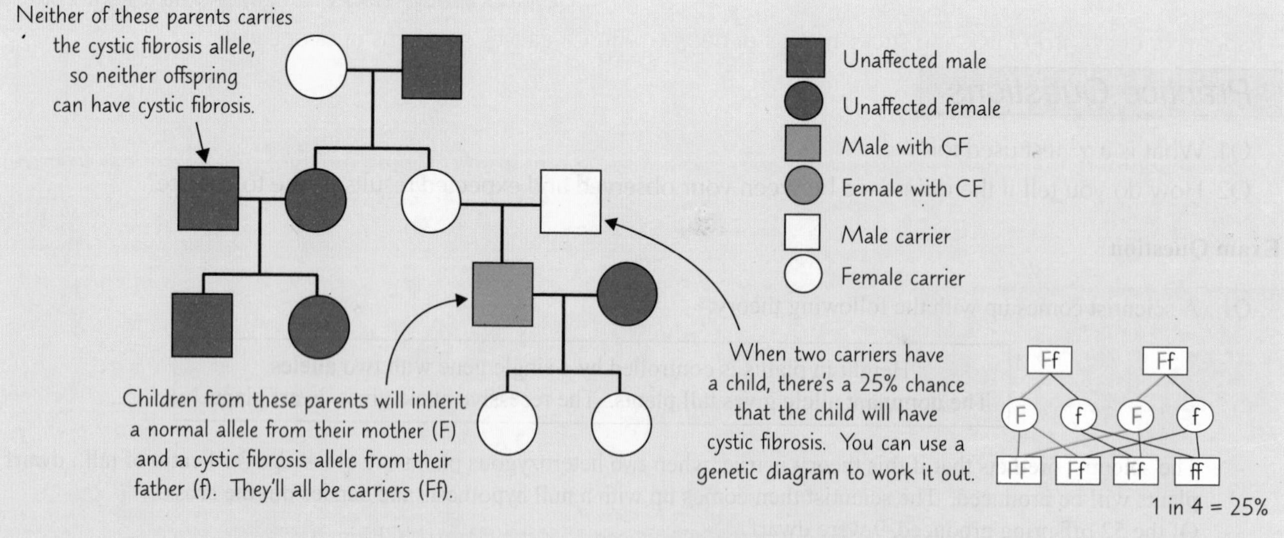

Neither of these parents carries the cystic fibrosis allele, so neither offspring can have cystic fibrosis.
Unaffected male
Unaffected female
Male with CF
Female with CF
Male carrier
Female carrier
Children from these parents will inherit a normal allele from their mother (F) and a cystic fibrosis allele from their father (f). They'll all be carriers (Ff).
When two carriers have a child, there's a 25% chance that the child will have cystic fibrosis. You can use a genetic diagram to work it out.
Ff
Ff
F
f
F
f
FF
Ff
Ff
ff
1 in 4 = 25%

Cystic Fibrosis Causes the Production of Thick Sticky Mucus

See page 31 for more on osmosis.

1) Cystic fibrosis is caused by a **mutation** in the **gene** that codes for the **CFTR** protein (**C**ystic **F**ibrosis **T**ransmembrane Conductance **R**egulator).
2) CFTR is a **channel protein** (see page 32). It transports **chloride ions** out of cells and into **mucus** — this causes water to move **into** the mucus by **osmosis**, which makes mucus **watery**.
3) **Mutant** CFTR protein is much **less efficient** at transporting chloride ions **out** of the cell, so **less water moves out by osmosis**. This makes the mucus of people with CF abnormally **thick** and **sticky**.
4) This thick and sticky mucus causes **problems** in the **respiratory**, **digestive** and **reproductive systems**.

Cystic Fibrosis

Cystic Fibrosis Affects the **Respiratory System...**

Everybody has **mucus** in their respiratory system — it helps **prevent lung infections** by trapping **microorganisms**. The mucus (with the microorganisms) is transported towards the throat by **cilia** (small **hair-like** structures that beat to move mucus along). In people with CF the mucus is abnormally **thick** and **sticky**, which causes some problems:

1) The cilia are **unable to move** the mucus towards the throat because it's so thick and sticky.
2) This means the **mucus builds up** in the **airways**.
3) Some airways can become completely **blocked** by the mucus — **gas exchange** can't take place in the area **below the blockage**.
4) This means that the **surface area** available for gas exchange is **reduced**, causing breathing difficulties.
5) People with CF are also more prone to **lung infections** as mucus containing microorganisms can't be removed.

See page 28 for more on gas exchange in the lungs.

People with CF can be given **antibiotics** to **kill** the **bacteria** trapped in mucus, and they can also have **physiotherapy** to help dislodge mucus and **improve gas exchange**.

...the **Digestive System...**

Everyone also has mucus in their digestive system. The abnormally thick mucus produced by people with CF can also cause **digestive problems** because:

1) The **tube** that connects the **pancreas** to the **small intestine** can become **blocked** with mucus — preventing **digestive enzymes** produced by the pancreas from **reaching** the small intestine. This reduces the ability of someone with CF to **digest food** and so **fewer nutrients** can be absorbed.
2) The mucus can cause **cysts** (**growths**) to form in the **pancreas**. These **inhibit** the **production** of **enzymes**, which also reduces the ability to digest food and absorb nutrients.
3) The mucus **lining** the **small intestine** is **abnormally thick** — this inhibits the **absorption** of nutrients.

...and the **Reproductive System**

Mucus is also secreted by the reproductive system — it helps to **prevent infections** and **transport sex cells** (sperm or eggs). The thick and sticky mucus of people with CF causes problems here because:

1) In some men with CF, the **tubes** connecting the **testicles** (where sperm are produced) to the **penis** are **absent** and can become **blocked** by the thick mucus in others. So, any **sperm** produced **can't reach the penis**.
2) In women, thickened **cervical mucus** can **prevent** the sperm from **reaching the egg**. The sperm has to travel through this mucus to reach the egg — thick mucus reduces the **motility** of the sperm, reducing its chances of **making it** to the egg.

Practice Questions

Q1 What is a genetic pedigree diagram?

Q2 Why do people with cystic fibrosis have abnormally thick and sticky mucus?

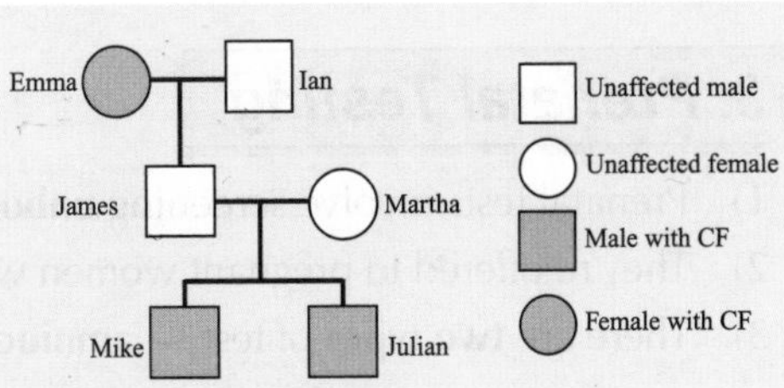

Exam Question

Q1 The genetic pedigree diagram above shows the inheritance of cystic fibrosis (CF) in one family.

a) Name one female who is homozygous for the CF allele and one individual who is a carrier. [2 marks]

b) If James and Martha have another child, what is the chance it will have CF? Show your working. [3 marks]

c)* Explain the effect of CF on the digestive system. [6 marks]

* You will be assessed on the quality of your written response in this question.

Pedigree Diagram — because your dog's worth it...

Pedigree diagrams aren't as scary as they look, just work through them slowly. And remember, with recessive disorders affected individuals are always homozygous, so any children they have will always have at least one recessive allele.

Genetic Screening

Most genetic disorders can only be treated, not cured, so it's important to be able to screen for these conditions.

There are Three Main Uses of Genetic Screening

Genetic screening involves analysing **DNA** to see if it contains **alleles** for genetic disorders.
The **three** main uses are:

1. Identification of Carriers

1) **Carrier testing** is offered to individuals with a **family history** of genetic disorders.
2) It shows whether people **without** a disorder **carry an allele** that can cause a disorder (e.g. CF).
3) Couples can be tested **before having children** to determine the **chances** of any **future** children having the disorder, e.g. if both parents are **carriers** there's a **25%** chance their child will have the disorder.
4) Carrier testing allows people to make **informed decisions** about things like **whether to have children** and whether to carry out **prenatal testing** if the woman is pregnant (see below).
5) Carrier testing raises **social** and **ethical issues**:

- Finding out you're a carrier may cause **emotional stress** or affect your ability to **find a partner**.
- The tests **aren't** always 100% **accurate** — they could give a **false result**. This means decisions could be based on **incorrect information**.
- Other genetic **abnormalities** may be found, which could cause **further stress**.
- There are concerns that the **results** of genetic tests could be used by **employers** or **life insurance companies** — resulting in **genetic discrimination**.

2. Preimplantation Genetic Diagnosis (PGD)

1) **PGD** is carried out on **embryos** produced by ***in vitro*** **fertilisation (IVF)**.
2) It involves **screening** embryos for genetic disorders **before** they're implanted into the woman.
3) The **advantages** of PGD are that it **reduces** the chance of having a baby with a genetic disorder — only embryos **without** the genetic disorders tested for will be implanted. Also, because it's performed **before implantation**, it avoids the issue of **abortion** that could be raised by **prenatal testing** (see below).
4) PGD also raises **social** and **ethical issues**:

- It can be used to find out **other characteristics** (e.g. **gender**, **eye colour**) — leading to concerns that **in the future**, embryos may be selected for other characteristics (**designer babies**).
- **False results** could provide **incorrect information**.

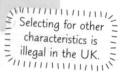

Selecting for other characteristics is illegal in the UK.

3. Prenatal Testing

1) Prenatal tests involve screening **unborn babies** (fetuses) for genetic disorders.
2) They're offered to pregnant women with a **family history** of genetic disease.
3) There are **two** types of test — **amniocentesis** and **chorionic villus sampling**.

Amniocentesis

1) This is usually carried out at **15-20 weeks** of pregnancy.
2) A sample of **amniotic fluid** (the fluid that surrounds the fetus) is obtained via the **abdomen** using a very fine **needle**.
3) This fluid contains fetal **cells**. The cells contain **DNA**, which can be **analysed**.
4) Amniocentesis has a **1% risk** of **miscarriage**.
5) Results aren't available until **2-3 weeks after** the sample is taken, although a **rapid test** (which only looks for a **few** of the **most common** disorders) can also be performed. The results of the rapid test are usually available in **3-4 days**.

Genetic Screening

Chorionic Villus Sampling (CVS)

1) CVS is usually performed at **11-14 weeks** of pregnancy.
2) Because it can take place **earlier** in a pregnancy than amniocentesis, an earlier **decision** to abort can be made, meaning that the procedure is less physically traumatic.
3) A sample of **cells** is taken from the **chorionic villi** (part of the fetus that connects it to its mother). The cells contain fetal **DNA**, which can be **analysed**.
4) This procedure is done via either the **abdomen** (using a fine **needle**) or the **vagina** (using a **catheter** — a thin flexible tube).
5) CVS has a **1-2% risk** of **miscarriage**, which is greater than with amniocentesis.
6) **Initial** results (which tell you whether any **obvious major issues** have been found) are available in a **few days**, but the results of more **in-depth** and **detailed** tests can take **two weeks** or **more**.

Testing Allows People to **Make Decisions**

1) Prenatal testing allows parents to make **informed decisions**. If the test is positive, the parents may decide to **have the child** or to have an **abortion**. The results can also help parents to **prepare for the future care** of the child — any **medical treatment** available could be started as soon as the child is born.
2) As with the other forms of testing, prenatal testing raises **social** and **ethical issues**:

- Prenatal tests slightly **increase** the risk of **miscarriage**.
- **False results** could provide **incorrect information**.
- Some people consider it **unethical** to **abort** a fetus because it has a genetic disorder.

Practice Questions

Q1 What is genetic screening?

Q2 Describe one ethical issue raised by prenatal testing.

Exam Questions

Q1 Which of the following is true about chorionic villus sampling (CVS)?

A It has a lower risk of miscarriage and can be carried out earlier than amniocentesis.
B It has a higher risk of miscarriage and is carried out later than amniocentesis.
C It has a higher risk of miscarriage and can be carried out earlier than amniocentesis.
D It has a lower risk of miscarriage and is carried out later than amniocentesis. [1 mark]

Q2 Duchenne muscular dystrophy is a genetic disorder caused by a recessive allele.
It is caused by a mutated gene, which normally codes for a protein needed for healthy muscle tissue.

a) Explain why an individual with a family history of Duchenne muscular dystrophy may be offered carrier testing. [3 marks]

b) Preimplantation genetic diagnosis is available for Duchenne muscular dystrophy.

i) Explain what preimplantation genetic diagnosis is. [1 mark]

ii) Describe one benefit of preimplantation genetic diagnosis. [1 mark]

iii) Describe two social or ethical issues raised by preimplantation genetic diagnosis. [2 marks]

Carrier testing — which bag has the strongest handles?

There's lots to learn when it comes to genetic screening. You need to understand the three main uses, the implications of each, and all the possible ethical issues. As with any ethics question in the exam, don't forget to cover both the advantages and the issues surrounding it (whatever your personal opinion). Chin up, kettle on, and back to it.

Eukaryotic Cells and Organelles

Ah, cells. Where would we be without them? There are two types of cell — prokaryotic and eukaryotic. This topic is about eukaryotic cells and their organelles (all the tiny bits and bobs that you can only see in detail with a fancy microscope)...

Organisms Can be ***Prokaryotes*** *or* ***Eukaryotes***

All living organisms are made of **cells** and share some **common features**.

1) Prokaryotic organisms are **prokaryotic cells** (i.e. they're single-celled organisms) and eukaryotic organisms are made up of **eukaryotic cells**.
2) Both types of cells contain **organelles**. Organelles are **parts** of cells — each one has a **specific function**.
3) If you examine a cell through an **electron microscope** (see page 62) you can see its **organelles** and the **internal structure** of most of them — this is known as the **cell ultrastructure**.

> 1) Eukaryotic cells are **complex** and include all **animal** and **plant cells.**
> 2) Prokaryotic cells are **smaller** and **simpler**, e.g. bacteria. See page 61 for more.

Animal *Cells are* ***Eukaryotic***

Eukaryotic cells are generally a **bit more complicated** than prokaryotic cells. You've probably been looking at **animal cell** diagrams for years, so hopefully you'll be familiar with some of the bits and pieces...

Animal Cell

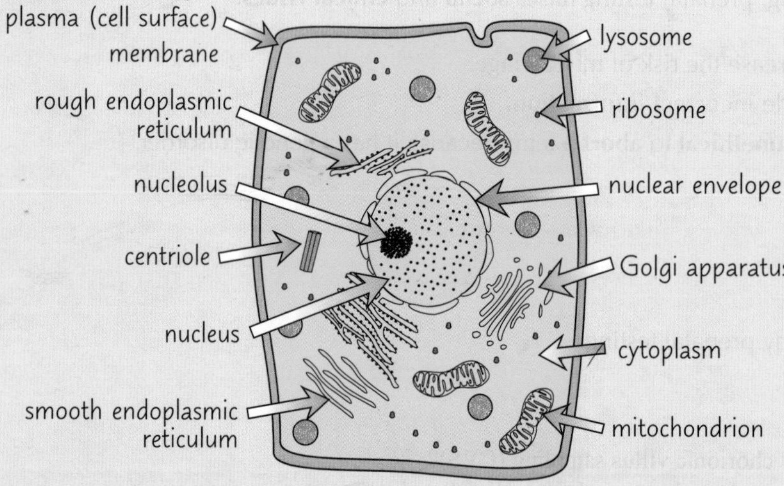

Plant cells also contain these organelles, along with a few different organelles that aren't found in animal cells — see pages 90-91.

You're expected to be able to recognise organelles from images taken through an electron microscope — so make sure you learn to recognise all the structures on pages 58-59.

Different Organelles *Have* ***Different Functions***

This giant table contains a big list of organelles — you need to know the **structure** and **function** of them all. Sorry. Most organelles are surrounded by **membranes**, which sometimes causes confusion — don't make the mistake of thinking that a diagram of an organelle is a diagram of a whole cell. They're not cells — they're **parts of** cells.

ORGANELLE	DIAGRAM	DESCRIPTION	FUNCTION
Nucleus	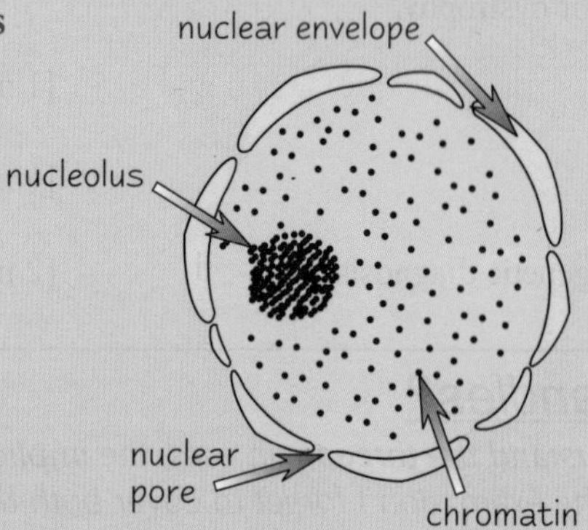	A large organelle surrounded by a **nuclear envelope** (double membrane), which contains many **pores**. The nucleus contains **chromatin** (which is made from **DNA** and proteins) and a structure called the **nucleolus**.	The nucleus **controls the cell's activities** (by controlling the transcription of DNA — see page 46). **DNA** contains instructions to make proteins — see page 44. The **pores** allow substances (e.g. RNA) to move between the nucleus and the cytoplasm. The **nucleolus** makes **ribosomes** (see next page).

Eukaryotic Cells and Organelles

ORGANELLE	DIAGRAM	DESCRIPTION	FUNCTION
Lysosome	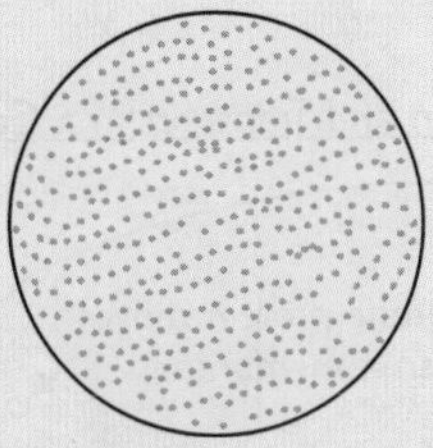	A **round organelle** surrounded by a **membrane**, with no clear internal structure.	Contains **digestive enzymes**. These are kept separate from the cytoplasm by the surrounding membrane, and can be used to **digest invading cells** or to **break down** worn out components of the cell.
Ribosome	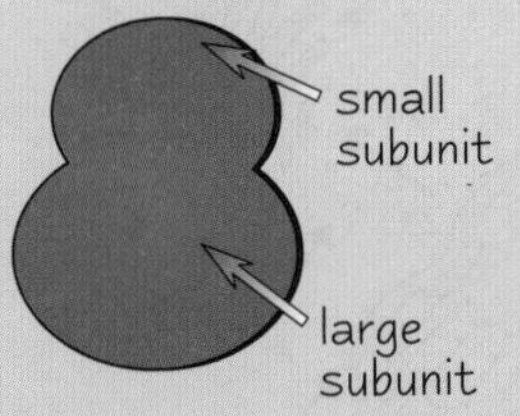	A **very small organelle** that either **floats free** in the cytoplasm or is attached to the **rough endoplasmic reticulum**. It's made up of **proteins** and **RNA** (see page 42). It's **not** surrounded by a membrane.	The **site** where **proteins** are made.
Rough Endoplasmic Reticulum (RER)	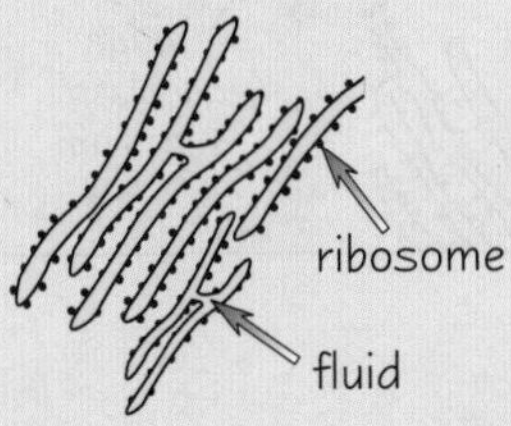	A system of membranes enclosing a fluid-filled space. The surface is **covered with ribosomes.**	**Folds** and **processes proteins** that have been made at the ribosomes.
Smooth Endoplasmic Reticulum (SER)	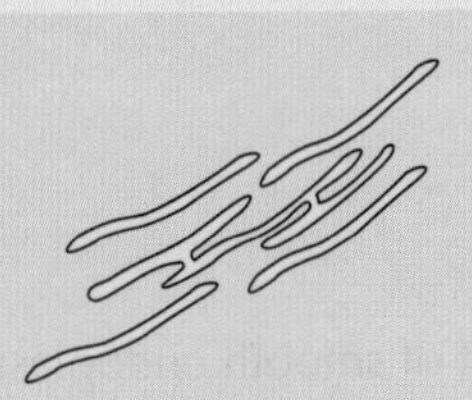	Similar to rough endoplasmic reticulum, but with no **ribosomes**.	**Synthesises** and **processes lipids.**
Golgi Apparatus	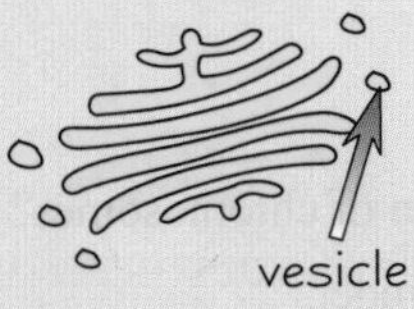	A group of fluid-filled, membrane-bound, **flattened sacs**. Vesicles are often seen at the edges of the sacs.	It **processes** and **packages** new lipids and proteins. It also **makes lysosomes.**
Mitochondrion	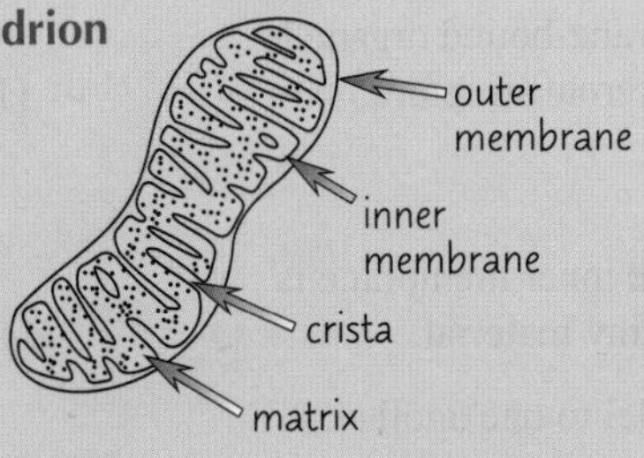	They're usually oval-shaped. They have a **double membrane** — the inner one is folded to form structures called **cristae.** Inside is the **matrix**, which contains enzymes involved in respiration.	The **site of aerobic respiration,** where **ATP** is produced. They're found in large numbers in cells that are very **active** and require a lot of **energy**.
Centriole	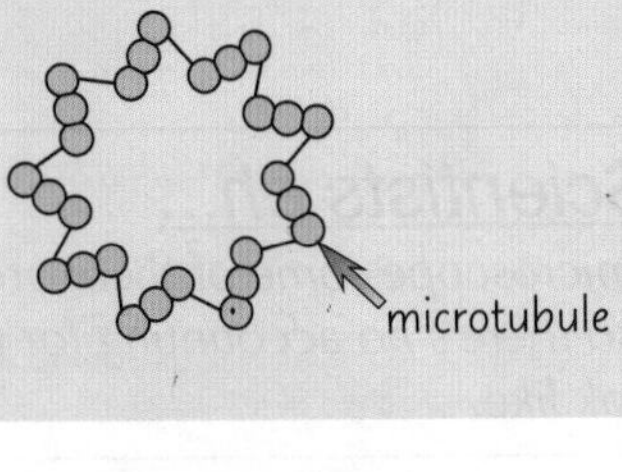	Small, **hollow cylinders**, made of **microtubules** (tiny protein cylinders). Found in animal cells, but only some plant cells.	Involved with the **separation of chromosomes** during cell division (see page 66).

Eukaryotic Cells and Organelles

Organelles are Involved in **Protein Production** and **Transport**

1) Proteins are made at the **ribosomes**.
2) The ribosomes on the **rough endoplasmic reticulum (ER)** make proteins that are **excreted** or attached to the **cell membrane**. The free ribosomes in the **cytoplasm** make proteins that **stay in the cytoplasm**.
3) New proteins produced at the rough ER are **folded** and **processed** (e.g. sugar chains are added) in the rough ER.
4) Then they're **transported** from the ER to the **Golgi apparatus** in **vesicles**.
5) At the Golgi apparatus, the proteins may undergo **further processing** (e.g. sugar chains are trimmed or more are added).
6) The proteins enter more **vesicles** to be transported around the cell. E.g. **extracellular enzymes** (like digestive enzymes) move to the cell surface and are **secreted**.

Protein Production and Transport in a Cell

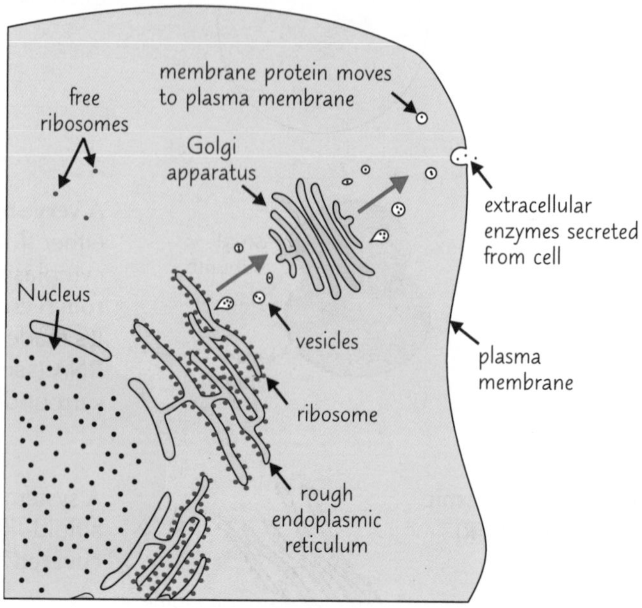

Practice Questions

Q1 Describe the structure of a nucleus.

Q2 What is the function of lysosomes?

Q3 How does the structure of rough endoplasmic reticulum differ from that of smooth endoplasmic reticulum?

Q4 What is the function of the smooth endoplasmic reticulum?

Exam Questions

Q1 Which of the following describes an organelle that is involved in the separation of chromosomes?

A A system of membranes enclosing a fluid-filled space. The surface is covered in ribosomes.

B A small, hollow cylinder, made up of microtubules.

C A small organelle consisting of two subunits. It is not surrounded by a membrane.

D A round, membrane-bound organelle with no clear internal structure. [1 mark]

Q2 a) Identify these two organelles from their descriptions.

i) An oval-shaped organelle surrounded by a double membrane. The inner membrane is folded and projects into the inner space, which is filled with a grainy material. [1 mark]

ii) A collection of flattened membrane 'sacs' arranged roughly parallel to one another. Small, circular structures are seen at the edges of these 'sacs'. [1 mark]

b) State the function of the two organelles that you have identified. [2 marks]

That's enough talk of fluid-filled sacs for my liking. Scientists eh...

'Organelle' is a very pretty-sounding name for all those blobs. Actually, under a microscope some of them are really quite fetching — well I think so anyway, but then my mate finds sheep fetching, so there's no accounting for taste. Anyway, you need to know the names of all the organelles and also what they look like.

Prokaryotic Cells

Now we're on to prokaryotic cells. They're much smaller than eukaryotic cells — and, luckily for both of us, so is the section on them in this book. Nevertheless, you need to know everything in it for your exams...

The Structure of ***Prokaryotic*** Cells is Different to ***Eukaryotic*** Cells

Remember, prokaryotic cells are **smaller** and **simpler** than eukaryotic cells (see page 58). **Bacteria** are examples of prokaryotic cells. You need to know the **structure** of a prokaryotic cell.

The **cytoplasm** of a prokaryotic cell has **no membrane-bound organelles** (unlike a eukaryotic cell). It has **ribosomes** — but they're **smaller** than those in a eukaryotic cell.

As with eukaryotic cells, the **plasma membrane** is mainly made of lipids and proteins (see p. 30). It controls the movement of substances into and out of the cell.

The **cell wall supports** the cell and prevents it from changing shape. It's made of a polymer called **murein.** Murein is a **glycoprotein** (a protein with a carbohydrate attached).

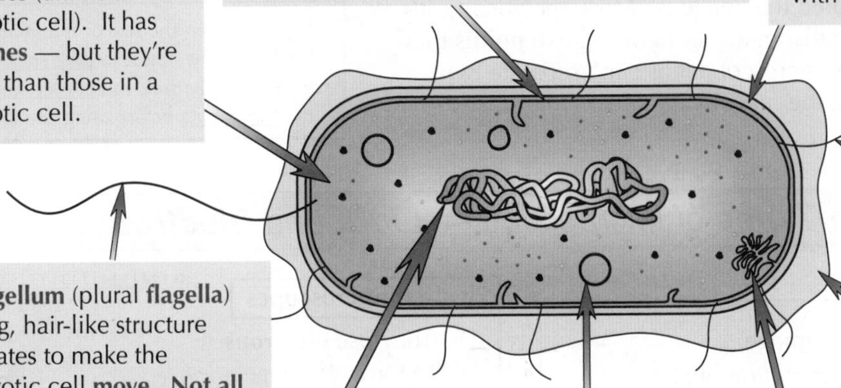

Some prokaryotes have short hair-like structures called **pili**. Pili help prokaryotes **stick** to other cells and can be used in the **transfer** of **genetic material** between cells.

The **flagellum** (plural **flagella**) is a long, hair-like structure that rotates to make the prokaryotic cell **move**. **Not all** prokaryotes have a flagellum. **Some** have **more than one**.

Some prokaryotes, e.g. bacteria, also have a **capsule** made up of secreted **slime**. It helps to **protect** bacteria from attack by cells of the immune system.

Unlike a eukaryotic cell, a prokaryotic cell **doesn't** have a nucleus. Instead, the **DNA** floats free in the cytoplasm. It's **circular DNA**, present as one long coiled-up strand. It's **not attached** to any **histone proteins** (see p. 77).

Plasmids are **small loops of DNA** that aren't part of the main circular DNA molecule. Plasmids contain genes for things like **antibiotic resistance**, and can be passed between prokaryotes. Plasmids are **not always** present in prokaryotic cells. **Some** prokaryotic cells have **several**.

Mesosomes are **inward folds** in the **plasma membrane**. Scientists are still debating what their **function** is. Some believe that they play a role in various **cellular processes** (e.g. respiration). However, others think that they're **not natural** features at all, and are just **artefacts** produced when the cells are being **prepared** for viewing with an **electron microscope**.

See pages 58-59 and 90-91 for more on organelles.

Practice Questions

Q1 What is a plasmid?

Q2 What is a flagellum?

Q3 What are pili?

Exam Questions

Q1 Which of the following structures can only be found in prokaryotic cells?

A Cytoplasm **B** Plasma membrane **C** Pili **D** Ribosome [1 mark]

Q2 Describe two ways in which DNA can be stored in a prokaryotic cell. [2 marks]

Prokaryotes — in favour of a good take-away...

You need to know the structures in prokaryotic cells and how these differ from those in eukaryotic cells. Make sure you spend plenty of time memorising them (see page 58 for more on eukaryotic cells). You could even make a song...

Looking at Cells and Organelles

You can use microscopes to look at all the lovely organelles you've been learning about...

Magnification is *Size*, *Resolution* is *Detail*

We all know that microscopes produce a **magnified image** of a sample, but **resolution** is just as important...

1) Magnification is how much **bigger** the image is than the specimen (the sample you're looking at). It's calculated using this formula:

$$\text{magnification} = \frac{\text{size of image}}{\text{size of real object}}$$

For example: If you have a magnified image that's 5 mm wide and your specimen is 0.05 mm wide, the magnification is: 5 ÷ 0.05 = **× 100**.

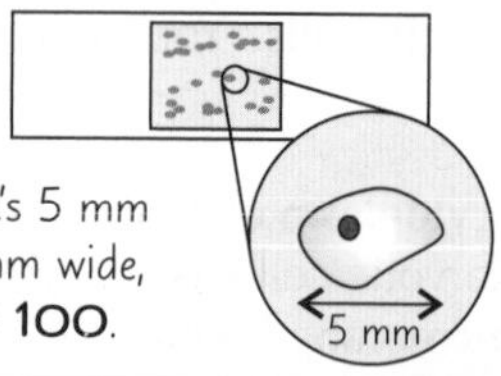

2) Resolution is how **detailed** the image is. More specifically, it's how well a microscope **distinguishes** between **two points** that are **close together**. If a microscope lens can't separate two objects, then increasing the magnification won't help.

If you're given the size of the image and the size of the object in different units in the exam, make sure you convert them into the same units before using the formula.

There are *Two Main Types* of Microscope — *Light* and *Electron*

Light microscopes

1) They use **light** to form an image.
2) They have a maximum resolution of about **0.2 micrometres** (μm). This means you can't use a light microscope to view organelles smaller than 0.2 μm. That includes **ribosomes**, the **endoplasmic reticulum** and **lysosomes**. You may be able to make out **mitochondria** — but not in perfect detail. You can also see the **nucleus**.
3) The maximum useful **magnification** of a light microscope is about **× 1500**.

Electron microscopes

1) They use **electrons** to form an image.
2) They have a **higher resolution** than light microscopes so give a **more detailed image** (and can be used to look at more organelles).
3) They have a maximum resolution of about **0.0002 micrometres** (μm). (About 1000 times higher than light microscopes.)
4) The maximum useful **magnification** of an electron microscope is about **× 1 500 000**.

A micrometre (μm) is 0.001 mm. To convert from μm to mm, divide by 1000.

Electron Microscopes are either *'Scanning'* or *'Transmission'*

Transmission electron microscopes (TEMs)

1) TEMs use **electromagnets** to focus a **beam of electrons**, which is then transmitted **through** the specimen.
2) **Denser** parts of the specimen absorb **more electrons**, which makes them look **darker** on the image you end up with.
3) TEMs are good because they give **high resolution images**, so you see the **internal structure** of **organelles** like mitochondria.
4) But they can only be used on **thin specimens**.

TEM image of a mitochondrion

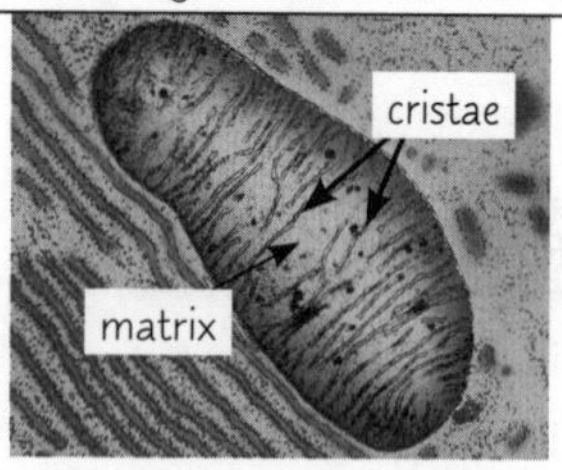

K.R. PORTER/SCIENCE PHOTO LIBRARY

Scanning electron microscopes (SEMs)

1) SEMs **scan** a beam of electrons across the specimen. This **knocks off** electrons from the **specimen**, which are gathered in a **cathode ray tube** to form an **image**.
2) The images you end up with show the **surface** of the specimen and they can be **3D**.
3) SEMs are good because they can be used on **thick specimens**.
4) But they give **lower resolution images** than TEMs.

SEM image of a mitochondrion

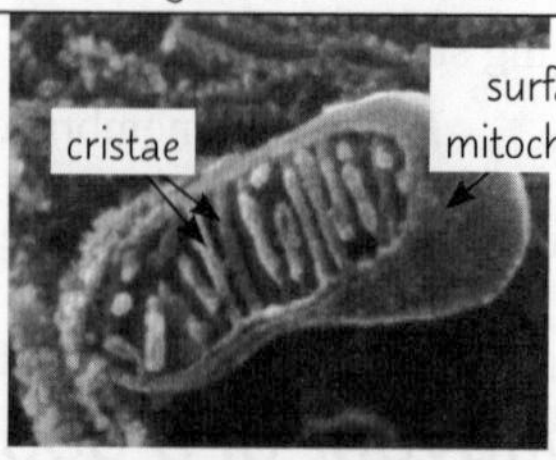

PROFESSORS P. MOTTA & T. NAGURO/ SCIENCE PHOTO LIBRARY

Looking at Cells and Organelles

Here's How to Use an *Eyepiece Graticule* and *Stage Micrometer...*

1) Sometimes, you might want to know the **size** of your specimen. When you're using a light microscope, you can use an **eyepiece graticule** and **stage micrometer** to do this — they're a bit like **rulers**.
2) An **eyepiece graticule** is fitted onto the **eyepiece** (the bit that you look down). It's like a transparent ruler with **numbers**, but **no units**.
3) The **stage micrometer** is placed on the **stage** (the platform where you put your slide). It's a microscope slide with an **accurate scale** (it has units) and it's used to work out the **value** of the divisions on the **eyepiece graticule** at a **particular magnification**.
4) This means that when you take the stage micrometer away and replace it with the slide containing your specimen, you'll be able to **measure** the size of the specimen. Here's an **example**:

Head to p. 10 for a recap on microscopes and how to use them.

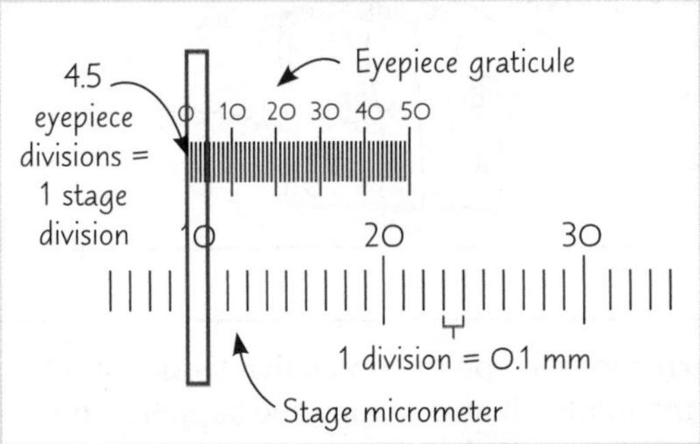

1) **Line up** the eyepiece graticule and the stage micrometer.
2) Each **division** on the stage micrometer is **0.1 mm** long.
3) At this magnification, **1 division** on the **stage micrometer** is the same as **4.5 divisions** on the **eyepiece graticule**.
4) To work out the size of **1 division** on the **eyepiece graticule**, you need to divide 0.1 by 4.5:
   1 division on eyepiece graticule = 0.1 ÷ 4.5 = **0.022 mm**
5) So if you look at an object under the microscope at this magnification and it's **20 eyepiece divisions** long, you know it measures:
   20 × 0.022 = **0.44 mm**

Remember: at a different magnification, 1 division on the stage micrometer will be equal to a different number of divisions on the eyepiece graticule — so the eyepiece graticule will need to be re-calibrated.

Practice Questions

Q1 What is the formula for calculating the magnification of an image?

Q2 How do you convert micrometers (μm) to millimetres (mm)?

Exam Questions

Q1 An insect is 0.5 mm long. In a book, a picture of the insect is 8 cm long. Calculate the magnification of the image. [2 marks]

Q2 An image from a light microscope shows a human cheek cell at × 100 magnification. The actual diameter of the cell is 59 μm. What is the diameter of the cell in the image? [2 marks]

Q3 The table shows the dimensions of some different organelles found in animal cells.

organelle	diameter / mm
lysosome	0.0001
mitochondrion	0.002
nucleus	0.005
ribosome	0.00002

a) Name those organelles in the table that would be visible using a good quality light microscope (max. resolution ≈ 0.2 μm)? [1 mark]

b) Which organelles would be visible using a transmission electron microscope (max. resolution ≈ 0.0002 μm)? [1 mark]

Q4 a) A microscope is set up with an eyepiece graticule and a stage micrometer. Each division on a stage micrometer is 10 μm long. At ×10 magnification, 1 division of the stage micrometer is equal to 6.5 divisions on the eyepiece graticule. Calculate the size of 1 division on the eyepiece graticule. Give your answer to the nearest 0.1 μm. [2 marks]

b) A specimen is viewed under this microscope at ×10 magnification. It is 14 eyepiece divisions long. Use your answer to part a) to calculate the specimen's length. Give your answer to the nearest μm. [2 marks]

A light microscope is better than a heavy one — for your back anyway...

OK, there's quite a bit of info on these pages, but the whole magnification thing isn't all that bad once you've given it a go. Just make sure you can use the formula to work out magnification, the size of the image and the size of the real object. There's more maths to do when measuring the size of a specimen with a graticule. Good job you love maths.

Cell Organisation

Multicellular organisms are made up of lots of different cell types, which are organised to work together — cells that carry out the same job are organised into tissues (e.g. epithelium), different tissues are organised into organs (e.g. the lungs) and organs work together as organ systems (e.g. the respiratory system).

Similar Cells are Organised into Tissues

A **tissue** is a group of similar cells that are **specially adapted** to **work together** to carry out a particular function. Here are some examples:

1) **Squamous epithelium** is a **single layer** of **cells** lining a surface. It's found in many places, including the alveoli in the lungs.

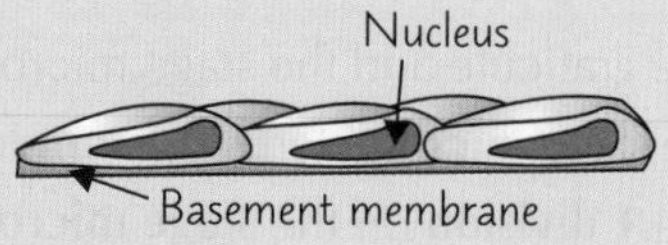

Epithelium is a tissue that forms a covering or a lining.

2) **Ciliated epithelium** is a layer of cells covered in **cilia** (tiny **hair-like** structures). It's found on surfaces where things need to be **moved** — in the trachea for instance, where the cilia waft mucus along.

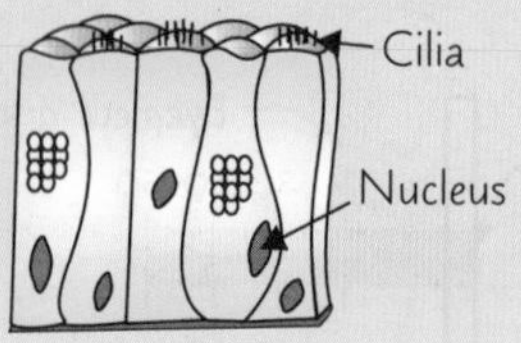

3) **Xylem tissue** is a plant tissue with two jobs — it **transports water** around the plant, and it **supports** the plant. It contains **xylem vessel cells** and **parenchyma cells**.

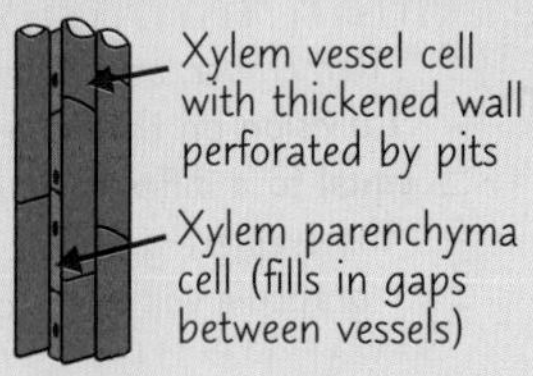

4) **Cartilage** is a type of **connective tissue** found in the **joints**. It also **shapes** and **supports** the **ears, nose** and **windpipe**.

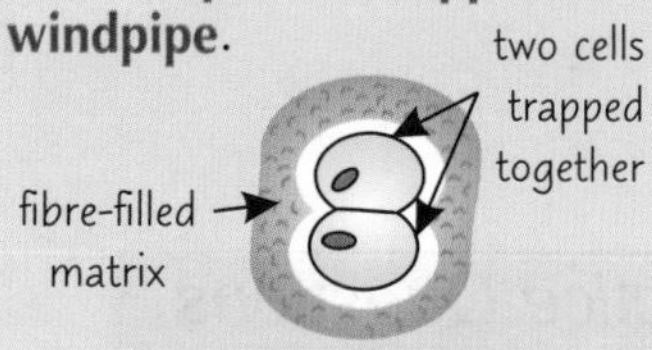

Tissues are Organised into Organs

An **organ** is a group of different tissues that **work together** to perform a particular function. Here are a couple of examples:

The leaf is an example of a plant organ. It's made up of the following **tissues**:

1) **Lower epidermis** — contains stomata (holes) to let air in and out for gas exchange.
2) **Spongy mesophyll** — full of spaces to let gases circulate.
3) **Palisade mesophyll** — most photosynthesis occurs here.
4) **Xylem** — carries water to the leaf.
5) **Phloem** — carries sugars away from the leaf.
6) **Upper epidermis** — covered in a waterproof waxy cuticle to reduce water loss.

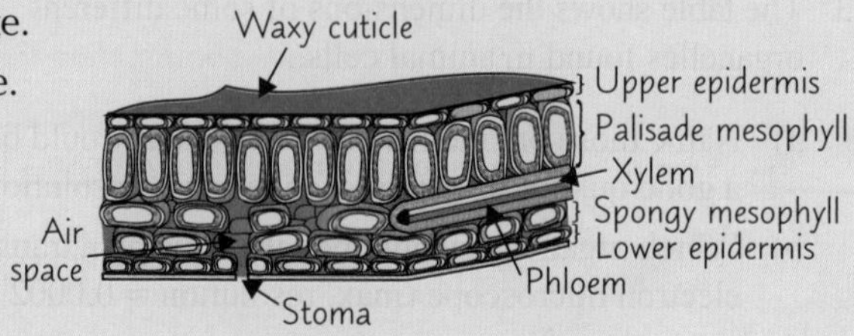

The lungs are an example of animal organs. They're made up of the following **tissues**:

1) **Squamous epithelium tissue** — surrounds the alveoli (where gas exchange occurs).
2) **Fibrous connective tissue** — helps to force air back out of the lungs when exhaling.
3) **Endothelium tissue** — makes up the wall of the capillaries, which surround the alveoli, and lines the larger blood vessels.

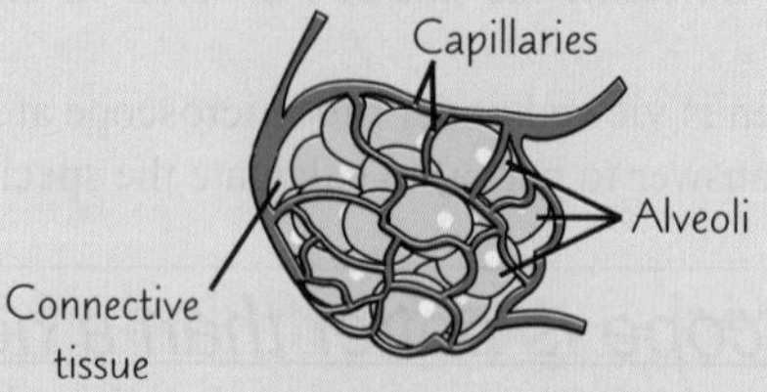

Cell Organisation

Different Organs Make up an Organ System

Organs work together to form **organ systems** — each system has a **particular function**.
Yup, you've guessed it, more examples:

1) The **respiratory system** is made up of all the organs, tissues and cells involved in **breathing**. The lungs, trachea, larynx, nose, mouth and diaphragm are all part of the respiratory system.

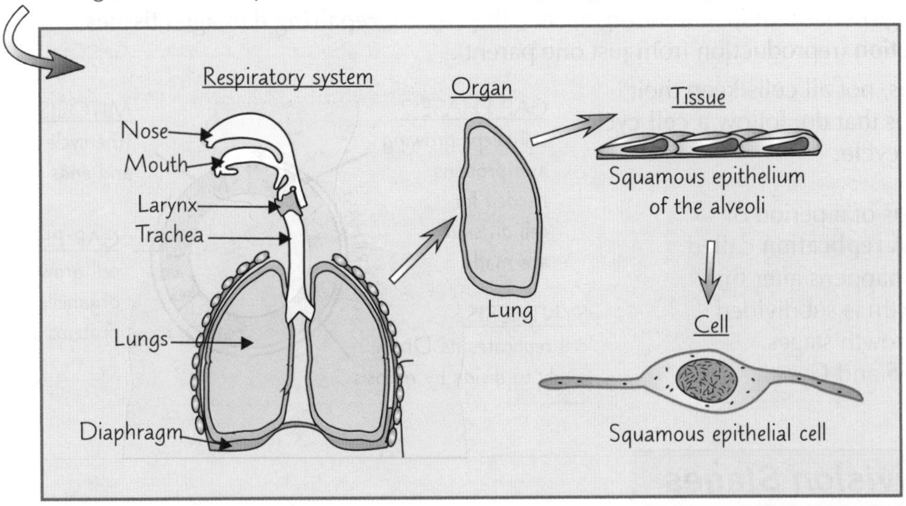

John and Fido — working together as part of an organ system.

2) The **circulatory system** is made up of the organs involved in **blood supply**. The heart, arteries, veins and capillaries are all parts of this system.

Practice Questions

Q1 Explain what is meant by the term tissue.

Q2 Name one organ found in plants and one organ found in animals.

Q3 Explain what is meant by the term organ system.

Exam Questions

Q1 The liver is made of hepatocyte cells, blood vessels (to provide nutrients and oxygen), and connective tissue (that holds the liver together).
Is the liver best described as a tissue, organ or an organ system? Explain your answer. [2 marks]

Q2 Which of the following statements about xylem tissue is correct?

A Xylem tissue is made up of a group of specialised cells.
B Xylem tissue is made up of a group of organs that work together.
C Xylem tissue is made up of a group of tissues that perform a particular function.
D Xylem tissue is made up of a group of organ systems. [1 mark]

Q3 Squamous epithelium in the alveoli is made up of a single layer of flat cells.
Squamous epithelium tissue, fibrous connective tissue and endothelium tissue make up the lungs.
The lungs are part of the respiratory system.

Using the lungs as an example, describe how the cells of multicellular organisms are organised in tissues, organs and organ systems. [3 marks]

Soft and quilted — the best kind of tissues...

So, similar cells group together to form tissues. Then, because they love being so helpful, tissues work together in an organ to perform a particular function. But even organs are better together — along comes the organ system. Mmmmmmmm it's always better when we're together... or something like that. You get the idea.

The Cell Cycle and Mitosis

If it wasn't for cell division, we'd still only be one cell big. If it wasn't for pies, my favourite jeans would still fit.

Mitosis is Cell Division that Produces Genetically Identical Cells

There are two types of cell division in **eukaryotes** — **mitosis** and **meiosis** (see page 70 for more on meiosis).

1) In **mitosis** a **parent cell** divides to produce **two genetically identical daughter cells** (they contain an **exact copy** of the **DNA** of the parent cell).
2) Mitosis is needed for the **growth** of multicellular organisms (like us), for **repairing damaged tissues** and for **asexual reproduction** (reproduction from just one parent).
3) In multicellular organisms, not all cells keep their ability to divide. The ones that do, follow a **cell cycle**. Mitosis is part of the cell cycle:

The cell cycle consists of a period of **cell growth** and **DNA replication** called **interphase**. **Mitosis** happens after that. Interphase (cell growth) is subdivided into three separate growth stages. These are called $\mathbf{G_1}$, **S** and $\mathbf{G_2}$.

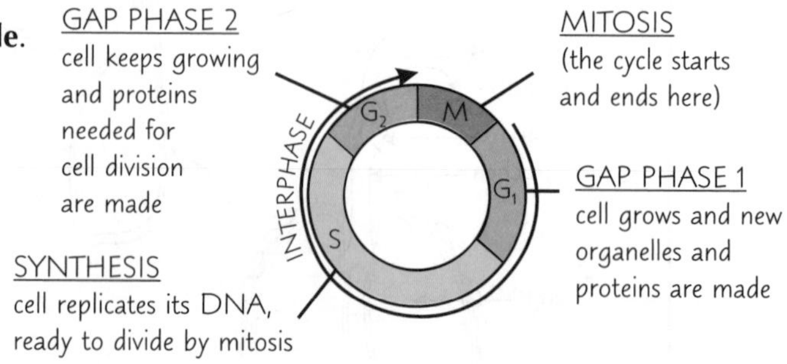

Mitosis has Four Division Stages

Mitosis is really one **continuous process**, but it's described as a series of **division stages** — prophase, metaphase, anaphase and telophase. **Interphase** comes **before** mitosis in the cell cycle.

Interphase — The cell carries out normal functions, but also prepares to divide. The cell's **DNA** is **unravelled** and **replicated**, to double its genetic content. The **organelles** are also **replicated** so it has spare ones, and its ATP content is increased (ATP provides the energy needed for cell division).

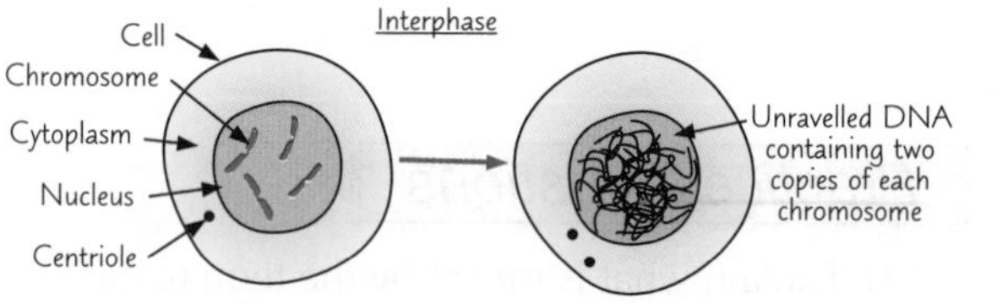

1) **Prophase** — The **chromosomes condense**, getting **shorter** and **fatter**. Tiny bundles of protein called **centrioles** start moving to opposite ends of the cell, forming a network of protein fibres across it called the **spindle**. The **nuclear envelope** (the membrane around the nucleus) **breaks down** and chromosomes lie free in the cytoplasm.

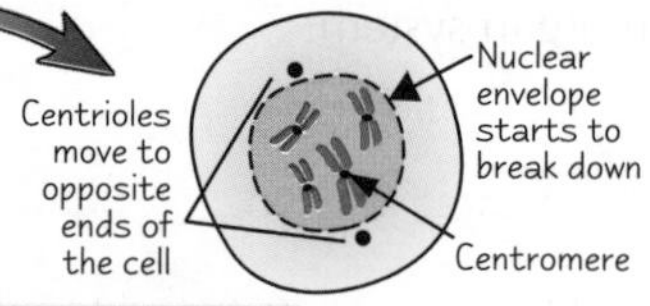

As mitosis begins, the chromosomes are made of two strands joined in the middle by a centromere. The separate strands are called chromatids. There are two strands because each chromosome has already made an identical copy of itself during interphase. When mitosis is over, the chromatids end up as one-strand chromosomes in the daughter cells.

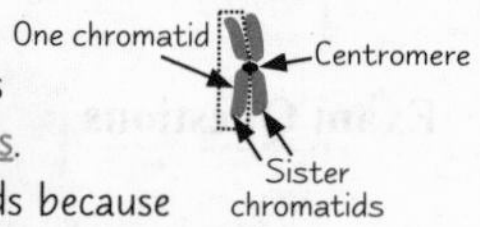

2) **Metaphase** — The chromosomes (each with two chromatids) **line up** along the middle of the cell and become **attached** to the **spindle** by their **centromere**.

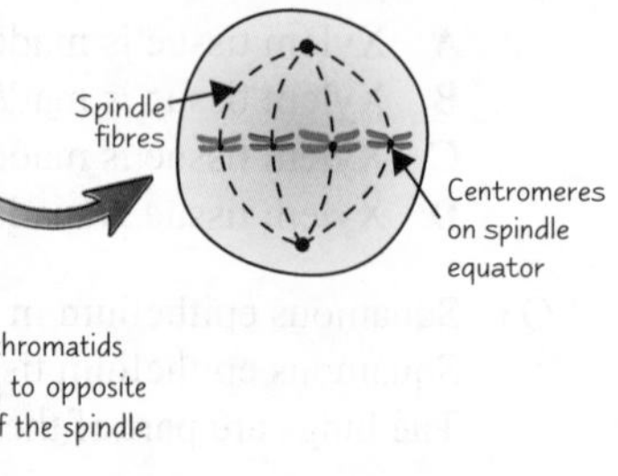

3) **Anaphase** — The **centromeres divide**, **separating** each pair of sister **chromatids**. The **spindles contract**, pulling chromatids to **opposite poles** (ends) of the **spindle**, centromere first. This makes the chromatids appear **v-shaped**.

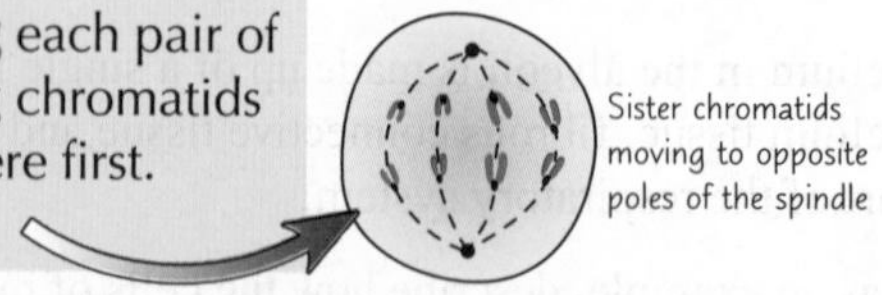

4) **Telophase** — The chromatids reach the **opposite poles** on the spindle. They **uncoil** and become **long** and **thin** again. They're now called **chromosomes** again. A **nuclear envelope** forms around each group of chromosomes, so there are now **two nuclei**. The **cytoplasm divides** (**cytokinesis**) and there are now **two daughter cells** that are **genetically identical** to the original cell and to each other. Mitosis is finished and each daughter cell starts the **interphase** part of the cell cycle to get ready for the next round of mitosis.

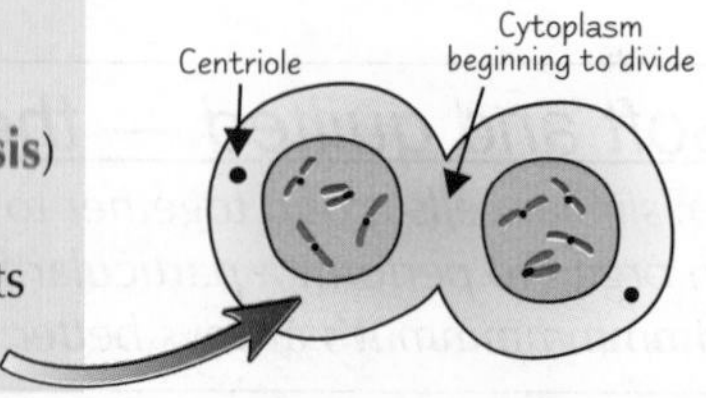

The Cell Cycle and Mitosis

Root Tips Can be *Stained* and *Squashed* to *Observe Mitosis*

You need to know how to **prepare** and **stain** a **root tip** in order to observe the **stages of mitosis**. Make sure you're wearing **safety goggles** and a **lab coat** before you start. You should also wear **gloves** when using **stains**.

Remind yourself how to prepare a slide on p. 10.

1) **Cut** 1 cm from the **tip** from a **growing root** (e.g. of an onion). It needs to be the **tip** because that's where **growth** occurs (and so that's where **mitosis** takes place).
   If you're using ethano-orcein to stain the cells, the tips will also need to be fixed in ethanoic acid.
2) **Prepare** a boiling tube containing **1 M hydrochloric acid** and put it in a **water bath** at **60 °C**.
3) **Transfer** the **root tip** into the **boiling tube** and incubate for about **5 minutes**.
4) Use a pipette to **rinse** the **root tip** well with **cold water**. Leave the tip to **dry** on a **paper towel**.
5) Place the root tip on a **microscope slide** and cut **2 mm** from the **very tip** of it. Get **rid of the rest**.
6) Use a **mounted needle** to **break** the tip **open** and **spread** the cells out thinly.
7) **Add** a small drop of **stain** and leave it for a few minutes. The stain will make the **chromosomes easier** to **see** under a microscope. There are loads of different stains, all with crazy names (**toluidine blue O, ethano-orcein, Feulgen stain...**)
   If you're using the Feulgen stain, you'll need an extra rinse.
8) **Place** a **cover slip** over the cells and **push** down firmly to **squash** the tissue. This will make the tissue **thinner** and allow **light** to pass through it. **Don't smear** the cover slip sideways (or you'll damage the chromosomes).
9) Now you can look at all the stages of mitosis under a **light microscope** (see page 10). You should see something that looks like the photograph on the right.

Take care when you're using sharp equipment.

Stained Root Cells

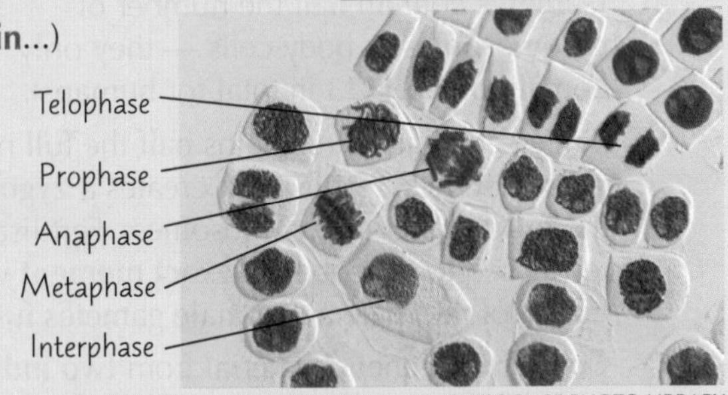

HERVE CONGE, ISM/SCIENCE PHOTO LIBRARY

The *Mitotic Index* is the *Proportion* of Cells *Undergoing Mitosis*

You can **calculate** the **mitotic index** of your cells using this **formula**:

$$\text{mitotic index} = \frac{\text{number of cells with visible chromosomes}}{\text{total number of cells observed}}$$

This lets you work out how quickly the **tissue** is growing. A **plant root tip** is constantly **growing**, so you'd expect a **high mitotic index** (i.e. **lots** of cells in **mitosis**).

Practice Questions

Q1 Give the main functions of mitosis.

Q2 List the four stages of mitosis.

Q3 Why do you need to squash the tissue when preparing a slide of plant root tip cells?

Exam Questions

Q1 The diagrams show cells at different stages of mitosis.

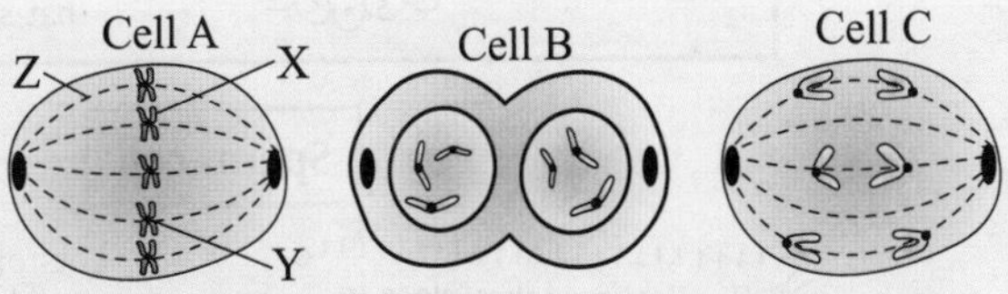

a) For each of the cells A, B and C, name the stage of mitosis. [3 marks]

b) Name the structures labelled X, Y and Z in cell A. [3 marks]

Q2 A sample of cells was prepared to observe mitosis. In total, 42 cells were observed. 32 of those had visible chromosomes. Calculate the mitotic index (the proportion of cells undergoing mitosis) for this sample. Give your answer to 2 decimal places. [2 marks]

Doctor, I'm getting short and fat — don't worry, it's just a phase...

Quite a lot to learn on these pages — but it's all important stuff, so no slacking. Mitosis is vital — it's how cells multiply and how organisms like us grow. Don't forget — the best way to learn is to get drawing those diagrams.

Gametes and Fertilisation

Ahh, now on to some really exciting stuff — gametes (sex cells to you and me) and fertilisation. I won't tell you any more because it's all explained on these pages. You have to read it though — don't just giggle at the rude diagram...

DNA is Passed to New Offspring by Gametes

1) **Gametes** are the male and female **sex cells** found in all organisms that reproduce **sexually**.
2) They join together at **fertilisation** to form a **zygote**, which divides and develops into a **new organism**.
3) In animals, the male gametes are **sperm** and the female gametes are **egg cells** (ova).
4) Normal body cells contain the **full number** of chromosomes. Humans have **two sets** of **23 chromosomes** — one set from the **male** parent and one from the **female** parent — giving each body cell a total of **46 chromosomes**.
5) **Gametes** contain **half** the number of chromosomes as body cells — they only contain **one set** (23 in total for humans).
6) Since each gamete contains **half** the full number of chromosomes, **fertilisation** creates a **zygote** with the **full** number of chromosomes. Fertilisation is the term used to describe the **exact moment** when the **nuclei** of the male and female gametes **fuse**.
7) **Combining** genetic material from **two individuals** makes offspring that are **genetically unique**.

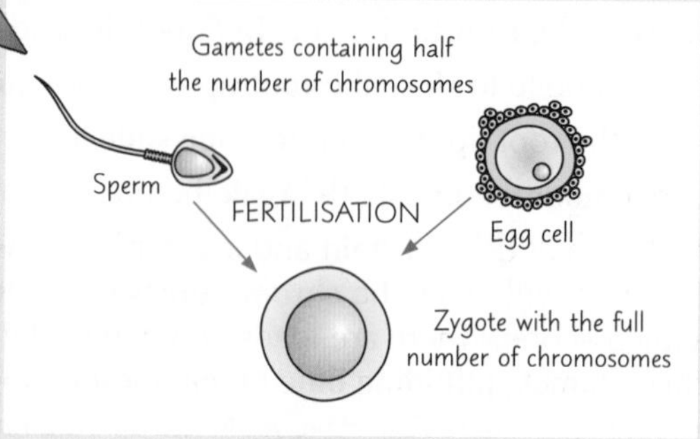
Gametes containing half the number of chromosomes
Sperm
FERTILISATION
Egg cell
Zygote with the full number of chromosomes

NB: you can't fertilise farmland with sperm.

Mammalian Gametes are Specialised for Their Function

Egg cells and sperm cells have all the **same organelles** as other **eukaryotic cells** (see pages 58-59), including a **nucleus** (which contains their genetic material) and a **cell membrane** (also known as a **plasma membrane**). But the structures of egg cells and sperm cells are also **specialised** for their **function** — bringing the **female** and **male DNA together** at **fertilisation** to form a **zygote**.

Egg cell

Egg cells are much larger than sperm.

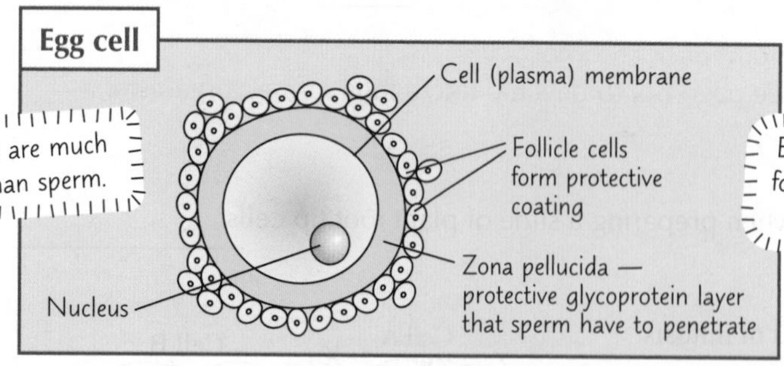
Cell (plasma) membrane
Follicle cells form protective coating
Zona pellucida — protective glycoprotein layer that sperm have to penetrate
Nucleus

Egg cells also contain huge food reserves to nourish the developing embryo.

Sperm cell

Respiration takes place in mitochondria. This releases energy in the form of ATP, which sperm use to swim.

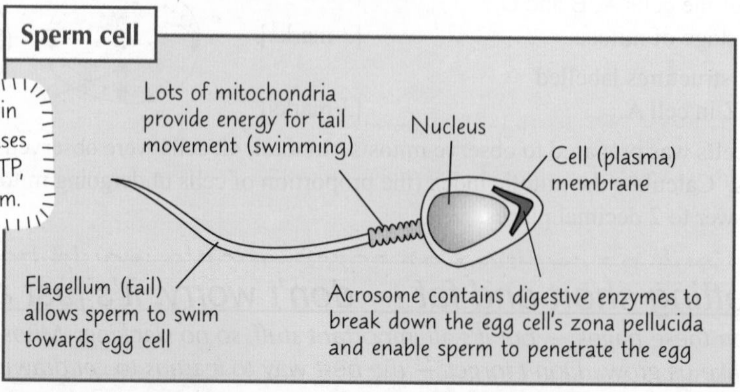
Lots of mitochondria provide energy for tail movement (swimming)
Nucleus
Cell (plasma) membrane
Flagellum (tail) allows sperm to swim towards egg cell
Acrosome contains digestive enzymes to break down the egg cell's zona pellucida and enable sperm to penetrate the egg

Gametes and Fertilisation

In *Mammals* Fertilisation Occurs in the *Oviduct*

1) In mammals, **sperm** are deposited high up in the female **vagina** close to the entrance of the **cervix**.
2) Once there, they have to make their way up through the **cervix** and **uterus**, and into one of the **oviducts**. The diagram on the right shows the **human** female reproductive system.
3) Once the sperm are in the oviduct, **fertilisation** may occur. Here's how it works:

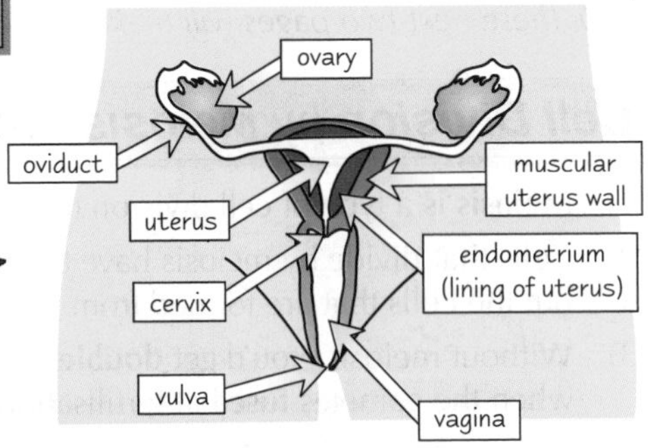

1) The **sperm swim** towards the **egg cell** in the oviduct.
2) Once **one** sperm makes contact with the **zona pellucida** of the egg cell (see previous page), the **acrosome reaction** occurs — this is where **digestive enzymes** are released from the acrosome of the sperm.
3) These enzymes **digest** the zona pellucida, so that the sperm can move through it to the cell membrane of the egg cell.

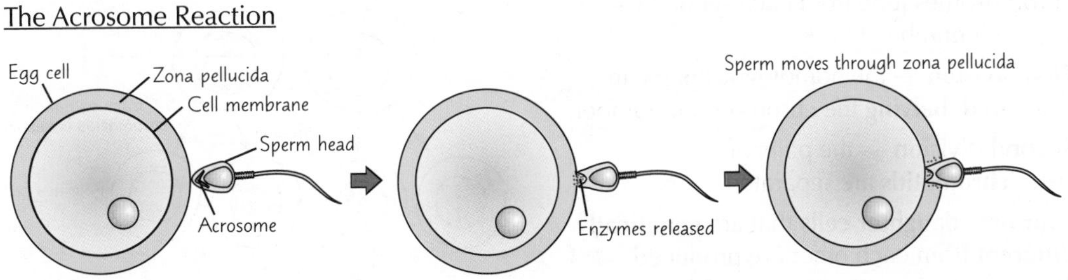

4) The sperm head **fuses** with the **cell membrane** of the egg cell. This triggers the **cortical reaction** — the egg cell releases the contents of vesicles called **cortical granules** into the space between the cell membrane and the zona pellucida.
5) The chemicals from the cortical granules make the zona pellucida **thicken**, which makes it **impenetrable** to other sperm. This makes sure that **only one** sperm fertilises the egg cell.
6) Only the **sperm nucleus** enters the egg cell — its **tail** is **discarded.**
7) The nucleus of the sperm **fuses** with the nucleus of the egg cell — this is **fertilisation.**

A **zygote** is now formed, which has the full number of chromosomes.
It immediately begins to divide by **mitosis** (see page 66) to develop into a fully formed organism.

Practice Questions

Q1 What is a gamete?

Q2 What is the zona pellucida?

Q3 Describe what happens in the acrosome reaction.

Exam Questions

Q1 Explain how sperm are specialised for their function. [3 marks]

Q2 Describe the process of fertilisation in mammals, following the acrosome reaction. [4 marks]

Reproduction isn't as exciting as some people would have you believe...

You don't need to learn the diagram of the female reproductive system — it's just there to give words like 'oviduct' and 'uterus' some sort of meaning when you're trying to learn what goes where. See, never say that I don't try my very best to help you. Now help yourself and get this stuff learnt — you'll be glad you put the effort in come exam time.

Meiosis and Inheritance

Right, now that you know what gametes are, I just know you're desperate to find out how they're formed. Luckily for you, these next two pages will make it all crystal clear (as long as you're wide awake with your learning head on first).

Cell Division by Meiosis Produces Gametes

1) **Meiosis** is a type of cell division that happens in the **reproductive organs** to produce **gametes**.
2) Cells that divide by meiosis have the **full number** of chromosomes to start with, but the cells that are formed from meiosis have **half the number**.
3) Without meiosis, you'd get **double** the number of chromosomes when the gametes **fused** at fertilisation. Not good.

You don't need to learn the stages of meiosis, just understand that it produces genetically different gametes.

Here's a brief overview of meiosis:

1) The DNA **replicates** so there are **two** identical copies of **each** chromosome, called **chromatids**.
2) The DNA condenses to form double-armed chromosomes, made from **two sister chromatids**.
3) The chromosomes arrange themselves into **homologous pairs** — pairs of **matching** chromosomes (one from each set of 23 — e.g. both number 1s).
4) **First division** — the homologous **pairs** are **separated, halving** the chromosome number.
5) **Second division** — the pairs of sister **chromatids** are separated.
6) **Four new daughter cells** that are **genetically different** from each other are produced. These are the **gametes**.

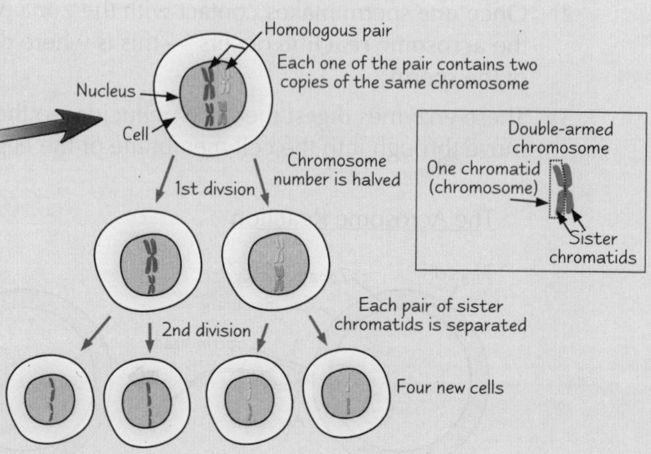
Homologous pair
Each one of the pair contains two copies of the same chromosome
Nucleus
Cell
Double-armed chromosome
One chromatid (chromosome)
Sister chromatids
1st divsion
Chromosome number is halved
2nd division
Each pair of sister chromatids is separated
Four new cells

Meiosis Produces Cells that are Genetically Different

Genetic variation is the **differences** that exist between **individuals' genetic material**. The reason that meiosis is so important is that it **creates** genetic variation — it makes gametes that are **genetically different** (non-identical). It does this in two ways:

1) Crossing over of chromatids

1) Before the first division of meiosis, **homologous pairs** of chromosomes come together and **pair up**.
2) Two of the **chromatids** in each homologous pair **twist around** each other.
3) The twisted bits **break off** their original chromatid and **rejoin** onto the other chromatid, **recombining** their genetic material.

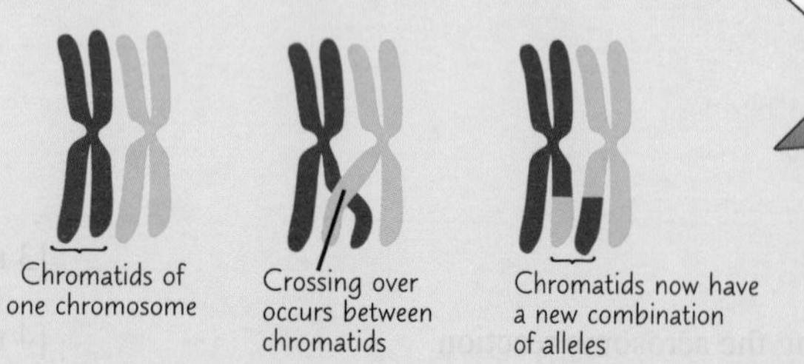
Chromatids of one chromosome
Crossing over occurs between chromatids
Chromatids now have a new combination of alleles

4) The chromatids still contain the **same genes** but they now have a **different combination** of **alleles**.
5) This means that each of the **four new cells** formed from meiosis contains chromatids with **different alleles**.

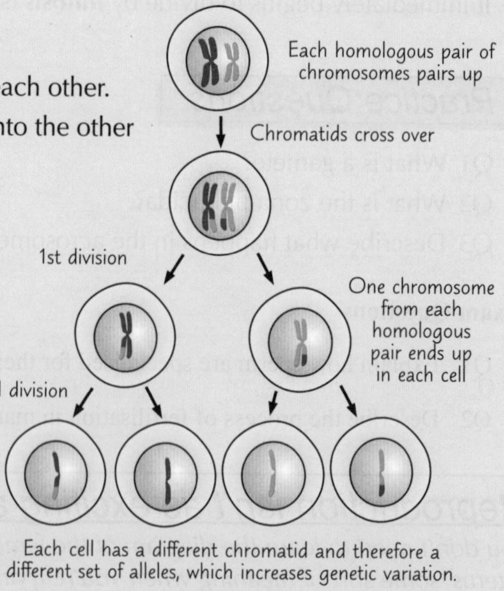
Each homologous pair of chromosomes pairs up
Chromatids cross over
1st division
One chromosome from each homologous pair ends up in each cell
2nd division
Each cell has a different chromatid and therefore a different set of alleles, which increases genetic variation.

Meiosis and Inheritance

2) Independent assortment of chromosomes

1) The four daughter cells formed from meiosis have completely **different combinations** of **chromosomes**.
2) All your cells have a **combination** of chromosomes from your parents, half from your mum (**maternal**) and half from your dad (**paternal**).
3) When the gametes are produced, different **combinations** of those maternal and paternal **chromosomes** go into each cell.
4) This is called **independent assortment** (separation) of the chromosomes.

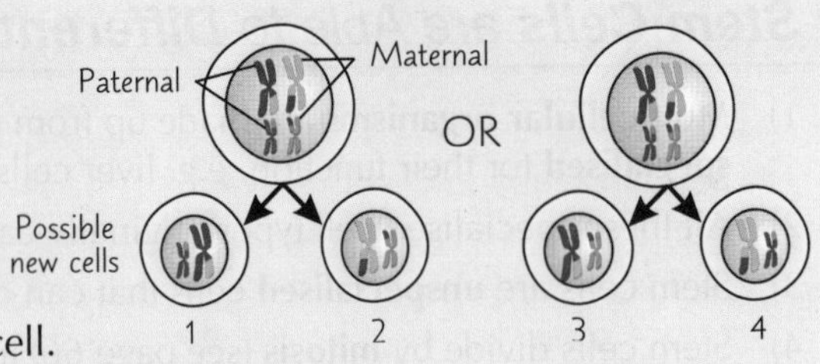

Some Genes are Linked

1) The **position** of a gene on a chromosome is called a **locus** (plural: **loci**). Independent assortment means that **genes** with loci on **different chromosomes** end up **randomly distributed** in the **gametes**.
2) But genes with loci on the **same chromosome** are said to be **linked** — because the genes are on the same chromosome, they'll stay together during **independent assortment** and their alleles will be **passed on to the offspring together**. The only reason this won't happen is if **crossing over** splits them up first.
3) The **closer together** the loci of two genes on a chromosome, the **more closely** they are said to be **linked**. This is because **crossing over** is **less likely** to split them up.

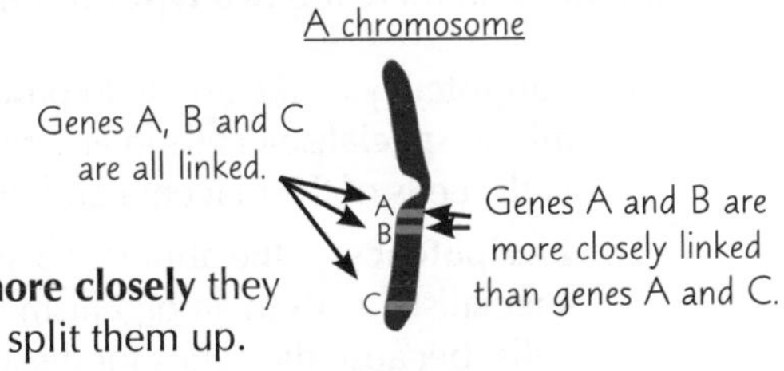

Some Characteristics are Sex-linked

1) A **characteristic** is said to be **sex-linked** when the **locus** of the **allele** that codes for it is on a **sex chromosome**.
2) In mammals, **females** have **two X** chromosomes (XX) and **males** have **one X** and **one Y** chromosome (XY).
3) The **Y chromosome** is **smaller** than the X chromosome and carries **fewer genes**. So most genes on the sex chromosomes are **only carried** on the X chromosome (called **X-linked** genes).
4) As **males** only have **one X chromosome**, they often only have **one allele** for sex-linked genes. So because they **only** have one copy, they **express** the **characteristic** of this allele even if it's **recessive**. This makes males **more likely** than females to show **recessive phenotypes** for genes that are sex-linked.
5) Genetic disorders caused by **faulty alleles** on sex chromosomes include **colour blindness** and **haemophilia**. The faulty alleles for both of these disorders are carried on the X chromosome — they're called **X-linked disorders**.

Look back at page 50 if you need a reminder of genetic terms such as 'recessive phenotype'.

Practice Questions

Q1 What name is given to the process that produces gametes?

Q2 What word is used to describe a gene's position on a chromosome?

Q3 What is a sex-linked characteristic?

Exam Questions

Q1 The genes for eye colour and wing length in fruit flies are linked.

a) What does it mean when two genes are linked? [1 mark]

b) Explain how the loci of the genes affects the likelihood that they will stay linked following meiosis. [2 marks]

Q2 a) Explain what crossing over is and how it leads to genetic variation. [3 marks]

b) Explain how independent assortment leads to genetic variation. [2 marks]

Some genes are linked... so are some sausages...

These pages are tricky, so use the diagrams to help you. The key thing to understand about meiosis is that it produces four genetically different daughter cells and that the genetic variation in the daughter cells occurs because of crossing over and independent assortment. Then there's just the linkage business to get your head around and you're sorted.

Cell Differentiation and Gene Expression

If I had to choose a favourite type of cell, I'd choose a stem cell and here's why...

Stem Cells are Able to Differentiate into Specialised Cells

1) **Multicellular organisms** are made up from many **different cell types** that are **specialised** for their function, e.g. liver cells, muscle cells, white blood cells.
2) **All** these specialised cell types originally came from **stem cells**.
3) Stem cells are **unspecialised** cells that can develop into **other types** of cell.
4) Stem cells divide by **mitosis** (see page 66) to become **new** cells, which then become **specialised**.
5) The **process** by which a cell becomes specialised is called **differentiation**.
6) All multicellular organisms have some form of stem cell.
7) In humans, some stem cells are found in the **embryo** (where they become all the **specialised cells** needed to form a **fetus**).
8) The ability of stem cells to differentiate into specialised cells is called **potency** and there are **two types** you need to know about:

> 1) **Totipotency** — the ability to produce **all cell types**, including all the **specialised cells** in an organism and **extraembryonic cells** (cells of the placenta and umbilical cord).
> 2) **Pluripotency** — the ability of a stem cell to produce all the **specialised cells** in an organism (but **not** extraembryonic cells, because the genes for these cell types have become inactivated — see below).

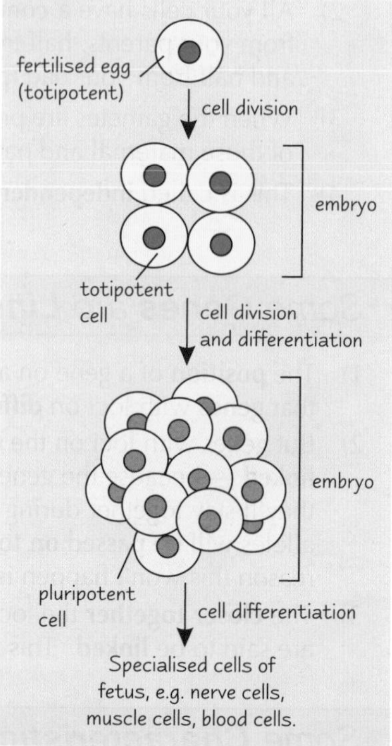

9) **Totipotent** stem cells are **only** present in mammals in the **first few cell divisions** of an **embryo**. After this point the **embryonic stem cells** become **pluripotent**. They can still specialise into **any** cell in the body, but **lose** the **ability** to become the cells that make up the **placenta** and **umbilical cord**.
10) Stem cells are also found in **some adult tissues** (where they become **specialised** cells that need to be **replaced**, e.g. stem cells in the intestines constantly replace intestinal epithelial cells). Adult stem cells are much **less flexible** than embryonic stem cells though — they can only develop into **some** cell types.
11) **Plants** also have **stem cells**. They're found in areas where the plant is **growing**, e.g. in **roots** and **shoots**.

Stem Cells Become Specialised Through Differential Gene Expression

A cell's **genome** is its **entire set of DNA**, including all the **genes** it contains. However, a cell **doesn't express** (make proteins from) **all the genes** in its genome. Stem cells become **specialised** because **different genes** in their DNA **become active** and get **expressed**:

> 1) **Stem cells** all contain the **same genes**, but not all of them are **expressed** because not all of them are **active**.
> 2) Under the **right conditions**, some **genes** are **activated** and others are **inactivated**.
> 3) **mRNA** is only **transcribed** from the **active genes**.
> 4) The mRNA from the active genes is then **translated** into **proteins**.
> 5) These proteins **modify** the cell — they determine the **cell structure** and **control cell processes** (including the activation of **more** genes, which produces more proteins).
> 6) **Changes** to the cell produced by these proteins cause the cell to become **specialised** (**differentiate**). These changes are **difficult** to **reverse**, so once a cell has specialised it **stays** specialised.

Transcription is when DNA is copied into mRNA. Translation is when proteins are produced using the code in mRNA. See pages 46-47 for more.

All of the girls expressed different jeans.

Example

Red blood cells contain lots of **haemoglobin** and have **no nucleus** (to make room for more haemoglobin). They are produced from a type of **stem cell** in the **bone marrow**. The stem cell produces a new cell in which the genes for **haemoglobin production** are **activated**. Other genes, such as those involved in **removing the nucleus**, are **activated** too. Many other genes are activated or inactivated, resulting in a specialised red blood cell.

Cell Differentiation and Gene Expression

Transcription Factors Can *Control* the *Expression* of *Genes*

1) **Gene expression** can be **controlled** by **altering** the rate of **transcription** of genes. E.g. **increased** transcription produces **more mRNA**, which can be used to make **more protein**.
2) This is controlled by **transcription factors** — proteins that **bind** to **DNA** and **activate** or **deactivate** genes by **increasing** or **decreasing** the **rate** of **transcription**.
3) Factors that **increase** the rate of transcription are called **activators** and those that **decrease** the rate are called **repressors**. **Activators** often work by helping **RNA polymerase bind** to the **DNA** and **begin** transcription. **Repressors** often work by **preventing** RNA polymerase from **binding** and so **stopping** transcription.
4) In **eukaryotes**, such as **animals** and **plants**, transcription factors bind to **specific DNA sites** near the **start** of their **target genes** — the genes they **control** the **expression** of. In **prokaryotes**, control of gene expression often involves transcription factors binding to **operons**.
5) An **operon** is a **section** of **DNA** that contains a cluster of **structural genes**, that are **transcribed together**, as well as **control elements** and sometimes a **regulatory gene**:
   - The **structural genes** code for **useful proteins**, such as **enzymes**.
   - The **control elements** include a **promoter** (a DNA sequence located **before** the structural genes that **RNA polymerase** binds to) and an **operator** (a DNA sequence that **transcription factors** bind to).
   - The **regulatory gene** codes for an **activator** or **repressor**.
6) You need to know about the ***lac* operon** in ***E. coli***:
   1) *E. coli* is a bacterium that **respires glucose**, but it can use **lactose** if glucose isn't available.
   2) The genes that produce the **enzymes** needed to **respire lactose** are found on an operon called the ***lac* operon**.
   3) The *lac* operon has **three structural genes** — ***lac*Z**, ***lac*Y** and ***lac*A**, which produce proteins that help the bacteria digest lactose (including **β-galactosidase** and **lactose permease**).

Lactose NOT present

The **regulatory** gene (*lac*I) produces the ***lac* repressor**, which is a **transcription factor** that **binds** to the **operator** site when there's **no lactose** present. This **blocks transcription** because RNA polymerase can't bind to the promoter.

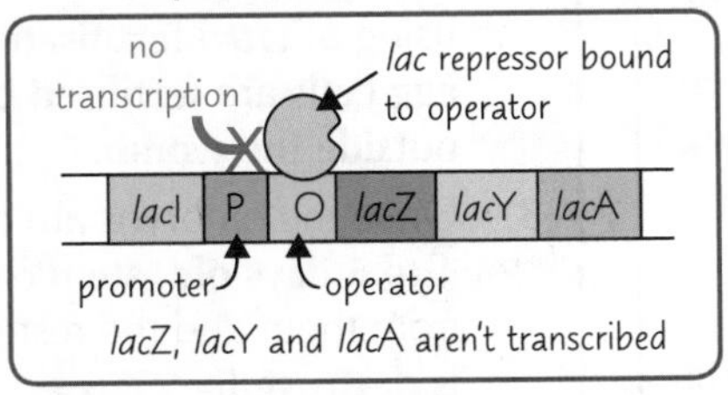

Lactose present

When **lactose is present**, it **binds** to the **repressor**, **changing** the repressor's **shape** so that it can **no longer bind** to the operator site. **RNA polymerase** can now **begin transcription** of the structural genes.

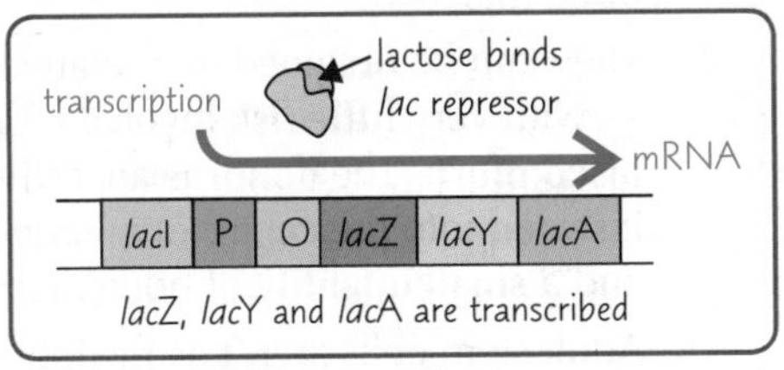

The *lac* operon controls a cell process in *E. coli*.

Practice Questions

Q1 What is the name of the process by which a stem cell becomes specialised?

Q2 What do the structural genes on the *lac* operon do?

Exam Question

Q1 During the development of an embryo, stem cells specialise to become all the different types of cell that make up the body. During very early development, stem cells are totipotent, but they soon become pluripotent.

a) Explain the difference between totipotent stem cells and pluripotent stem cells. [3 marks]

b)* Describe how differential gene expression results in the production of specialised cells from stem cells. [6 marks]

* You will be assessed on the quality of your written response in this question.

And you thought differentiation was just boring maths stuff...

Stem cells are pretty amazing when you think about it — they can differentiate to become any cell in the whole body. Totipotent stem cells are the coolest cells though — they can divide and differentiate into a whole organism.

Stem Cells in Medicine

These pages are about how stem cells can be used in medicine to replace damaged cells. It's got me thinking... perhaps I could grow another brain from some of my stem cells — then I'd be twice as clever.

Stem Cells *Could be Used to* ***Treat*** *Some* ***Diseases***

1) **Stem cells** can develop into **any** specialised cell type, so scientists think they could be used to **replace damaged tissues** in a **range** of **diseases.**
2) Some stem cell therapies **already exist**. For example, the treatment for **leukaemia** (a cancer of the bone marrow) kills all the **stem cells** in the bone marrow, so **bone marrow transplants** can be given to patients to **replace** them.
3) Scientists are **researching** the use of stem cells as a **treatment** for lots of conditions, including:
   - **Spinal cord injuries** — stem cells could be used to repair damaged **nerve tissue.**
   - **Heart disease** and **damage caused by heart attacks** — stem cells could be used to replace damaged heart tissue.
4) People who make **decisions** about the **use** of stem cells in medicine and research have to consider the **potential benefits** of stem cell therapies:
   - They could **save** many **lives** — e.g. many people waiting for organ transplants **die** before a **donor organ** becomes available. Stem cells could be used to **grow organs** for those people awaiting transplants.
   - They could **improve** the **quality of life** for many people — e.g. stem cells could be used to replace damaged cells in the eyes of people who are **blind**.

Human ***Stem Cells*** *Can Come from* ***Adult Tissue*** *or* ***Embryos***

1) In order to **use stem cells** in medicine and research, scientists have to get them from somewhere.
2) There are **two** potential **sources** of human stem cells:

1 Adult stem cells

1) These are obtained from the **body tissues** of an **adult.** For example, adult stem cells are found in **bone marrow.**
2) They can be obtained in a relatively **simple operation** — with very **little risk** involved, but quite **a lot** of **discomfort**. The **donor** is anaesthetised, a **needle** is **inserted** into the centre of a **bone** (usually the hip) and a **small quantity** of bone marrow is **removed.**
3) Adult stem cells **aren't** as **flexible** as embryonic stem cells — they can only develop into a **limited** range of cells.
4) However, if a **patient** needs a stem cell transplant and their **own** adult stem cells can be used (from elsewhere in their body) there's **less risk of rejection.**

2 Embryonic stem cells

1) These are obtained from **early embryos.**
2) Embryos are created in a **laboratory** using ***in vitro*** **fertilisation** (IVF) — **egg cells** are **fertilised** by sperm **outside the womb.**
3) Once the embryos are approximately **4 to 5 days old, stem cells** are **removed** from them and the rest of the embryo is **destroyed.**
4) Embryonic stem cells can develop into **all types** of specialised cells.

Rejection of transplants occurs quite often and is caused by the patient's immune system recognising the cells as foreign and attacking them.

3) Obtaining stem cells from **embryos** created by IVF raises **ethical issues** because the procedure results in the **destruction** of an embryo that's **viable** (could become a fetus if placed in a womb).
4) Many people believe that at the moment of **fertilisation** a **genetically unique individual** is formed that has the **right** to **life** — so they believe that it's **wrong** to **destroy** embryos.
5) Some people have **fewer objections** to stem cells being **obtained** from **egg cells** that **haven't** been fertilised by sperm, but have been **artificially activated** to start dividing. This is because the cells **couldn't survive** past a few days and **wouldn't** produce a fetus if placed in a womb.
6) Some people think that **scientists** should **only use** adult stem cells because their production **doesn't** destroy an embryo. But adult stem cells **can't** develop into all the specialised cell types that embryonic stem cells can.
7) The decision-makers in **society** have to take into account **everyone's views** when making decisions about **important scientific work** like stem cell research and its use in medicine.

Stem Cells in Medicine

Society Makes **Decisions** About the **Use** of **Stem Cells** in **Medicine**

1) Embryonic stem cells could be really **useful** in **medicine**, but **research** into their use raises many **ethical issues** (see previous page).
2) **Society** has to consider all the arguments **for** and **against** stem cell research before allowing it to go ahead.
3) To help society make these decisions, **regulatory authorities** have been established to consider the **benefits** and **ethical issues** surrounding embryonic stem cell research.
4) The work of regulatory authorities includes:

   1) Looking at proposals of **research** and deciding if they should be **allowed**, taking the **ethical issues** surrounding the work **into account** — this ensures that any research involving embryos is carried out for a **good reason**. This also makes sure research isn't unnecessarily **repeated** by different groups.

   2) **Licensing** and **monitoring centres** involved in embryonic stem cell research — this ensures that only **fully trained staff** carry out the research. These staff will understand the **implications** of the research and **won't** waste precious resources, such as embryos. This also helps to **avoid unregulated research**.

   3) Producing **guidelines** and **codes of practice** — this ensures all scientists are working in a **similar manner** (if scientists don't use similar methods their results can't be compared). It also ensures that the scientists are using an **acceptable source** of stem cells and that the **methods** they use to **extract** the cells are **controlled**. This includes regulating the **maximum age** of an **embryo** that can be used as a source of stem cells.

   4) **Monitoring developments** in scientific research and advances — this ensures that any changes in the field are **regulated appropriately** and that all the **guidelines** are **up to date** with the latest in scientific understanding.

   5) Providing **information** and **advice** to governments and professionals — this helps to **promote** the science involved in embryo research, and it helps **society** to **understand** what's involved and why it's important.

Just like a regulatory authority, you'll need to consider all the benefits and issues of stem cell research when asked about it.

Practice Questions

Q1 Describe how stem cells could be used to treat a range of diseases.

Q2 Name two potential sources of human stem cells.

Q3 Give three ways in which regulatory authorities help society to consider the benefits and ethical issues of embryonic stem cell research.

Exam Question

Q1 Stem cell research is permitted in the UK, but it is regulated by a number of authorities.

a) Give one potential benefit of using stem cells in medicine. [1 mark]

b) Embryonic stem cells can be used for research.

i) Explain one benefit of using embryonic stem cells for research rather than adult stem cells. [2 marks]

ii) State two reasons why some people are opposed to using stem cells from embryos. [2 marks]

Stem cells — I think they prove that we all evolved from plants...

Stem cells have the potential to cure or relieve the symptoms of some diseases, but as you've seen, there are some issues surrounding embryonic stem cells. Scientists are working towards producing stem cells that are as flexible as embryonic stem cells (i.e. can become any cell type) but that have come from other sources (e.g. skin or bone marrow).

Variation

Ever wondered why no two people are exactly alike? No, well nor have I, actually, but it's time to start thinking about it. Variation is the differences that exist between individuals — it's partly due to genes and partly due to differences in the environment.

Variation in *Phenotype* can be *Continuous* or *Discontinuous*

Phenotype is the characteristics displayed by an organism.

Continuous variation

This is when the individuals in a population vary **within a range** — there are **no distinct categories**. For example:

Height — you could be any height within a range.

Mass — you could be any mass within a range.

Skin colour — any shade from very dark to very pale.

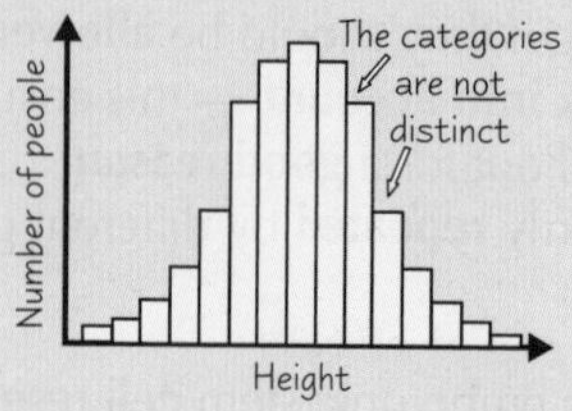

Discontinuous variation

This is when there are two or more **distinct categories** — each individual falls into **only one** of these categories.

For example:

Blood group — you can be group A, group B, group AB or group O, but nothing else.

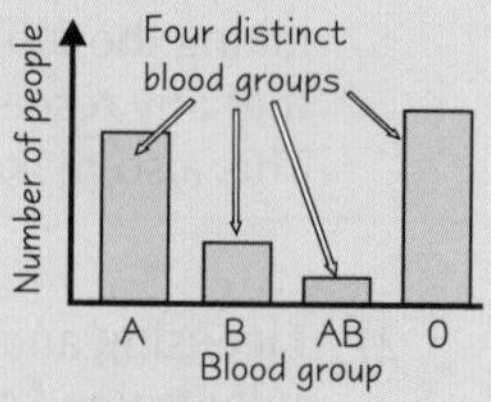

Variation in *Phenotype* is Influenced by *Variation* in *Genotype (Genes)*...

1) Individuals of the same species have **different genotypes** (different combinations of alleles).
2) This **variation** in **genotype** results in **variation** in **phenotype** — the **characteristics** displayed by an organism. For example, in humans there are six different combinations of blood group alleles, which can produce one of four different blood groups.
3) Some characteristics are controlled by only **one gene** — they're called **monogenic**. They tend to show **discontinuous variation**, e.g. blood group.
4) Most characteristics are controlled by a **number of genes** at **different loci** — they're said to be **polygenic**. They usually show **continuous variation**, e.g. height.

Different alleles for the **same gene** are found in the **same position** on **chromosomes**. This position is called the **locus**.

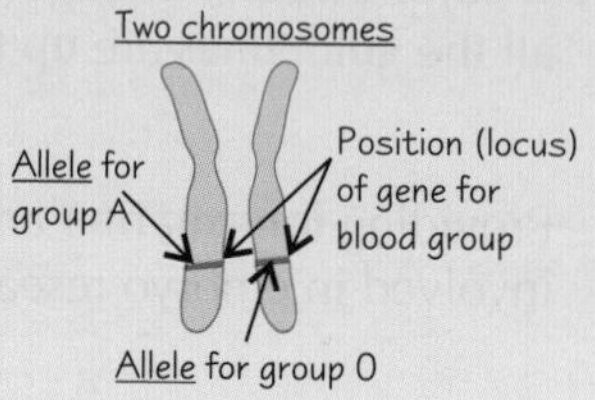

...and the *Environment*

1) Some characteristics are **only influenced** by **genotype**, e.g. blood group.
2) **Most** characteristics are influenced by **both** genotype and the environment, e.g. weight.
3) Here are a few examples of how the **environment interacts** with an organism's **genotype** to produce its **phenotype**:

1) Height is **polygenic** and affected by **environmental factors**, especially **nutrition**. E.g. **tall parents** usually have **tall children**, but if the children are **undernourished** they **won't** grow to their **maximum height** (because **protein** is required for **growth**).

2) Monoamine Oxidase A (MAOA) is an **enzyme** that breaks down **monoamines** (a type of **chemical**) in **humans**. **Low levels** of MAOA have been linked to **mental health problems**. MAOA production is controlled by a **single gene** (it's **monogenic**), but taking **anti-depressants** or **smoking tobacco** can **reduce** the amount produced.

3) Cancer is the **uncontrolled division of cells** that leads to lumps of cells (**tumours**) forming. The **risk of developing** some cancers is affected by **genes**, but **environmental factors** such as **diet** can also **influence** the risk.

4) Animal hair colour is **polygenic**, but the environment also plays a part in **some** animals. E.g. some **arctic animals** have **dark hair** in **summer** but **white hair** in **winter**. **Environmental factors** like decreasing temperature **trigger** this change but it **couldn't** happen if the animal **didn't** have the **genes** for it.

Variation

Changes in the Environment Can Cause Changes in Gene Expression

1) In **eukaryotes**, **epigenetic control** can determine **whether** certain genes are expressed, **altering** the **phenotype**.
2) Epigenetic control **doesn't** alter the **base sequence** of **DNA**. It works by **attaching** or **removing** chemical groups **to** or **from** the **DNA**. This alters how **easy** it is for the **enzymes** and other proteins needed for **transcription** to **interact** with and **transcribe** genes.
3) **Epigenetic changes** to gene expression play a **role** in lots of normal **cellular processes**. They can also occur in **response** to **changes** in the **environment** — e.g. pollution and availability of food.

Increased Methylation of DNA Represses a Gene

1) One method of **epigenetic control** is **methylation** of **DNA** — this is when a **methyl group** is **attached** to the **DNA** coding for a **gene**.
2) The group always attaches at a **CpG site**, which is where a **cytosine** and **guanine** base are **next to** each other in the DNA.
3) **Increased** methylation **changes** the **DNA structure**, so that the **proteins** and **enzymes** needed for transcription **can't bind to** the gene — so the gene is **not expressed** (i.e. it's **repressed** or **inactivated**).

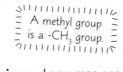

A methyl group is a $-CH_3$ group.

Modification of Histones Also Affects Gene Expression

Histones are **proteins** that DNA **wraps around** to form **chromatin**, which makes up **chromosomes**. Chromatin can be **highly** condensed or **less** condensed. How **condensed** it is affects the **accessibility** of the **DNA** and whether or not the **proteins** and **enzymes** needed for transcription can **bind** to it.

Epigenetic modifications to histones include the **addition** or **removal** of **acetyl** groups:

1) When histones are **acetylated**, the chromatin is **less condensed**. This means that the proteins involved in transcription can bind to the DNA, allowing genes to be **transcribed** (i.e. the genes are **activated**).

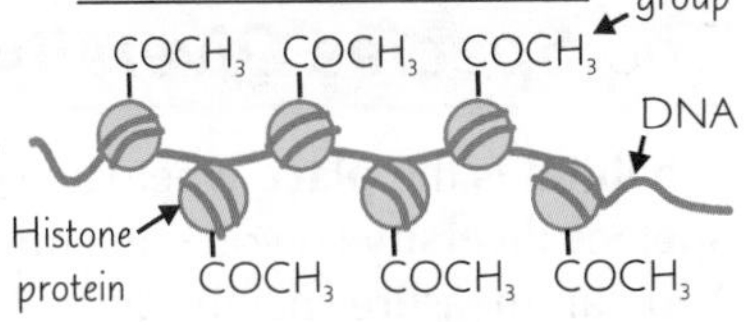

2) When **acetyl groups** are **removed** from the histones, the chromatin becomes **highly condensed** and genes in the DNA **can't** be **transcribed** because the transcription proteins **can't** bind to them — the genes are **repressed**.

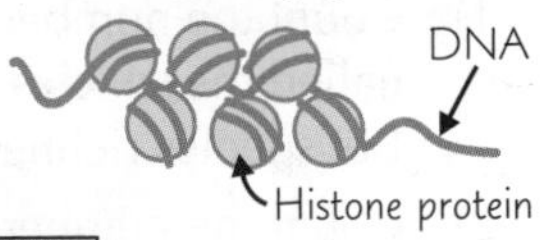

Epigenetic Changes Can be Passed On After Cell Division

1) When a cell **divides** and **replicates**, **epigenetic changes** to its gene expression may be **passed on** to the resulting **daughter cells**. For example, **methyl groups** are usually **removed** from DNA during the production of gametes, but some **escape the removal process** and end up in the sperm or egg cells.
2) If epigenetic changes get passed on, it means that certain **genes** that are **activated** or **deactivated** in the **original cell** will also be **activated** or **deactivated** in the **daughter cells**.
3) If an epigenetic change occurred in **response** to a **change** in the **environment**, this means that the **daughter cells** will be **equipped** to deal with the **changed environment** in the same way as the **original cell** was.

Practice Questions

Q1 Give one example of continuous and one example of discontinuous variation.

Exam Question

Q1 Some cancers can be caused by epigenetic modifications to histones associated with genes related to cell division.
a) What are histones? [1 mark]
b) Describe how histone modifications can affect the transcription of the genes that the histones are associated with. [2 marks]

Histones are great, but hisrhythm is way off...

Remember that variation can be continuous or discontinuous and can be affected by both genetic and environmental factors. Epigenetic changes can also affect gene expression and can even be passed on. Whoever would've thought...

Biodiversity and Endemism

Bet you've noticed how there are loads of different living things in the world — well that's biodiversity in a nutshell. What's even more nutty is that scientists quite like to measure it. There's no accounting for taste...

Biodiversity is the Variety of Organisms

1) **Biodiversity** is the **variety** of **living organisms** in an **area**. It includes:
   - **Species diversity** — the number of **different species** and the **abundance** of each species in an **area.** For example, a wood could contain many different species of plants, insects, birds and mammals.
   - **Genetic diversity** — the variation of **alleles within a species** (or a population of a species). For example, human blood type is determined by a gene with three different alleles.

A population is a group of organisms of the same species living in a particular area.

2) **Endemism** is when a species is **unique** to a **single place** (isn't naturally found anywhere else in the world) — e.g. the **giant tortoise** is **endemic** to the Galapagos Islands — it can only be found there.
3) **Natural selection**, leading to **adaptation** and **evolution** (see pages 81-82), has **increased biodiversity** on Earth over time. But **human activities**, such as farming and deforestation, are **reducing species diversity** — causing **biodiversity** to fall as a result.
4) **Conservation** is needed to **help maintain** biodiversity (see pages 88-89). It is also really important for endemic species because they're particularly **vulnerable to extinction**. They're only found in one place, so if their habitat is threatened they can't usually migrate and their **numbers** will **decline**.

Mr Tiddles was endemic to blue silk sheets — he could only be found there.

The Species Diversity in a Habitat can be Measured

A **habitat** is the **place** where an organism **lives**, e.g. a rocky shore or a field. It's important to be able to **measure species diversity** so you can **compare different habitats**, or study how a habitat has **changed over time**. You can measure species diversity in different ways:

1) Count the number of **different species** in an area. The number of different species in the area is called the **species richness**. The **higher** the number of species, the **greater** the species richness. But species richness gives **no indication** of the **abundance** of each species.
2) Count the number of **different species** <u>**and**</u> the number of **individuals in each species**. Then use an **index of diversity** (worked out with a fancy equation — see page 80) to **calculate** the species diversity.

When measuring species diversity, it's usually **too time-consuming** to count every individual organism in a habitat. Instead, a **sample** of the population is taken. **Estimates** about the whole habitat are based on the sample. Here's what sampling involves:

1) Choose an area to **sample** — a small area within the habitat being studied.
2) To avoid **bias** in your results, the sample should be **random**. For example, if you were investigating the species of plants in a field you could pick random sample sites by dividing the field into a **grid** and using a **random number generator** to select coordinates.
3) **Count** the number of individuals of **each species** in the sample area. How you do this depends on **what** you're counting, for example:
   - For plants you'd use a **quadrat** (a frame which you place on the ground).
   - For flying insects you'd use a **sweepnet** (a net on a pole).
   - For ground insects you'd use a **pitfall trap** (a small pit that insects can't get out of).
   - For aquatic animals you'd use a **net**.
4) **Repeat** the process — take as many samples as possible. This gives a better indication of the **whole habitat**.
5) Use the results to **estimate** the **total number of individuals** or the **total number of different species** (the species richness) in the habitat being studied.
6) When sampling **different habitats** and comparing them, always use the **same sampling technique**.

Biodiversity and Endemism

The Genetic Diversity within a Species can also be Measured

You can measure diversity **within a species** by looking at **genetic diversity**.

1) Diversity within a species is the **variety** shown by **individuals** of that species (or within a population of that species).
2) Individuals of the **same species** vary because they have **different alleles** (different versions of the same gene, see page 50).
3) Genetic diversity is the **variety of alleles** in the **gene pool** of a species (or population).
4) The **gene pool** is the **complete set of alleles** in a species (or population).
5) The **greater the variety** of alleles, the **greater** the genetic diversity. For example, animals have different alleles for **blood group**. In humans there are **three alleles** for blood group, but gorillas have **only one**, so humans show **greater genetic diversity** for blood group than gorillas.
6) You can investigate the **changes** in the genetic diversity of a population over time, or how two populations of the same species show **different diversity**.

To measure the genetic diversity of a species you can look at **two things**:

1 Phenotype

1) Phenotype describes the **observable characteristics** of an **organism.**
2) **Different alleles** code for slightly **different versions** of the same characteristics.
3) By looking at the different phenotypes in a population of a species, you can get an idea of the **diversity of alleles** in that population.
4) The **larger the number** of different phenotypes, the **greater** the genetic diversity.
5) For example, humans have **different eye colours** due to **different alleles**. Humans in northern Europe show a **variety** of blue, grey, green or brown eyes. Outside this area, eye colour shows **little variety** — they're **usually brown**. There's **greater genetic diversity** in eye colour in northern Europe.

2 Genotype

1) Samples of an organism's DNA can be taken and the sequence of **base pairs analysed.**
2) The **order of bases** in different alleles is **slightly different**, e.g. the allele for brown hair will have a slightly different order of bases than the allele for blonde hair.
3) By sequencing the DNA of individuals of the same species, you can look at **similarities** and **differences** in the alleles within a species.
4) You can measure the **number of different alleles** a species has for one characteristic to see how **genetically diverse** the species is. The **larger the number** of different alleles, the **greater** the genetic diversity.
5) You can also look at the **heterozygosity index** (see below).

The Heterozygosity Index Measures Genetic Diversity

You can measure **genetic diversity within** a species using the **heterozygosity index**. Heterozygotes have **two different alleles** at a particular **locus** (the position of a gene on a chromosome). A **higher proportion** of **heterozygotes** in a population means that the population has **greater genetic diversity**. The **heterozygosity index** (H) can be **calculated** using the following **formula**:

$$H = \frac{\textbf{number of heterozygotes}}{\textbf{number of individuals in the population}}$$

EXAMPLE

The fruit fly has **many different alleles** which code for eye colour. In a particular **population** of **456** fruit flies, **276** were found to be **heterozygous** at the locus for eye colour.
Calculate the **heterozygosity index** for the flies at the locus for eye colour.

$$H = \frac{\text{number of heterozygotes}}{\text{number of individuals in the population}} = \frac{276}{456} = \mathbf{0.61}$$

You can find an **average** value for H at many loci — this can be used to estimate genetic diversity in the **whole genome** of the population.

Biodiversity and Endemism

Biodiversity Can be **Measured** Using an **Index** of **Diversity**

1) As you might remember from page 78, an **index of diversity** is a way of **measuring** species diversity. It's calculated using an equation that takes **both** the **number** of species (species richness) and the **abundance** of each species (population sizes) into account.
2) You can **calculate** an index of diversity (D) using this formula:

$$D = \frac{N(N-1)}{\sum n(n-1)}$$

Where...
N = **Total number** of organisms of **all** species
n = **Total number** of organisms of **one** species
Σ = **'Sum of'** (i.e. added together)

The **higher** the **number**, the **more diverse** the area is. If all the individuals are of the **same species** (i.e. no biodiversity) the **index is 1**.

3) By calculating the **index of diversity**, you can **compare** the **species diversity** in **different habitats**. Here's an example:

There are 3 different species of flower in this field — a red species, a white and a blue.
There are 11 organisms altogether, so N = 11.
There are 3 of the red species, 5 of the white and 3 of the blue.
So the species diversity index of this field is:

$$D = \frac{11\,(11-1)}{3\,(3-1) + 5\,(5-1) + 3\,(3-1)} = \frac{110}{6 + 20 + 6} = \mathbf{3.44}$$

When calculating the bottom half of the equation you need to work out the n(n–1) bit for each different species then add them all together.

In another field there are the same 3 species of flower and 11 organisms altogether, but in this field there are 9 of the red species, 1 of the white and 1 of the blue.

The species diversity index of this field is:

$$D = \frac{11\,(11-1)}{9\,(9-1) + 1\,(1-1) + 1\,(1-1)} = \frac{110}{72 + 0 + 0} = \mathbf{1.53}$$

Although both fields have the **same number** of **species**, the second field has **lower species diversity** compared to the **first field** because the **abundance** of the white and blue species in this field is **lower**.

Practice Questions

Q1 What is endemism?

Q2 What is species richness?

Q3 What does the heterozygosity index (H) measure?

Exam Question

Site 1 — No Field Margins		Site 2 — Enhanced Field Margins	
Bombus lucorum	15	*Bombus lucorum*	35
Bombus lapidarius	12	*Bombus lapidarius*	25
Bombus pascuorum	24	*Bombus pascuorum*	34
		Bombus ruderatus	12
		Bombus terrestris	26

Q1 A study was conducted to investigate the impact of introducing enhanced field margins on the diversity of bumblebees. Enhanced field margins are thick bands of land around the edges of fields that are not farmed, but instead are planted with plants that are good for wildlife. Scientists studied two wheat fields, one where the farmer sowed crops right to the edge of the field and another where the farmer created enhanced field margins. The scientists counted the number of bees of different species at each site. Their results are shown in the table above.

a) What two things does an index of diversity take into account when measuring biodiversity? [2 marks]

b) The index of diversity (D) for site 1 was found to be 2.85.
Use the data in the table and the formula on the right to calculate the index of diversity for site 2. $D = \frac{N(N-1)}{\sum n(n-1)}$ [3 marks]

c) What conclusions can be drawn from the findings of this study? [2 marks]

Species richness — goldfish and money spiders top the list...

I know endemism sounds like some sort of disease, but it's not so bad. Knowing these terms is important for your exams — so write out the definitions for biodiversity, endemism, etc. a few times. As for the formulae for the heterozygosity index and the index of diversity — be prepared to use them and to say what the numbers they churn out actually mean.

Adaptation and Evolution

Every species has a role in the environment where it lives. All the variation between organisms means that some organisms are better adapted to their role than others, which can lead to evolution by natural selection...

A **Niche** is the **Role** of a **Species Within Its Habitat**

Remember, a habitat is where an organism lives.

1) The **niche** a species occupies within its habitat includes:
   - Its **interactions** with **other living organisms** — e.g. the organisms it eats, and those it's eaten by.
   - Its **interactions** with the **non-living environment** — e.g. the oxygen an organism breathes in, and the carbon dioxide it breathes out.
2) Every species has its own **unique niche** — a niche can only be occupied by **one species**.
3) It may **look like** two species are filling the **same niche** (e.g. they're both eaten by the same species), but there'll be **slight differences** (e.g. variations in what they eat).
4) If **two species try** to occupy the **same niche**, they will **compete** with each other. One species will be **more successful** than the other, until **only one** of the species is **left**.
5) Here are a couple of examples of niches:

Common Pipistrelle Bat

This bat lives throughout Britain on **farmland**, **open woodland**, **hedgerows** and **urban areas**. It feeds by **flying** and catching **insects** using **echolocation** (**high-pitched sounds**) at a **frequency** of around **45 kHz**.

Soprano Pipistrelle Bat

This bat lives in Britain in **woodland** areas, close to **lakes** or **rivers**. It feeds by **flying** and catching **insects** using **echolocation**, at a **frequency** of **55 kHz**.

It may **look like** both species are filling the **same niche** (e.g. they **both eat insects**), but there are **slight differences** (e.g. they use **different frequencies** for their echolocation).

Organisms Can be **Adapted** to their **Niche** in **Three Ways**

1) Adaptations are features that **increase** an organism's chance of **survival** and **reproduction**.
2) They can be **behavioural**, **physiological** or **anatomical**:

Behavioural adaptations

Ways an organism **acts** that increase its chance of survival. For example:
- **Possums** sometimes **'play dead'** — if they're being threatened by a **predator** they play dead to **escape attack**. This **increases** their chance of **survival**.
- **Scorpions dance** before **mating** — this makes sure they attract a mate of the **same species**, increasing the likelihood of **successful mating**.

Bob and Sue were well adapted to hiding in candyfloss shops.

Physiological adaptations

Processes inside an organism's body that increase its chance of survival. For example:
- **Brown bears hibernate** — they **lower their rate of metabolism** (all the chemical reactions taking place in their body) over **winter**. This **conserves energy**, so they don't need to look for **food** in the months when it's scarce — **increasing** their chance of **survival**.
- **Some bacteria** produce **antibiotics** — these **kill** other species of bacteria in the area. This means there's **less competition**, so they're **more likely** to **survive**.

Anatomical (structural) adaptations

Structural features of an organism's body that increase its chance of survival. For example:
- **Otters** have a **streamlined shape** — making it easier to **glide** through the **water**. This makes it easier for them to **catch prey** and **escape predators**, increasing their chance of **survival**.
- **Whales** have a **thick layer** of **blubber** (fat) — this helps to keep them **warm** in the cold sea. This increases their chance of survival in places where their **food** is found.

Adaptation and Evolution

Adaptations Become More Common by Evolution

Useful adaptations become more common in populations of species because of **evolution** by **natural selection**:

1) **Mutations** (see page 50) can introduce **new alleles** into a population, so individuals within a population show **variation** in their **phenotypes** (characteristics). Some of these alleles determine **characteristics** that can make the individual **more likely** to **survive**.
2) **Selection pressures** such as **predation**, **disease** and **competition** create a **struggle for survival.**
3) Individuals **without** the advantageous alleles **don't survive**. This means there are **fewer individuals** and **less competition** for **resources**.
4) Individuals with **better adaptations** (characteristics that give a selective advantage, e.g. being able to run away from predators faster) are **more likely** to **survive**, **reproduce** and **pass on** their advantageous alleles to their **offspring**.
5) Over time, the **number** of individuals with the advantageous alleles **increases**.
6) Over generations this leads to **evolution** as the frequency of the advantageous alleles in the population increase and the favourable adaptations become **more common**.

A selection pressure is anything that affects an organism's chance of survival and reproduction.

Natural selection is one process by which evolution occurs.

Charles Darwin came up with the original theory of evolution by natural selection. Over time the theory has become **increasingly accepted** as more **evidence** has been found to support it, and no evidence has been shown to disprove it. Evidence increases scientists' **confidence** in a theory — the more evidence there is, the more chance of something becoming an **accepted scientific explanation** (see page 2).

Here's an example to show you how natural selection leads to evolution:

Peppered Moths

1) Peppered moths show **variation** in **colour** — there are **light** ones (with alleles for light colour) and **dark** ones (with alleles for dark colour, which arose from **mutations**).
2) Before the 1800s, there were **more light moths** than dark moths.
3) During the 1800s, **pollution** had **blackened** many of the trees.
4) Dark coloured moths were now **better adapted** to this environment — the alleles for dark colour made them better **camouflaged** from predators.

That colour is marvellous on you, really darling.

5) The light coloured moths were **more susceptible** to **predation** (the selection pressure) as they **stood out** against the **blackened** tree bark, meaning that they were **less likely** to survive. This meant the dark moths had **less competition** for resources (such as food).
6) So the dark moths were more likely to **survive**, reproduce and **pass on** the **alleles** for their dark colouring to their offspring.
7) Over time, the **frequency** of the **alleles** for **dark colour** in the population **increased** and the **dark moths** became **more common**.

Speciation is the Development of a New Species

1) A **species** is defined as a group of **similar organisms** that can **reproduce** to give **fertile offspring**.
2) **Speciation** is the development of a **new species**.
3) It occurs when **populations** of the **same species** become **reproductively isolated** — the **changes** in the alleles and phenotypes of the populations **prevent** them from **successfully breeding together**. These changes include:
   - **Seasonal changes** — individuals from the same population develop different **flowering** or **mating** seasons, or become **sexually active** at **different times** of the year.
   - **Mechanical changes** — changes in **genitalia** prevent successful mating.
   - **Behavioural changes** — a group of individuals develop **courtship rituals** that **aren't attractive** to the main population.
4) A population could become **reproductively isolated** due to **geographical isolation** (see next page) or **random mutations** that introduce **new alleles** to the population, resulting in the changes mentioned above.

Janice's courtship ritual was still successful in attracting mates.

Adaptation and Evolution

Geographical Isolation can lead to Speciation

1) Geographical isolation happens when a **physical barrier divides** a population of a species — **floods**, **volcanic eruptions** and **earthquakes** can all cause barriers that isolate some individuals from the main population.
2) **Conditions** on either side of the barrier will be slightly **different**. For example, there might be a **different climate** on each side.
3) Because the environment is different on each side, **different characteristics** will become **more common** due to **natural selection** (because there are **different selection pressures**):

- Because different **characteristics** will be **advantageous** on each side, the **allele frequencies** will change in each population, e.g. if one allele is more advantageous on one side of the barrier, the frequency of that allele on that side will **increase**.
- **Mutations** will take place **independently** in each population, also changing the **allele frequencies**.
- The changes in allele frequencies will lead to changes in **phenotype frequencies**, e.g. the advantageous characteristics (**phenotypes**) will become more common on that side.

Remember, an organism's phenotype is the characteristics that it displays.

4) Eventually, the different populations will have become **genetically distinct**. Individuals from the different populations will have changed so much that they won't be able to breed with one another to produce **fertile** offspring — they'll have become **reproductively isolated**.
5) The two groups will have become separate **species**.

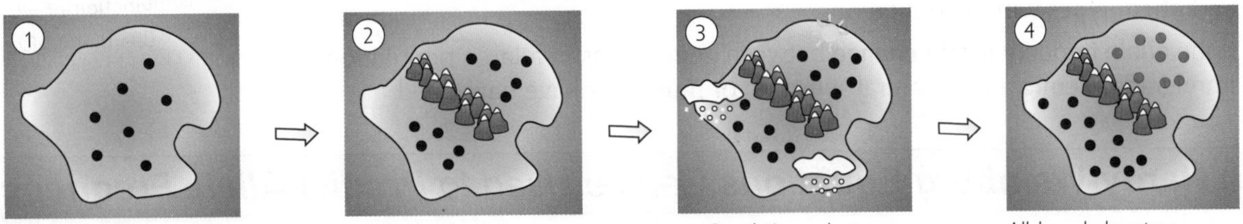

1 Population of individuals ● = individual organism → 2 Physical barriers stop interbreeding between populations. → 3 Populations adapt to new environments. → 4 Allele and phenotype frequency change leading to development of new species.

Practice Questions

Q1 What is meant by the term niche?

Q2 What is meant by the term adaptation?

Q3 Describe the differences between behavioural, physiological and anatomical adaptations.

Exam Questions

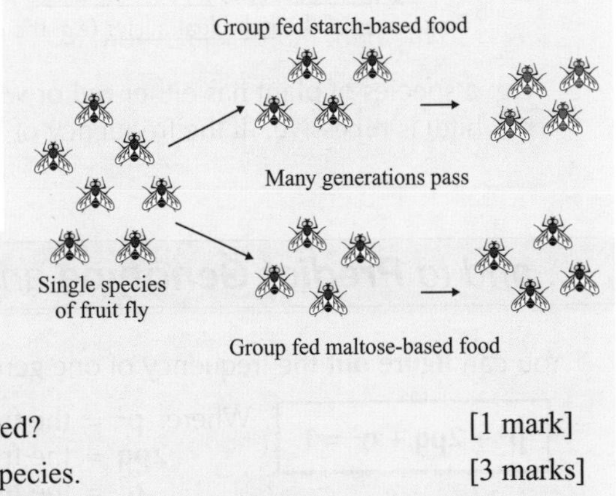

Q1 The diagram shows an experiment conducted with fruit flies. One population was split in two and each population was fed a different food. After many generations the two populations were placed together and it was observed that they were unable to breed together.

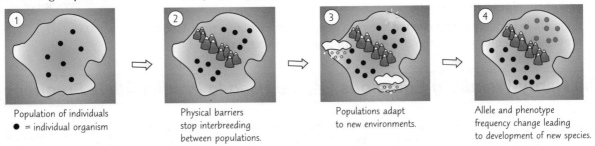

a) What evidence shows that the formation of a new species occurred? [1 mark]

b) Explain why the experiment resulted in the formation of a new species. [3 marks]

Q2 Tawny owls show variation in colour. There are light grey owls and darker brown owls. Before the 1970s there were more grey owls than brown owls in Finland. Since then, climate change has been causing a decrease in the amount of snowfall in Finland. During this period, the darker brown owls have become more common. Explain how natural selection has led to the brown owls becoming more common. [5 marks]

I've evolved to revise for hours and still not remember things...

Basically, natural selection leads to adaptation and evolution — if an organism has alleles that make it better adapted, it's more likely to survive, reproduce and pass on those advantageous alleles, increasing their frequency in the population. If a population gets split up for any reason, the organisms might even evolve into separate species. Niche... I mean nice.

The Hardy-Weinberg Principle

Natural selection affects the frequency of alleles in a population — so by calculating the allele frequencies for a population, you can see whether the population is changing. That's where those fellows Hardy and Weinberg come in...

Evolution** is a **Change** in **Allele Frequency

Remember, a population is a group of organisms of the same species living in a particular area.

1) How **often** an **allele occurs** in a population is called the **allele frequency**. It's usually given as a **percentage** of the total population, e.g. 35%, or a **number**, e.g. 0.35.
2) The **frequency** of an **allele** in a population **changes** over time — this is **evolution** (see p. 82).
3) **New alleles** are usually generated by **mutations** in **genes** (see page 50).
4) The **allele frequencies** of a population can be **calculated** using the **Hardy-Weinberg equations** (see below) and used to see if the population is **changing** over time (see next page).

*The **Hardy-Weinberg Principle** Predicts **Allele Frequencies Won't Change***

1) The **Hardy-Weinberg principle** predicts that the **frequencies** of **alleles** in a population **won't change** from **one generation** to the **next**.
2) But this prediction is **only true** under **certain conditions** — it has to be a **large population** where there's **no immigration**, **emigration**, **mutations** or **natural selection**. There also needs to be **random mating** — all possible genotypes can breed with all others.
3) The **Hardy-Weinberg equations** (see below) are based on this principle. They can be used to **estimate the frequency** of particular **alleles**, **genotypes** and **phenotypes** within populations.
4) If the allele frequencies **do change** between generations in a large population then immigration, emigration, natural selection or mutations have happened.

Remember, the genotype of an organism is the combination of alleles it has (page 50).

*The **Hardy-Weinberg Equations** Can be Used to **Predict Allele Frequency**...*

When a gene has two alleles, you can **figure out** the frequency of one of the alleles of the gene if you **know the frequency of the other allele**, using this equation:

Make sure you learn this equation — you might not get given it in the exams.

$$p + q = 1$$

Where: p = the **frequency** of the **dominant** allele
q = the **frequency** of the **recessive** allele

The total frequency of all possible alleles for a characteristic in a certain population is 1.0. So the frequencies of the individual alleles (e.g. the dominant one and the recessive one) must add up to 1.0.

E.g. a species of plant has either **red** or **white** flowers. Allele **R** (red) is **dominant** and allele **r** (white) is **recessive**. If the frequency of **R** is **0.4**, then the frequency of **r** is: 1 – 0.4 = **0.6**.

*... and to **Predict Genotype** and **Phenotype Frequency***

You can **figure out** the frequency of one genotype if you **know the frequencies of the others**, using this equation:

$$p^2 + 2pq + q^2 = 1$$

Where: p^2 = the **frequency** of the **homozygous dominant genotype**
$2pq$ = the **frequency** of the **heterozygous genotype**
q^2 = the **frequency** of the **homozygous recessive genotype**

The total frequency of all possible genotypes for one characteristic in a certain population is 1.0. So the frequencies of the individual genotypes must add up to 1.0.

E.g. if there are **two alleles** for **flower colour** (R and r), there are **three possible genotypes** — **RR**, **Rr** and **rr**. If the frequency of genotype **RR** (p^2) is **0.34** and the frequency of genotype **Rr** ($2pq$) is **0.27**, the frequency of genotype **rr** (q^2) must be: 1 – 0.34 – 0.27 = **0.39**.

Genotype frequencies can then be used to work out **phenotype frequencies** (the frequencies of observable traits).

E.g. the frequency of **red flowers** is equal to the genotype frequencies of **RR** and **Rr** added together (0.34 + 0.27 = **0.61**) and the frequency of **white flowers** is equal to the genotype frequency of **rr** (**0.39**).

The Hardy-Weinberg Principle

Sometimes You Need to Use **Both Hardy-Weinberg Equations**

EXAMPLE

The **frequency** of **cystic fibrosis** (genotype ff) in the UK is currently approximately **1 birth in every 2500**. From this information you can estimate the **percentage** of people in the UK that are cystic fibrosis **carriers** (Ff). To do this you need to find the **frequency** of **heterozygous genotype Ff**, i.e. **2pq**, using **both** equations:

$p + q = 1$ $\qquad$ $p^2 + 2pq + q^2 = 1$

First calculate q:
Frequency of cystic fibrosis (homozygous recessive, ff) is 1 in 2500
$ff = q^2 = 1 \div 2500 = 0.0004$
So, $q = \sqrt{0.0004} = 0.02$

Next calculate p:
Using $p + q = 1$, $p = 1 - q$
$p = 1 - 0.02 = 0.98$

Then calculate 2pq:
$2pq = 2 \times 0.98 \times 0.02 = 0.039$

The **frequency** of **genotype Ff** is **0.039**, so the **percentage** of the UK population that are **carriers** is **3.9%**.

Allele Frequencies Show if a **Population** is **Changing** Over **Time**

EXAMPLE

If the **frequency** of **cystic fibrosis** is measured **50 years later** it might be found to be **1 birth in 3500**. From this information you can estimate the **frequency** of the **recessive allele** (f) in the population, i.e. **q**.

To calculate q:
Frequency of cystic fibrosis (homozygous recessive, ff) is 1 in 3500
$ff = q^2 = 1 \div 3500 = 0.00029$
So, $q = \sqrt{0.00029} = 0.017$

The frequency of the recessive allele is now **0.017**, compared to **0.02** currently (see above).
As the frequency of the allele has **changed** between generations the **Hardy-Weinberg principle doesn't apply** so there must have been some **factors** affecting **allele frequency**, e.g. **immigration**, **emigration**, **mutations** or **natural selection**.

Practice Questions

Q1 What is the relationship between allele frequency in a population and evolution?

Q2 What conditions are needed for the Hardy-Weinberg principle to apply?

Q3 Which term represents the frequency of the heterozygous genotype in the Hardy-Weinberg equation $p^2 + 2pq + q^2$?

Exam Questions

Q1 A breed of dog has either a black or brown coat. Allele B (black) is dominant and allele b (brown) is recessive. The frequency of the recessive allele is 0.23. The Hardy-Weinberg equation is $p^2 + 2pq + q^2 = 1$.
Find the frequency of the heterozygous (Bb) genotype. [1 mark]

Q2 Cleft chins are controlled by a single gene with two alleles. The allele coding for a cleft chin (T) is dominant over the allele coding for a non-cleft chin (t). In a particular population the frequency of the homozygous dominant genotype for cleft chin is 0.14. The Hardy-Weinberg equation is $p^2 + 2pq + q^2 = 1$.

a) What is the frequency of the recessive allele in the population? [1 mark]

b) What is the frequency of the homozygous recessive genotype in the population? [1 mark]

c) What percentage of the population have a cleft chin? [1 mark]

This stuff's surely not that bad — Hardly worth Weining about...

Not many of you will be thrilled with the maths content on these pages, but don't worry. Make sure you know what to use each Hardy-Weinberg equation for and what the different terms mean, so you can plug the numbers you're given into the right places. Don't forget to take a calculator into the exam with you either, or you'll be really, really sad.

Classification

All species need names. This is where classification comes in — it's about naming and organising species into groups.

Classification is All About Grouping Together Similar Organisms

Taxonomy is the science of classification. It involves **naming** organisms and **organising them** into **groups** based on their **similarities** and **differences**. This makes it **easier** for scientists to **identify** them and to **study** them.

1) There are **eight** levels of groups (called taxonomic groups) used in classification.
2) **Similar organisms** are first sorted into one of three **very large** groups called **domains**, e.g. animals, plants and fungi are in the Eukaryota domain. Then they're sorted into **kingdoms**, e.g. all animals are in the animal kingdom.
3) **Similar** organisms from that kingdom are then grouped into a **phylum**. **Similar** organisms from each phylum are then grouped into a **class**, and **so on** down the eight levels of the hierarchy.

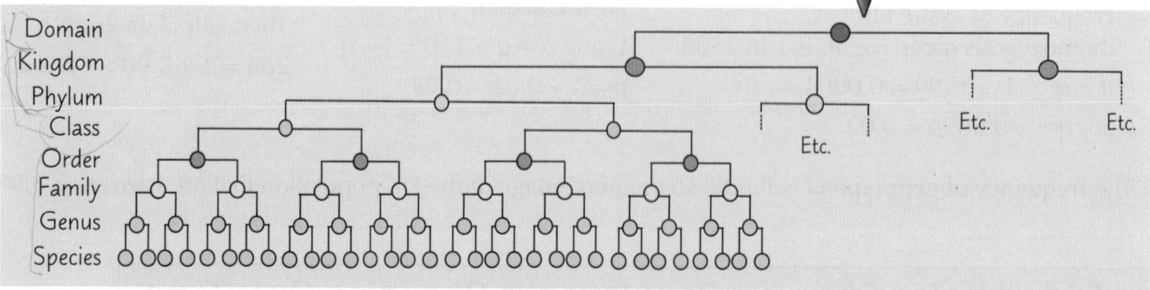

4) As you move **down** the hierarchy, there are **more groups** at each level but **fewer organisms** in each group.
5) The hierarchy **ends** with **species** — the groups that contain only **one type** of organism (e.g. humans, dogs, *E. coli*).
6) Species in the **same genus** can be **very similar**, with similar **phenotypes** and **genotypes**, but they're **separate** species because they **can't breed together** to produce **fertile offspring** (see p. 82). This is the **species concept**.

> All species are given a **unique scientific name** in **Latin** to **distinguish** them from similar organisms. In this **binomial** (**two-word**) system, the **first** word is the **genus** name and the **second** word is the **species** name — e.g. humans are *Homo sapiens*. Giving organisms a scientific name enables scientists to **communicate** about organisms in a standard way that **minimises confusion** — all scientists, in all countries, will call a species by the **same name**.

7) The classification of organisms is based on their **phenotypes**, **genotypes** and how **related** they are.

- Early classification systems **only** used **observable phenotypes** to place organisms into groups, e.g. whether they lay eggs or can fly. But scientists don't always agree on the **relative importance** of different features and groups based **solely** on **physical features** may not show how **related** organisms are. For example, **sharks** and **whales look** quite similar and they both **live** in the **sea**. But they're **not** actually **closely related**. Whales are **mammals** and sharks are **cartilaginous fish** — two completely **different classes**.
- **New technologies** that have enabled organisms' **genotypes** to be determined have resulted in **new discoveries** being made and the **relationships** between organisms being **clarified**. For example, skunks **were** classified in the family **Mustelidae** (e.g. weasels and badgers) until their **DNA sequence** was found to be significantly different to other members of that family. So they were reclassified into the family **Mephitidae**.

Organisms Can be Placed into One of Five Kingdoms

See pages 58-61 for more on prokaryotes and eukaryotes. Remember — eukaryotic cells have DNA contained within a nucleus.

All organisms can be placed into one of **five kingdoms** based on their **general features**:

KINGDOM	EXAMPLES	FEATURES
Prokaryotae (Monera)	bacteria	prokaryotes, unicellular (single-celled), no nucleus, less than 5 μm
Protoctista	algae, protozoa	eukaryotic cells, usually live in water, single-celled or simple multicellular organisms
Fungi	moulds, yeasts, mushrooms	eukaryotic, chitin cell wall, saprotrophic (absorb substances from dead or decaying organisms)
Plantae	mosses, ferns, flowering plants	eukaryotic, multicellular, cell walls made of cellulose, can photosynthesise, contain chlorophyll, autotrophic (produce their own food)
Animalia	nematodes (roundworms), molluscs, insects, fish, reptiles, birds, mammals	eukaryotic, multicellular, no cell walls, heterotrophic (consume plants and animals)

Classification

New Scientific Data Can Lead to New Taxonomic Groupings

1) **New data** about a species can influence the way it is **classified** (see previous page).
2) New data has to be **evaluated** by other scientists though (to check that experiments or studies were **designed properly** and that the conclusions are **fair**). Scientists can share their new discoveries in **meetings** and **scientific journals**. If scientists generally agree with the new data, it can lead to an **organism** being **reclassified** or lead to changes in the **classification system structure**.
3) This shows the **tentative nature** of scientific knowledge — it's always changing based on new data (see page 2).

EXAMPLE — Three Domains vs Five Kingdoms

1) A new, **three domain** classification system has been proposed based on **new data**.
2) The new data came from **molecular phylogeny**:
   - **Phylogeny** is the study of the **evolutionary history** of groups of **organisms**.
   - Phylogeny tells us **which species are related** to which and how **closely related** they are.
   - **Molecular phylogeny** looks at **molecules** (**DNA** and **proteins**) to see how **closely related** organisms are, e.g. **more closely related** organisms have **more similar molecules**.
3) This new system classifies organisms in a **different way**:
   1) In the **older**, **five kingdom** system of classification, all organisms are placed into **one** of five kingdoms.
   2) In the **new**, **three domain** system all organisms are placed into one of three **domains** — **large superkingdoms** that are **above** the kingdoms in the **taxonomic hierarchy** (see previous page).

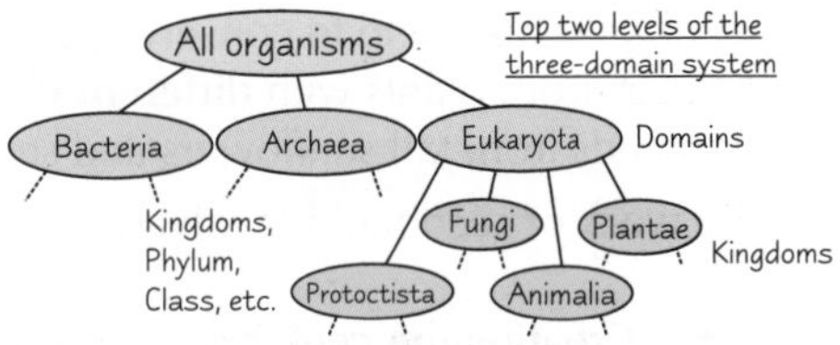

   3) Organisms that were in the kingdom **Prokaryotae** (unicellular organisms **without a nucleus**) are separated into two domains — the **Archaea** and **Bacteria**. Organisms from the **other four** kingdoms (organisms with cells that **contain a nucleus**) are placed in the third domain — **Eukaryota**.
   4) The **Prokaryotae** were **reclassified** into **two domains** because **molecular phylogeny** suggested that archaea and bacteria are **more distantly related** than originally thought.

Practice Questions

Q1 What is taxonomy?

Q2 Why should new data relating to the DNA sequence of a species be evaluated before that species is reclassified?

Q3 What is molecular phylogeny?

Q4 Name the three domains in the three domains classification system.

Exam Question

Q1 The brown trout is a species of fish and is part of the Salmonidae family. Its Latin name is *Salmo trutta*.

a) Complete the table below for the classification of the brown trout. [2 marks]

Domain		Phylum				Genus	Species
Eukaryota	Animalia	Chordata	Actinopterygii	Salmoniformes			

b) The brook trout is another member of the Salmonidae family. Rarely, a brook trout and a brown trout are able to mate to produce offspring known as tiger trout. Tiger trout are unable to reproduce. Explain how you know that a brook trout and a brown trout are different species. [1 mark]

Phylum — I thought that was the snot you get with a cold...

So classification systems can change if any new data rears its ugly mug... Just imagine thinking you were a prokaryote, then waking up one morning and discovering you'd been reclassified as an archaeon — it's enough to give anyone issues. But don't forget that any new data has to be evaluated by other scientists before it's accepted, to check it's OK.

Conservation of Biodiversity

Places like zoos and seedbanks help preserve biodiversity through conservation — they help species that are endangered get out of the woods, or back into the woods, depending on how you look at it...

Zoos and Seedbanks Help Conserve Endangered Species

Remember, biodiversity is the variety of organisms in an area (see p. 78).

1) The **extinction** of a **species**, or the loss of **genetic diversity** within a species, causes a **reduction** in **global biodiversity**.
2) Some species have **already become extinct** (e.g. the dodo) and there are lots of **endangered species** — species that are at **risk of extinction** because of a **low population** or a **threatened habitat.**
3) **Conservation** involves the **protection** and **management** of endangered species.
4) **Zoos** and **seedbanks** help to conserve endangered species and conserve genetic diversity.

Seedbanks Store Seeds from Plants That are Endangered

1) A **seedbank** is a **store** of lots of **seeds** from lots of **different species** of **plant**.
2) They help to conserve biodiversity by storing the seeds of **endangered** plants.
3) If the plants become extinct in the wild the stored seeds can be used to **grow new plants**.
4) Seedbanks also help to conserve **genetic diversity**. For some species they store a **range** of seeds from plants with **different characteristics** (and so **different alleles**), e.g. seeds from tall sunflowers and seeds from short sunflowers.
5) The **work** of seedbanks involves:
   - Creating the **cool, dry conditions** needed for storage. This means seeds can be stored for **a long time**.
   - **Testing** seeds for **viability** (the **ability** to grow into a plant). Seeds are **planted, grown** and **new seeds** are harvested to put back into storage.
6) There are **advantages** and **disadvantages** to using seedbanks:

Polly had enough seeds in the bank for a fancy new perch.

Advantages

1) It's **cheaper** to store seeds than to store **fully grown plants.**
2) **Larger numbers** of seeds **can be stored** than grown plants because they need **less space**.
3) **Less labour** is required to look after seeds than plants.
4) Seeds can be **stored anywhere**, as long as it's cool and dry. Plants would need the **conditions** from their **original habitat**.
5) Seeds are **less likely** to be damaged by **disease, natural disaster** or **vandalism** than plants.

Disadvantages

1) Testing the seeds for **viability** can be **expensive** and **time-consuming.**
2) It would be **too expensive** to store **all types** of seed and **regularly** test them all for viability.
3) It may be **difficult to collect** seeds from some plants as they may grow in **remote locations.**

Zoos have Captive Breeding Programmes to Help Endangered Species

1) Captive breeding programmes involve breeding animals in **controlled environments**.
2) Species that are **endangered**, or already **extinct in the wild**, can be **bred together** in zoos to help **increase their numbers**, e.g. pandas are bred in captivity because their numbers are **critically low** in the wild.
3) There are some problems with captive breeding programmes though. →
   1) Animals can have **problems breeding** outside their **natural habitat**, which can be hard to **recreate** in a zoo. For example, pandas do not reproduce as successfully in captivity as they do in the wild.
   2) Many people think it's **cruel** to keep animals in captivity, even if it's done to prevent them becoming extinct.

Conservation of Biodiversity

Organisms from Zoos and Seedbanks can be Reintroduced to the Wild

1) The **reintroduction** of plants grown from seedbanks or animals bred in zoos can **increase** their **numbers in the wild**, helping to **conserve** their numbers or bring them **back** from the **brink of extinction**.
2) This could also help **organisms** that rely on these plants or animals for **food**, or as part of their **habitat**.
3) The reintroduction of plants and animals also contributes to **restoring habitats** that have been **lost**, e.g. rainforests that have been cut down.
4) Reintroducing organisms to the wild can cause problems though:

Example

The Californian condor was **nearly extinct** in the wild (only 22 birds were left). Thanks to **captive breeding programmes** there are now around 300, half of which have been **reintroduced** to the wild.

1) Reintroduced organisms could bring **new diseases** to habitats, **harming** other organisms **living there**.
2) Reintroduced animals may not **behave as they would** if they'd been **raised in the wild**. E.g. they may have problems **finding food** or **communicating** with wild members of their species.

Seedbanks and Zoos Contribute to Scientific Research

Seedbanks

1) Scientists can study how plant species can be **successfully grown** from seeds. This is useful for **reintroducing** them to the wild.
2) Seedbanks can be used to grow endangered plants for use in **medical research**, as **new crops** or for **new materials**. This means we don't have to **remove** endangered plants from the wild.
3) A **disadvantage** is that **only** studying plants from seeds in a seedbank limits the data to **small, interbred populations**. So the information gained may not be **representative** of wild plants.

Zoos

1) Research in zoos **increases knowledge** about the **behaviour**, **physiology** and **nutritional needs** of animals. This can **contribute** to conservation efforts in the wild.
2) Zoos can carry out research that's **not possible** for some species **in the wild**, e.g. **nutritional** or **reproductive studies.**
3) A **disadvantage** is that animals **in captivity** may **act differently** to those in the wild.

Zoos and Seedbanks Help to Educate People about Conserving Biodiversity

Educating people about endangered species and reduced biodiversity helps to **raise public awareness** and **interest** in conserving biodiversity:

1) Zoos let people get **close** to organisms, **increasing** their **enthusiasm** for conservation work.
2) Seedbanks contribute to education by **providing training** and setting up **local seedbanks** all round the world. For example, the **Millennium Seed Bank Project** aims to conserve seeds in their **original country**.

Practice Questions

Q1 What is conservation?

Q2 Suggest two advantages of storing seeds in a seedbank, rather than storing grown plants.

Exam Question

Q1 The sand lizard is a threatened species in the UK. Captive breeding and reintroduction programmes are being used to increase their numbers in the wild. Give four problems that could be involved with the captive breeding and reintroduction of sand lizards to the wild. [4 marks]

The bank of seeds — high interest rates and 0% on branch transfers...

Zoos do a bit more than you thought — in fact they're just a front for all the covert operations to support conservation. Well, they're not that covert — there's a page here all about them actually. Sigh, I do try and make life more exciting...

Plant Cell Structure

Plants aren't everybody's cup of tea, but they should be — without them we'd be stuck. We get loads of useful stuff from plants, but before we delve into that there are a few important bits and pieces you need to know...

Plant Cells *Have* ***Different Organelles*** *from* ***Animal Cells***

For more on animal organelles see p. 58-59.

You know all about the organelles in animal cells — well plant cells are a little bit different.
Plant cells contain most of the organelles that animal cells do, **plus a few extras** that **animal cells don't have**:

ORGANELLE	DIAGRAM	DESCRIPTION	FUNCTION
Cell wall	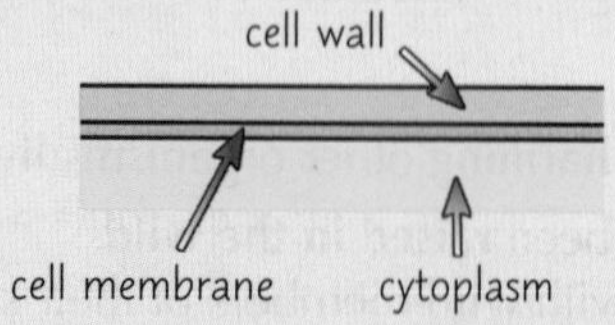	A rigid structure that surrounds **plant cells.** It's made mainly of the carbohydrate **cellulose.**	**Supports** plant cells.
Middle lamella	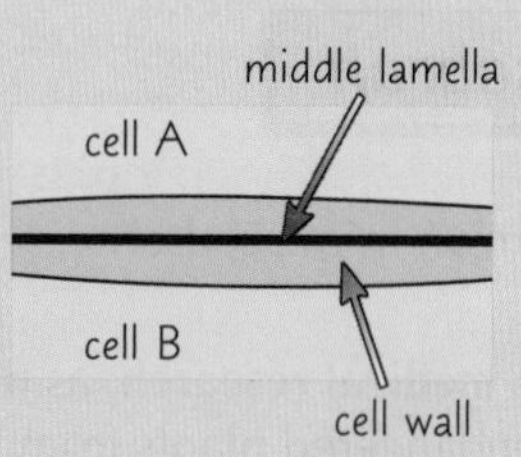	The **outermost layer** of the cell.	This layer acts as an **adhesive**, sticking adjacent plant cells together. It gives the plant **stability.**
Plasmodesmata	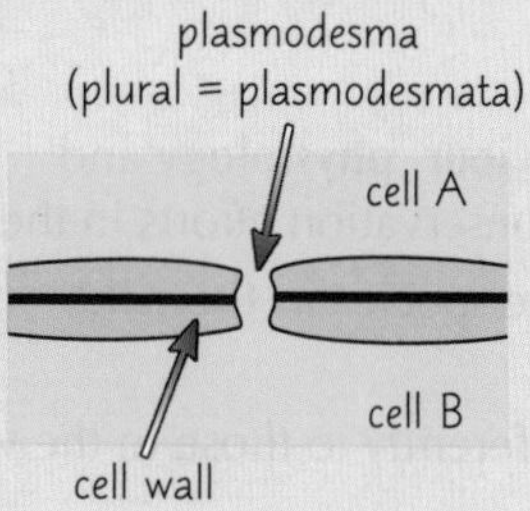	**Channels** in the cell walls that **link** adjacent cells together.	Allow **transport** of **substances** and **communication** between cells.
Pits	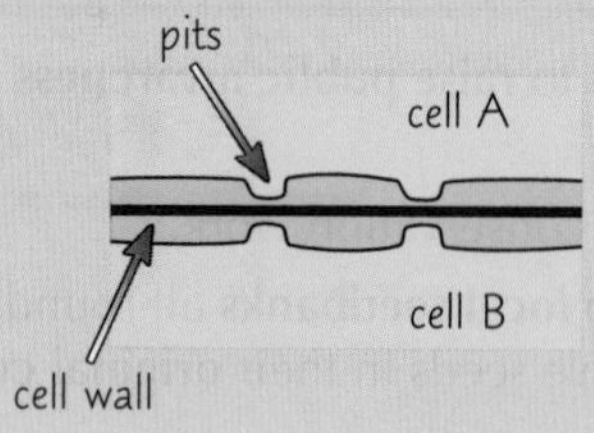	Regions of the cell wall where the wall is **very thin.** They're arranged in **pairs** — the pit in one cell is lined up with the pit in the adjacent cell.	Allow **transport** of **substances** between cells.
Chloroplast	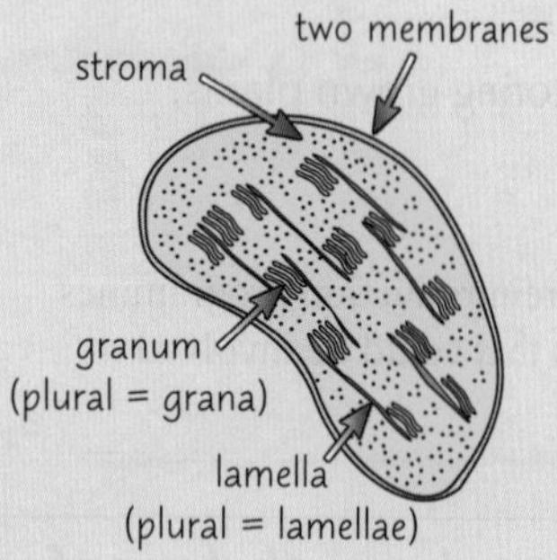	A small, **flattened** structure. It's surrounded by a **double membrane**, and also has membranes inside called **thylakoid membranes.** These membranes are stacked up in some parts of the chloroplast to form **grana.** Grana are linked together by lamellae — thin, flat pieces of thylakoid membrane.	The **site** where **photosynthesis** takes place. Some parts of photosynthesis happen in the **grana**, and other parts happen in the **stroma** (a thick fluid found in chloroplasts).

Plant Cell Structure

ORGANELLE	DIAGRAM	DESCRIPTION	FUNCTION
Amyloplast	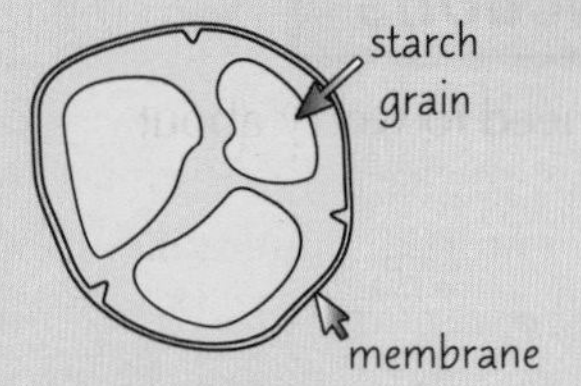	A small organelle enclosed by a **membrane**. They contain **starch granules.**	**Storage of starch grains.** They also convert starch back to glucose for release when the plant requires it.
Vacuole and Tonoplast	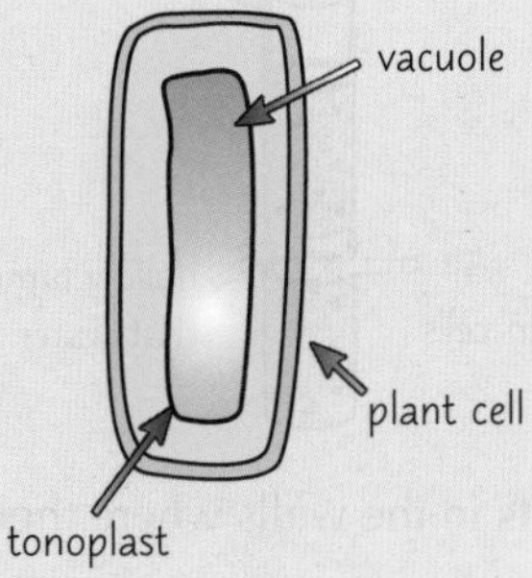	The vacuole is a **compartment** surrounded by a **membrane** called the **tonoplast.**	The vacuole contains the **cell sap**, which is made up of water, enzymes, minerals and waste products. Vacuoles keep the cells **turgid** — this stops plants wilting. They're also involved in the **breakdown** and **isolation** of unwanted chemicals in the cell. The tonoplast controls what **enters** and **leaves** the vacuole.

You need to be able to recognise the different organelles in images taken with electron microscopes.

Practice Questions

Q1 What is the function of the middle lamella?

Q2 Which two organelles allow transport of substances between plant cells?

Q3 Describe the structure of pits in a plant cell.

Q4 Name the membrane that surrounds the vacuole.

Exam Questions

Q1 The image on the right shows a plant organelle as seen under a transmission electron microscope. Which of the following describes its function?

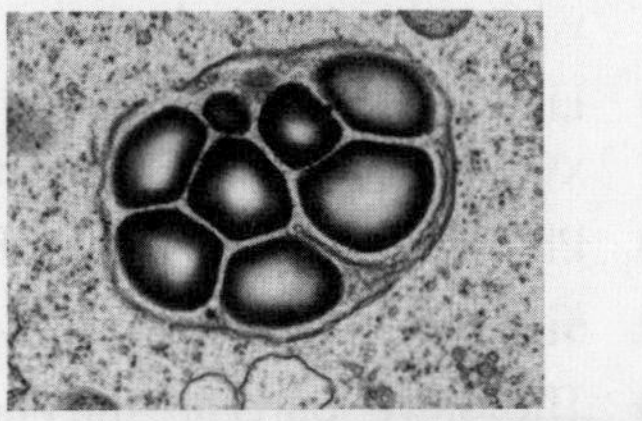

Biophoto Associates/SCIENCE PHOTO LIBRARY

A It keeps the cell turgid and is involved in the breakdown and isolation of unwanted chemicals in the cell.

B It transports substances between cells.

C It is the site where photosynthesis takes place.

D It stores starch grains and converts starch back to glucose for release when the plant requires it. [1 mark]

Q2 The image on the right shows a plant organelle as seen under a transmission electron microscope.

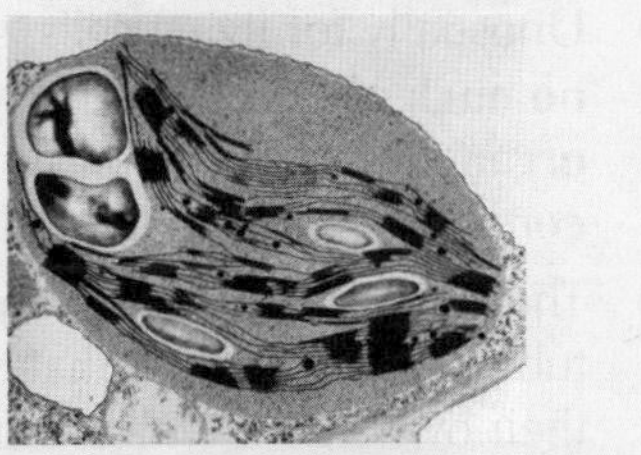

Biophoto Associates/SCIENCE PHOTO LIBRARY

a) Identify the organelle. [1 mark]

b) State the function of the organelle. [1 mark]

Esmerelda... the cells! the cells!

I know this table of organelles looks pretty daunting, but I'm afraid you've got to learn it — scribble down one diagram at a time and write out its description and function 'til you know it like the back of your hand. Then think back to the table of animal organelles on pages 58-59 and make you sure you can compare the two. So many organelles...

Plant Stems

Two whole pages on plant stems... just what I always dreamed of...

Different Parts of **Plant Stems** have **Different Functions**

Plant stems are made up of loads of different things — the only bits you need to worry about are **xylem vessels**, **sclerenchyma fibres** and **phloem tissue**.

Xylem vessels

1) The function of xylem vessels is to **transport water** and **mineral ions** up the plant, and **provide support**.
2) They're very **long**, **tube-like** structures formed from **dead cells**, joined end to end. The tubes are found together in **bundles**.
3) The cells are **longer** than they are **wide**, they have a **hollow lumen** (they contain **no cytoplasm**) and have **no end walls**.
4) This makes an **uninterrupted tube**, allowing water and mineral ions to pass up through the middle easily.
5) Their walls are **thickened** with the woody substance **lignin** (see page 94), which helps to **support** the plant.
6) **Water** and **mineral ions** move **into** and **out of** the vessels through **pits** in the walls where there's **no lignin**.

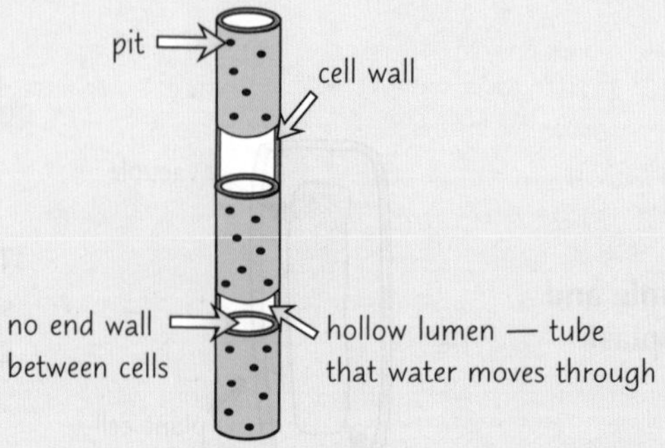

Sclerenchyma fibres

1) The function of sclerenchyma fibres is to provide **support** — they are not involved in transport.
2) Like xylem vessels, they're also made of bundles of **dead cells** that run vertically up the stem.
3) The cells are **longer** than they are **wide**, and have a **hollow lumen** but, unlike xylem vessels, they do have **end walls**.
4) Their cell walls are also **thickened** with **lignin**, but they don't contain pits. They have more **cellulose** (see page 94) than other plant cells.

Phloem tissue

1) The function of phloem tissue is to **transport organic solutes** (mainly sugars like sucrose) from where they're made in the plant to where they're needed. This is known as **translocation**.
2) Like xylem, phloem is formed from cells arranged in **tubes**. But unlike xylem, it's purely a **transport tissue** — it **isn't** used for support as well.
3) Phloem tissue contains different types of cells including **sieve tube elements** and **companion cells**.
4) **Sieve tube elements** are **living cells** and are joined **end to end** to form **sieve tubes**.
5) The '**sieve**' parts are the **end walls**, which have lots of **holes** in them to allow **solutes** to pass through.
6) Unusually for living cells, sieve tube elements have **no nucleus**, a **very thin** layer of **cytoplasm** and **few organelles**. The cytoplasm of adjacent cells is **connected** through the holes in the sieve plates.
7) The **lack** of a **nucleus** and **other organelles** in sieve tube elements means that they **can't survive** on their own. So there's a **companion cell** for **every** sieve tube element.
8) Companion cells carry out the living functions for **both** themselves and their sieve cells. For example, they provide the **energy** for the **active transport** of solutes.

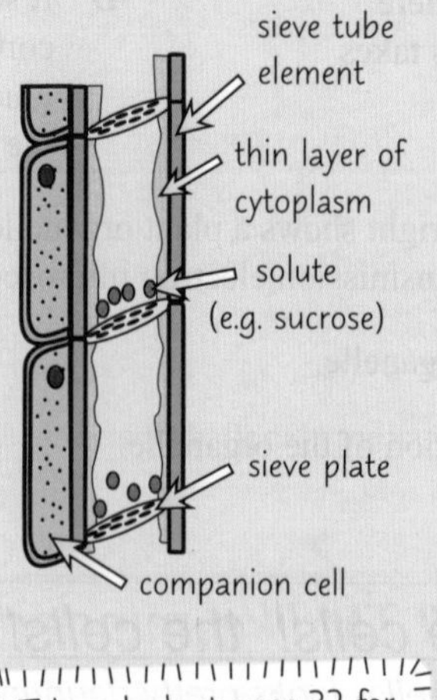

Take a look at page 32 for more on active transport.

Plant Stems

Xylem and *Phloem* are Found in *Vascular Bundles*

1) Xylem vessels, phloem tissue and sclerenchyma fibres are found throughout the plant, but you only need to know about their **position** in the **stem**.
2) In the stem, **xylem vessels** group together with **phloem tissue** to form **vascular bundles**. **Sclerenchyma fibres** are usually **associated** with the vascular bundles.
3) The position of the xylem, phloem and sclerenchyma fibres in the stem are shown in the **cross-sections** below:

This is a **transverse cross-section**. Transverse means the sections cut through each structure at a **right angle** to its **length**.

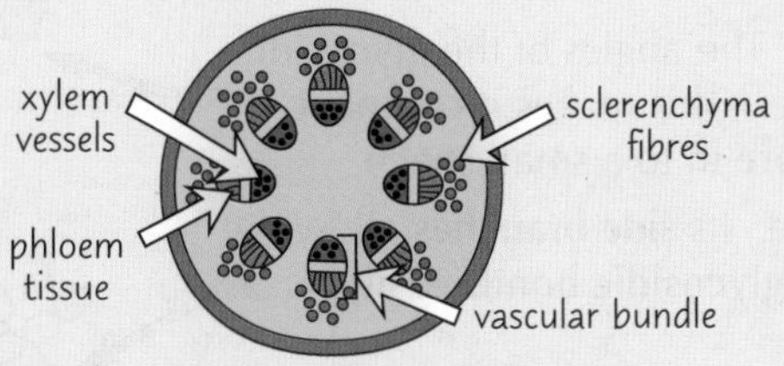

This is a **longitudinal** cross-section. **Longitudinal** cross-sections are taken **along the length** of a structure.

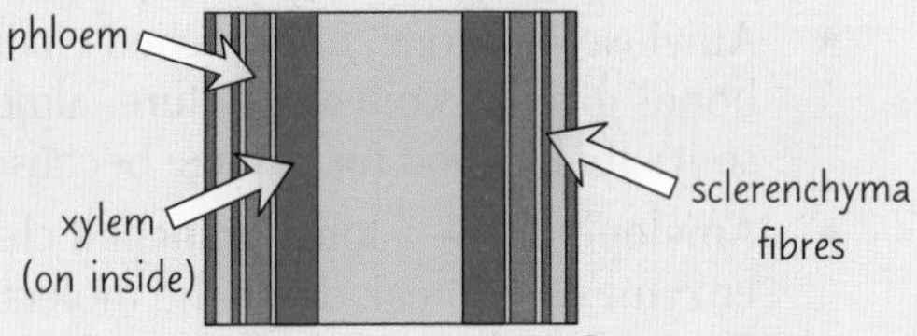

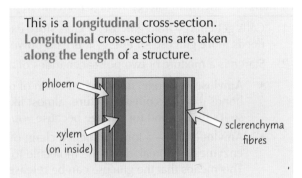

You May Need to *Dissect Plant Stems*

You can **look at** part of a **plant stem** under a **light microscope** and **identify** xylem vessels, sieve cells (phloem tissue) and sclerenchyma fibres. You might be given a **pre-prepared slide** to look at or you could **dissect the stem** and **prepare a section of tissue** yourself. If you're dissecting the plant stem yourself, you can use this method:

1) Use a **scalpel** (or razor blade) to cut a **cross-section** of the stem (transverse or longitudinal). Cut the sections as **thinly** as possible — thin sections are better for viewing under a microscope.
   Be careful when using sharp equipment — make sure you're cutting away from yourself and that any blades are free from rust.
2) Use **tweezers** to gently place the cut sections in **water** until you come to use them. This stops them from **drying out**.
3) Transfer each section to a dish containing a **stain**, e.g. **toluidine blue O (TBO)**, and leave for one minute. TBO stains **lignin blue-green**, so will let you see the positions of the xylem vessels and sclerenchyma fibres. The phloem cells and the rest of the tissue should appear **pinkish purple**.
4) **Rinse off** the sections in water and **mount** each one onto a **slide** (see page 10).
5) Place your prepared slide under a **microscope** and adjust the microscope until you get a **clear image** of your sample. Make a **labelled drawing** that shows the positions of the xylem vessels, phloem sieve tubes and sclerenchyma fibres.

There's more about how to use microscopes on page 10.

Practice Questions

Q1 What is the name of the substance that thickens the walls of xylem vessels?

Q2 What is the function of companion cells?

Exam Question

Q1 The image on the right shows a cross-section of a plant stem as seen under a light microscope.

a) Identify the structures labelled X and Y. [2 marks]

b) Describe the functions of structures X and Y. [2 marks]

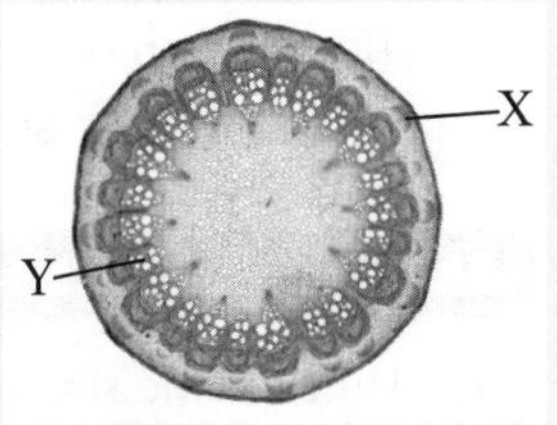

Sieve tube — WLTM like-minded cell for long-term companionship...

Sieve tube elements sound a bit feeble to me — not being able to survive on their own, and all that. Anyway, some of the structures and functions of the cell types covered here are quite similar, so it's important you learn them properly. You don't want to mix up your sieve tube elements with your sclerenchyma fibres in the exam — you'd never forgive yourself...

Starch, Cellulose and Plant Fibres

I know these pages don't have the most stimulating title, but they're actually pretty interesting... honest...

*The **Structures** of **Starch** and **Cellulose** Determine Their **Functions***

You might remember some stuff about the structure of **starch** from Topic 1.
Well you need to know about it for Topic 4 as well — but now you've got to **compare** it to **cellulose**, another polysaccharide. Cellulose is made of similar stuff, but has a **different function**.

1) **Starch** — the main **energy storage material** in **plants**

1) Cells get **energy** from **glucose**. Plants **store** excess glucose as **starch** (when a plant **needs more glucose** for energy it **breaks down** starch to release the glucose).
2) Starch is a mixture of **two** polysaccharides of **alpha-glucose** — **amylose** and **amylopectin**:
   - **Amylose** — a long, **unbranched chain** of α–glucose. The angles of the glycosidic bonds give it a **coiled structure**, almost like a cylinder. This makes it **compact**, so it's really **good for storage** because you can **fit more in** to a small space.
   - **Amylopectin** — a long, **branched chain** of α–glucose. Its **side branches** allow the **enzymes** that break down the molecule to get at the **glycosidic bonds easily**. This means that the glucose can be **released quickly**.
3) Starch is **insoluble** in water, so it doesn't cause water to enter cells by **osmosis** (which would make them swell). This makes it good for **storage**.

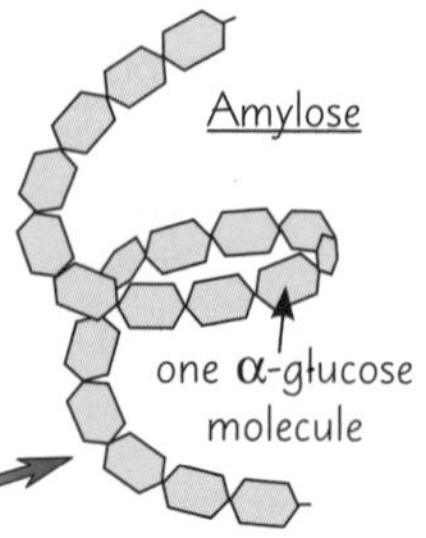

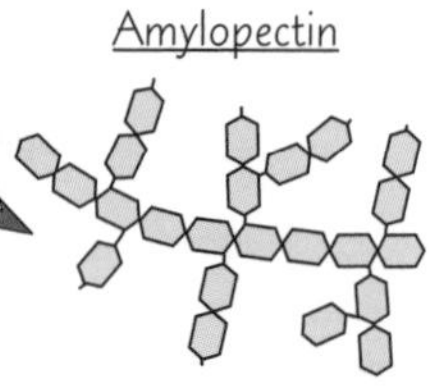

See page 22 for more on glycosidic bonds.

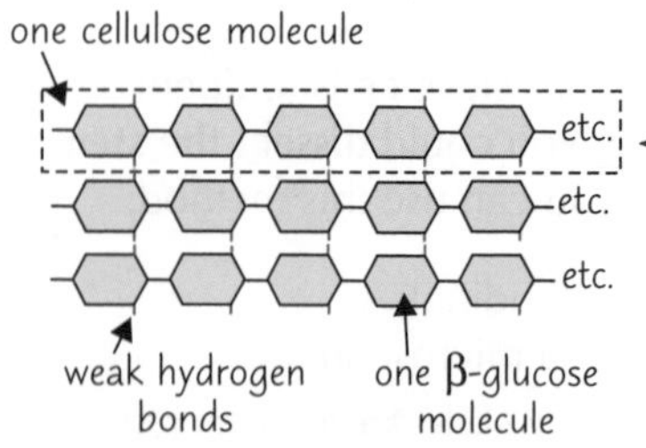

2) **Cellulose** — the major component of **cell walls** in **plants**

1) Cellulose is made of **long**, **unbranched** chains of **β-glucose**, joined by **1-4 glycosidic bonds**.
2) The glycosidic bonds are **straight**, so the cellulose chains are straight.
3) Between **50 and 80** cellulose chains are **linked together** by a large number of **hydrogen bonds** to form **strong threads** called **microfibrils**. The strong threads mean cellulose provides **structural support** for cells (e.g. they strengthen plant cell walls).

Plant Fibres** are **Useful** to **Humans** Because They're **Strong

1) Plant fibres are made up of **long tubes** of **plant cells**, e.g. sclerenchyma fibres and xylem vessels are made of tubes of dead cells (see page 92).
2) They're **strong**, which makes them useful for loads of things, e.g. **ropes** or **fabrics** like hemp.
3) They're strong for a **number of reasons**, but you only need to know **two**:

The arrangement of cellulose microfibrils in the cell wall

1) The cell wall contains **cellulose microfibrils** in a **net-like arrangement**.
2) The strength of the microfibrils and their arrangement in the cell wall gives plant fibres **strength**.

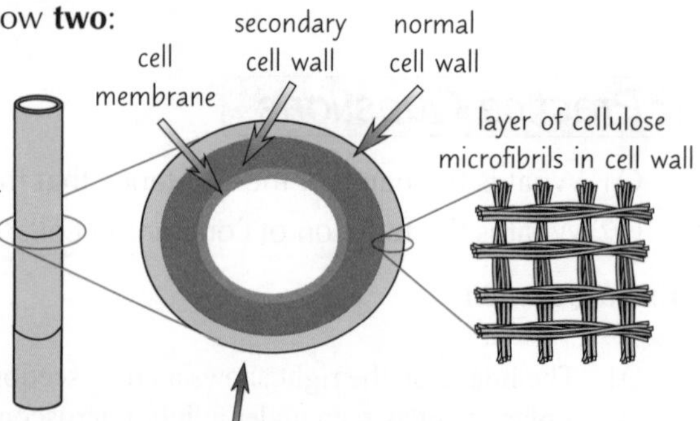

The secondary thickening of cell walls

1) When some structural plant cells (like sclerenchyma and xylem) have finished growing, they produce a **secondary cell wall** between the normal cell wall and the cell membrane.
2) The secondary cell wall is **thicker** than the normal cell wall and usually has **more** of a woody substance called **lignin**.
3) The growth of a secondary cell wall is called **secondary thickening**.
4) Secondary thickening makes plant fibres even **stronger**.

Starch, Cellulose and Plant Fibres

You Can Measure the *Tensile Strength* of *Plant Fibres*

I don't know Dave, we usually use weights to test tensile strength...

The **tensile strength** of a fibre is the **maximum load** it can take before it **breaks**. Knowing the tensile strength of plant fibres can be really important, especially if they're going to be used for things like ropes (e.g. a rock climber would want to know the rope they're using is going to hold their weight).
Here's how you'd find out the tensile strength of a plant fibre:

1) Attach the fibre to a **clamp stand** and **hang** a **weight** from the other end.
2) Keep **adding weights**, one at a time, until the **fibre breaks**.
3) Record the **mass needed** to break the fibre — the **higher** the mass, the **higher** the tensile strength.
4) **Repeat** the experiment with different samples of the same fibre and calculate the **mean** of the results. This reduces the effect of **random error** and so increases the **precision** of the results (see page 100).
5) The fibres being tested should always be the **same length**.
6) Throughout the experiment all **other variables**, like temperature and humidity, must be kept **constant**.
7) You also need to take **safety measures** when doing this experiment, e.g. wear goggles to protect your eyes, and leave the area where the weights will fall clear so they don't squish your toes.

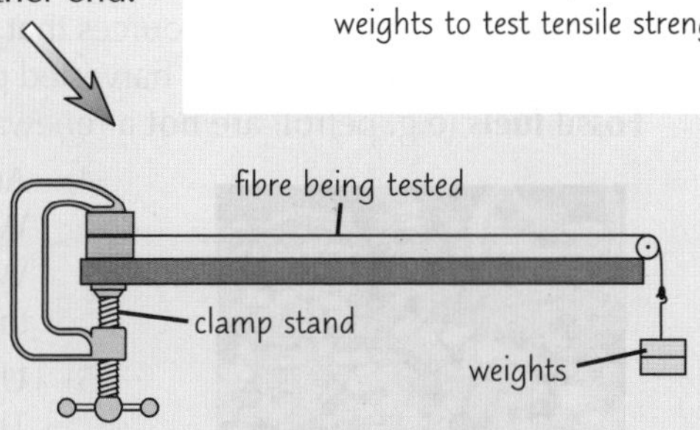

Practice Questions

Q1 Name the two polysaccharides that starch is made up from.
Q2 Compare the structure and function of starch and cellulose.
Q3 What is meant by tensile strength?

Exam Questions

Q1 The physical properties of plant fibres can make them useful to humans.

a) Describe the arrangement of cellulose microfibrils in a plant cell wall, and explain how this relates to the properties of plant fibres. [2 marks]

b) Describe secondary thickening of plant cell walls, and explain how this relates to the properties of plant fibres. [2 marks]

Q2 A group of students investigated the tensile strength of four different plant fibres. Their results are displayed in the table on the right.

	fibre A	fibre B	fibre C	fibre D
mean mass which caused fibre to break / kg	3.5	220.0	52.7	17.2

a) Describe a method they could have used to obtain these results. [3 marks]

b) Give two variables they should have kept constant in their investigation. [2 marks]

c) Based on the results, which fibre would be most suitable to make a climbing rope? Explain your answer. [1 mark]

The world's strongest plant — live from the Bahamas...

Well at least there are a few pretty pictures on these pages to look at. Anyway, it's not so bad — basically plant fibres are really strong and there are lots of reasons, but you just need to know about how the cell walls are strong, which makes the plant fibres super strong. They're strong to the finish, 'cos they eats their spinach...

Sustainability and Plant Minerals

As you saw on page 94, you can use plants to make ropes and fabrics. But there are plenty of other things you can make from plants, like plastics, fuel and castles of mashed potatoes. Making things from plants is also sustainable, which is nice...

Sustainable Practices Don't Deplete Resources

1) Sustainability is all about **using resources** in a way that meets the **needs** of the **present generation** without messing it up for **future generations** (i.e. not using something up so there's none left).
2) To **make products sustainably** you have to use **renewable resources**.
3) Renewable resources are resources that can be **used indefinitely** without **running out**, e.g. **plants** are a renewable resource because harvested plants can be **regrown** (so there'll be plenty for future generations). **Fossil fuels** (e.g. petrol) are **not** a renewable resource — once you've used it all there's no more.

If only Amy's sweets were a renewable resource...

4) An example of a **sustainable practice** is replacing trees after logging. Whenever a tree is cut down, a **new one** is planted in its place. When the tree is fully grown the process can **begin again** — the environment isn't **significantly damaged** in the long term.
5) **Unsustainable practices** can't continue indefinitely. The **resources** would eventually **run out**.
6) An example of an unsustainable practice is the use of **fossil fuels** to make oil-based plastics like polythene.

Using *Plant Fibres* and *Starch* can *Contribute* to *Sustainability*

Plant fibres

1) **Ropes** and **fabrics** can be made of **plastic**, which is made from **oil**. They can also be made from **plant fibres** (see page 94).
2) Making products from plant fibres is **more sustainable** than making them from oil — **less fossil fuel** is **used up**, and crops can be **regrown** to **maintain the supply** for future generations.
3) Products made from plant fibres are **biodegradable** — they can be broken down by **microbes**, unlike most oil-based plastics (which can't be broken down and remain in the environment for many years).
4) Plants are **easier to grow** and **process** (to extract the fibres) than extracting and processing oil. This makes them **cheaper** and it's easier to do in developing countries (as less technology and expertise is needed).

One disadvantage of making ropes from plant fibres is that they're generally not as strong as ropes made of plastic.

Starch

1) Starch is found in **all plants** — crops such as **potatoes** and **corn** are particularly rich in starch.
2) **Plastics** are usually made from **oil**, but some can be made from **plant-based** materials, like **starch**. These plastics are called **bioplastics**.
3) Making plastics from starch is **more sustainable** than making them from oil because less fossil fuel is used up and the **crops** from which the starch came from can be **regrown**.
4) **Vehicle fuel** is also usually made from **oil**, but you can make fuel from **starch**. E.g. **bioethanol** is a fuel that can be made from starch.
5) Making fuel from starch is **more sustainable** than making it from oil because, you guessed it, **less fossil fuel** is used up and the **crops** from which the starch came from can be **regrown**.

The potatoes were getting worried about all this talk of using more starch — you could see it in their eyes.

Sustainability and Plant Minerals

Plants **Need Water** and **Inorganic Ions**

Plants need **water** and **inorganic ions** (**minerals**) for a number of different functions. They're absorbed through the **roots** and travel through the plant in the xylem. If there isn't enough water or inorganic ions in the soil, the plant will show **deficiency symptoms**, like stunted growth. You need to know why plants need water and these three minerals:

- **Water** is needed for **photosynthesis**, to **transport minerals**, to maintain **structural rigidity** (water exerts pressure in cell vacuoles — see page 91) and to **regulate temperature** (water evaporating from leaves helps cool plants down).
- **Magnesium ions** are needed for the production of **chlorophyll** — the **pigment** needed for **photosynthesis**.
- **Nitrate ions** are needed for the production of **DNA**, **proteins** (including enzymes) and **chlorophyll**. They're required for **plant growth**, **fruit production** and **seed production**.
- **Calcium ions** are important components in plant **cell walls**. They're required for **plant growth**.

You Can **Investigate Plant Mineral Deficiencies** in the **Lab**

Here's how to **investigate mineral deficiency** in a plant using calcium ions as an example (you could do the same experiment with any of the minerals mentioned above):

1) Make up three **nutrient broths** containing all the essential minerals, but vary the concentration of **calcium ions**. Make up one broth with a **high** concentration, one with a **medium** concentration and one with a **low** concentration of calcium ions.
2) Split 9 test tubes into **three groups** and fill the tubes of each group with one of the three broths.
3) Take 9 seedlings of the **same plant**, e.g. germinated mung beans (they should be the **same age**). For each seedling, measure its **mass** using a balance and record it. Then put it gently into the top of one of the test tubes so that the **root is suspended** in the nutrient broth. You will have to **support** the seedling to stop it from falling into the test tube, e.g. by putting cotton wool inside the opening of the tube.
4) **Cover the outside** of each test tube in aluminium foil so that **no light** can get to the nutrient broth and cause other organisms, such as algae, to grow.
5) Place all the tubes near a **light source**, e.g. on a windowsill, and leave them for the same amount of time, e.g. **2 weeks**. You may have to **top up** the nutrient broth in each tube during this time to ensure the roots stay suspended in the liquid.
6) Carefully **remove** each plant from its test tube and **blot it dry**. Measure and record the **new mass** of each plant, then calculate the **mean change in mass** of the plants for each nutrient broth. It's good to note down any **visual differences** between the groups too.
7) During the experiment it's important to keep all other **variables the same**, e.g. the amount of light the plants receive.

Don't forget to label each of your tubes with the preparation of nutrient broth it contains and the starting mass of the seedling.

You could use a similar method to investigate the effect on **plant growth** when plants are **completely deficient** in one mineral — instead of varying the concentration of one mineral in each broth, you would use broths containing **all the nutrients** apart from **the nutrient you were testing**. In this experiment you would also need two **control broths** — one **containing all** the nutrients and one **lacking all** the nutrients.

Practice Questions

Q1 What does it mean if a product is made sustainably?

Q2 Give two advantages of using plant fibres rather than oil-based plastics to make rope.

Q3 Name two products, other than rope, that can be made from plants.

Exam Question

Q1 A student wants to investigate both the effects of magnesium ion deficiency and nitrate ion deficiency on plant growth. Describe four different broths she would need to prepare for her investigation to produce valid results. [2 marks]

Potatoes, good for plastics and fuel — we'll be eating them next...

Renewable resources are great — they'll never run out (like my bad jokes — plenty more where they came from...). There's another experiment to learn here, but look at it like this — it could get you some easy marks in the exams.

Drugs from Plants and Drug Testing

A lot of drugs come from plants. Nowadays it's seen as a good idea to test drugs before we use them. But back in the olden days drug testing tended to be a bit hit and miss...

Some Plants Have **Antimicrobial Properties**

Some plants have **antimicrobial properties** — they **kill** or **inhibit the growth** of microorganisms, which is why they're useful components of drugs. You need to know how to investigate the antimicrobial properties of plants using **aseptic techniques** — here's an example:

1) Take **extracts** from the plants **you want to test**. To do this you need to **dry** and **grind** each plant, then soak them in **ethanol** (this will extract the antimicrobial substances, as they're soluble in ethanol).
2) **Filter off** the **liquid bit** (the ethanol containing the dissolved plant extract).
3) You need some **bacteria** to test the plant extract on — you're likely to use bacteria that's been grown in **broth** (a mixture of distilled water, bacterial culture and nutrients). Use a **wire inoculation loop** to **transfer** the bacteria from the broth to an **agar plate** — a **Petri dish** containing **agar jelly**. **Spread** the **bacteria** over the plate using the loop.
4) Dip **equally-sized** discs of **absorbent paper** in the plant extracts, so they absorb the same volume of liquid.
5) You also need to do a **control disc** soaked only in ethanol (to make sure it isn't the ethanol or the paper that's inhibiting bacterial growth).
6) Place the paper discs on the agar plate — make sure they're spread out. Tape the **lid on**, **invert**, and **incubate** the plate at about **25 °C** — this temperature is high enough for the bacteria to grow well, but low enough to prevent the growth of unwanted **human pathogens** (disease-causing microbes that could make you ill). Incubate for **24-48 hours** to allow the bacteria to **grow**, forming a 'lawn'.
7) Where the bacteria **can't grow** there'll be a **clear patch** in the lawn of bacteria. This is called a **clear zone**.
8) The size of a **clear zone** tells you how well the antimicrobial plant extract is working. The **larger** the zone, the **more** effective the plant extract is. You can measure the size of the clear zone by measuring the **diameter** or by working out the **area** using the formula: area = πr^2 ('r' stands for radius).

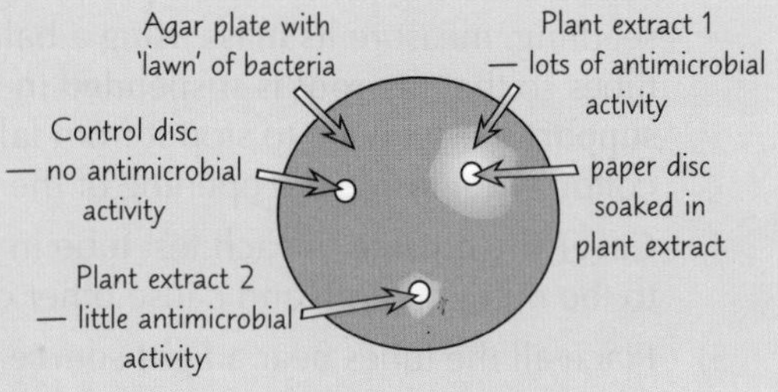

You should <u>repeat</u> the experiment at least <u>twice</u> more and take the <u>mean</u> of your results.

Make sure you keep all other variables (e.g. agar composition, temperature, etc.) constant.

Make Sure the **Conditions** are Right for **Bacterial Growth**

To test antimicrobial properties, the **conditions** need to be right for bacteria to **survive and reproduce**. For example:

1) Bacteria need a source of **nutrients** so they can respire and grow.
2) If they rely on aerobic respiration, they'll need a supply of **oxygen** too.
3) The **temperature** and **pH** of the environment are also important — if either of these factors is too high or too low it can affect **enzyme activity**, meaning metabolic processes (e.g. respiration) can't take place normally.

Always Use **Aseptic Techniques** to **Prevent Contamination** of Microbial Cultures

Aseptic techniques are used to **prevent contamination** of cultures by **unwanted** microorganisms. This is important because contamination can affect the **growth** of the microorganism that you're **working** with. It's also important to avoid contamination with **human pathogens**. When carrying out the investigation above, you need to use the following **aseptic techniques**:

- **Close windows** and **doors** to prevent draughts disturbing the air.
- Regularly **disinfect** work surfaces to minimise contamination.
- Work **near** a **Bunsen flame**. **Hot air rises**, so any microbes in the air should be drawn away from your culture.
- **Sterilise** the **wire inoculation loop before** and **after** each use by passing it through a **hot** Bunsen burner **flame** for 5 seconds. This will kill any microbes on the loop.
- Briefly **flame** the neck of the glass **container of broth** just after it's **opened** and just before it's **closed** — this causes air to move out of the container, preventing **unwanted** organisms from **falling in**.
- **Sterilise** all glassware before and after use, e.g. in an **autoclave** (a machine which steams equipment at high pressure).

Drugs from Plants and Drug Testing

Testing Drugs Used to be *Trial and Error*

Before **new drugs** become available to the general public they need to be **tested** — to make sure they **work** and don't have any horrible **side effects**. In the past, drug testing was a lot **less scientific** than modern clinical trials (see below) and a bit more dangerous for the participants...

Example — William Withering's digitalis soup

1) **William Withering** was a scientist in the 1700s. He discovered that an extract of **foxgloves** could be used to treat **dropsy** (swelling brought about by heart failure). This extract contained the drug **digitalis**.
2) Withering made a **chance observation** — a patient suffering from dropsy made a good recovery after being treated with a **traditional remedy** containing foxgloves. Withering knew foxgloves were **poisonous**, so he started testing **different versions** of the remedy with **different concentrations** of digitalis — this became known as his **digitalis soup**.
3) **Too much** digitalis **poisoned** his patients, while **too little** had **no effect**.
4) It was through this crude method of **trial and error** that he discovered the right amount to give to a patient.

Modern Drug Testing is **More Rigorous**

Nowadays **drug testing protocols** are much more **controlled**. Before a drug is tried on any live subjects, computers are used to **model** the **potential effects**. Tests are also carried out on **human tissues** in a **lab**, then they're tested on **live animals** before **clinical trials** are carried out on **humans**. During clinical trials new drugs undergo **three phases of testing**. This involves three different stages, with more people at each stage:

<u>Phase 1</u> — This involves testing a new drug on a **small group** of **healthy individuals**. It's done to find out things like **safe dosage**, if there are any **side effects**, and how the body **reacts** to the drug.

<u>Phase 2</u> — If a drug passes Phase 1 it will then be tested on a **larger group of people** (this time **patients**) to see **how well** the drug actually **works**.

<u>Phase 3</u> — During this phase the drug is **compared** to **existing treatments**.
It involves testing the drug on **hundreds**, or even **thousands**, of patients.
Using a large sample size makes the results of the test more **reliable**.
Patients are randomly split into two groups — one group receives the **new treatment** and the other group receives the **existing treatment**. This allows scientists to tell if the new drug is **any better** than existing drugs.

Drugs that pass all three phases are considered for clinical use.

Using **placebos** and a **double blind study design** make the results of clinical trials **more valid**.

Placebos

In Phase 2 clinical trials the patients are split into **two groups**. One group is given the drug and the other is given a **placebo** — an **inactive substance** that looks exactly like the drug but doesn't actually do anything. Patients often show a **placebo effect** — where they show some improvement because they **believe** that they're receiving treatment. Giving half the patients a placebo allows researchers to see if the **drug actually works** (if it improves patients more than the placebo does).

Double blind study design

Phase 2 and 3 clinical trials are usually **double blind** — **neither** the **patients** nor the **doctors** know who's been given the new drug and who's been given the placebo (or old drug). This **reduces bias** in the results because the **attitudes** of the patients and doctors **can't affect the results**. E.g. if a doctor knows someone has received the real drug, they may think they've improved more than they actually have — but if they don't know this can't happen.

Practice Questions

Q1 Describe how modern drug testing differs from historic drug testing.

Exam Question

Q1* It has been suggested that an extract of a plant has stronger antimicrobial properties against bacterial species X than mouthwash Y.
Devise an investigation that would give valid results to show whether this suggestion is true. [6 marks]

* You will be assessed on the quality of your written response in this question.

Digitalis soup — like Alphabetti Spaghetti with numbers...

Drug testing these days is really quite complicated, what with all this three phase testing and placebos. Though if you ask me, anything that's double blind just sounds like a recipe for disaster. Anyway, you've got to know this stuff...

Planning an Experiment

As well as doing practical work in class, you can get asked about it in your exams too. Harsh I know. You need to be able to plan the perfect experiment and suggest improvements to ones other people have planned.

Before You Start Planning, Be Clear on What You're Trying to Find Out

Like all scientists, you should start off by making a **prediction** or **hypothesis** — a **specific testable statement**, based on theory, about what will happen in the experiment. You then need to **plan** a good experiment that will provide **evidence to support the prediction** — or help **disprove it**.

A Good Experiment Gives Results that are:

1) **Precise** — precise results **don't vary** much **from the mean**. Precision is **reduced** by **random error**.
2) **Repeatable and reproducible** — repeatable means if the **same person** repeats the experiment using the same methods and equipment, they will get the same results. Reproducible means if **someone different** does the experiment, using a slightly different method or piece of equipment, the results will be the same. Repeatable and reproducible results give **reliable** data.
3) **Valid** — valid results **answer the original question**. To get valid results you need to **control all the variables** to make sure you're only testing the thing you want to.
4) **Accurate** — accurate results are **really close** to the **true answer**.

You need to be able to **design** a good experiment. Here are some things you'll need to consider:

1) **Only one variable should be changed** — Variables are **quantities** that have the **potential to change**, e.g. pH. In an experiment you usually **change one variable** and **measure its effect** on another variable.
   - The variable that you **change** is called the **independent variable**.
   - The variable that you **measure** is called the **dependent variable**.
2) **All the other variables should be controlled** — When you're investigating a variable you need to keep everything else that could affect it **constant**. This means you can be sure that **only** your **independent** variable is **affecting** the thing you're measuring (the dependent variable).
3) **Negative controls should be used** — Negative controls are used to **check** that only the independent variable is affecting the dependent variable. Negative controls **aren't expected** to have **any effect** on the experiment.
4) **The experiment should be repeated at least three times and a mean should be calculated** — this reduces the effect of **random error** on your experiment, which makes your results **more precise**. Doing repeats and getting similar results each time also shows that your data is **repeatable** and makes it more likely to be **reproducible**.

EXAMPLE: Investigating the effect of **temperature** on **enzyme activity**.

1) Temperature is the **independent** variable.
2) Enzyme activity is the **dependent** variable.
3) pH, volume, substrate concentration and enzyme concentration should all **stay the same** (and the quantities should be recorded to allow someone else to reproduce the experiment).
4) The experiment should be **repeated** at least **three times** at each temperature used.
5) A **negative control**, containing everything used **except the enzyme**, should be measured at each temperature used. No enzyme activity should be seen with these controls.

Select Appropriate Apparatus, Equipment and Techniques

1) When you're **planning** an experiment you need to decide what it is you're going to **measure** and **how often** you're going to take measurements. E.g. if you're investigating the **rate of an enzyme-controlled reaction**, you could measure how fast the **product appears** or how quickly the **substrate** is **used up**. You could take measurements at, e.g. 30 second intervals or 60 second intervals.
2) Then you need to choose the most **appropriate** apparatus, equipment and techniques for the experiment. E.g.

- The **measuring apparatus** you use has to be **sensitive** enough to measure the changes you're looking for. For example, if you need to measure **small changes in pH**, a **pH meter** (which can measure pH to several decimal places) would be more sensitive than indicator paper.
- The **technique** you use has to be the most **appropriate** one for your **experiment**. E.g. if you want to investigate plant cells undergoing mitosis, it's best to prepare a **stained squash slide** so you see the chromosomes clearly under the microscope (see page 67).

Planning an Experiment

You Need to Know How to Use **Apparatus** and **Techniques Correctly**

Examiners could ask you about a **whole range** of different apparatus and techniques. Make sure you know how to use all the instruments and equipment you've come across in class and can carry out all the techniques too. Here are some **examples** of equipment you should be able to use:

- **Measuring cylinders** and **graduated pipettes** — These have a **scale** so you can measure specific **volumes**. Whichever one you use, make sure you read the volume from the **bottom** of the **meniscus** when it's at **eye level**.

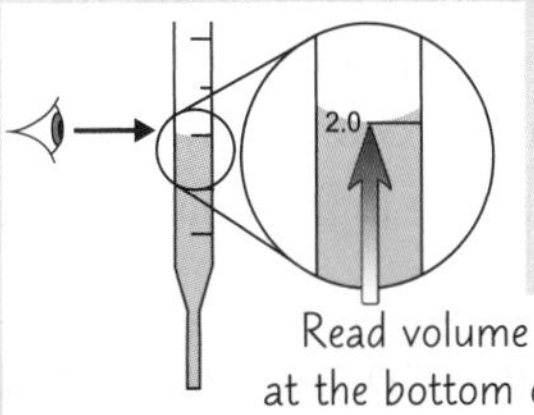

The meniscus is the curved upper surface of the liquid inside the pipette.

- **Water baths** — Make sure you **allow time** for water baths to **heat up** before starting your experiment. Don't forget that your **solutions** will need **time** to get to the **same temperature** as the water before you start the experiment too. Also, remember to **check** the **temperature** of the water bath with a **thermometer** during the investigation to make sure it **doesn't change.**
- **Data logger** — Decide **what** you are **measuring** and what **type** of **data logger** you will need, e.g. temperature, pH. Connect an **external sensor** to the data logger if you need to. Decide **how often** you want the data logger to take readings depending on the **length** of the **process** that you are measuring.

For some experiments you need several solutions of **different**, **known concentrations**. These can be prepared using a **serial dilution** technique — this gives solutions that differ in concentration by a chosen **scale factor**. Here's an example...

This is how you'd make **six serial dilutions** of a vitamin C solution (see page 21), starting with an initial vitamin C concentration of **60 mg cm^{-3}** and **diluting** each solution by a **scale factor** of **2**.

1) Line up six **test tubes** in a rack.
2) Add **10 cm^3** of the initial **60 mg cm^{-3} vitamin C solution** to the first test tube and **5 cm^3 of distilled water** to the other five test tubes.
3) Then, using a pipette, draw **5 cm^3** of the solution from the **first** test tube, add it to the distilled water in the **second** test tube and **mix** the solution **thoroughly**. You now have **10 cm^3** of solution that's **half as concentrated** as the solution in the first test tube (it's **30 mg cm^{-3}**).
4) Repeat this process **four more times** to create solutions of **15 mg cm^{-3}**, **7.5 mg cm^{-3}**, **3.75 mg cm^{-3}** and **1.875 mg cm^{-3}**.

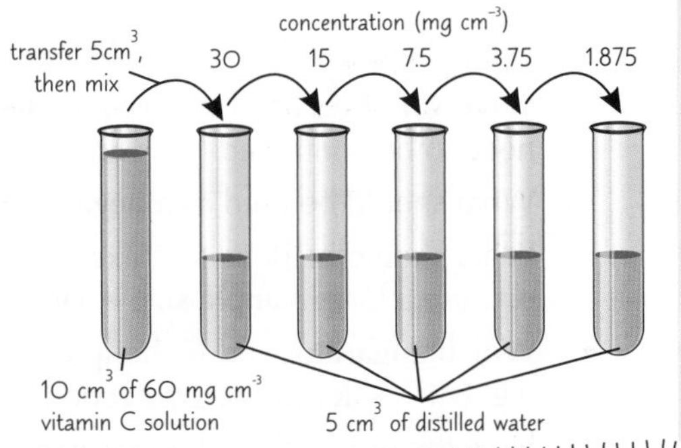

You don't have to dilute solutions by a scale factor of 2. E.g. to dilute by a factor of 10, take 1 cm^3 from your original sample and add it to 9 cm^3 of water.

Make sure you know how to do **all** the **practical investigations** described in this book. You should be able to **apply** the techniques described to **different contexts**. For example, **serial dilutions** can be used to make up **vitamin C solutions** of different concentrations (as described above). You could also use serial dilutions when investigating the effect of **substrate concentration** on **enzyme activity**, to prepare solutions of varying substrate concentration.

Risk Assessments Help You to **Work Safely**

1) When you're planning an experiment, you need to carry out a **risk assessment**. To do this, you need to identify:
   - All the **dangers** in the experiment, e.g. any hazardous chemicals, microorganisms or naked flames.
   - **Who** is at **risk** from these dangers.
   - What can be done to **reduce** the **risk**, such as wearing goggles or gloves or working in a fume cupboard.
2) You should also make sure you **dispose** of **waste materials safely**. E.g. **agar plates** that have been used to grow **microbes** should be **sterilised** before disposal to prevent potentially harmful bacteria spreading.
3) You also need to consider any **ethical issues** in your experiment. For example, if you're using **living animals** (e.g. insects) you must treat them with **respect**. This means **handling them carefully** and keeping them away from **harmful chemicals, extreme heat sources** and other things that might cause them **physical discomfort**.

Planning an Experiment

Record Your Data in a Table

It's a good idea to draw a table to **record** the **results** of your experiment in.

1) When you draw a table, make sure you **include** enough **rows** and **columns** to **record all of the data** you need to. You might also need to include a column for **processing** your data (e.g. working out an average).
2) Make sure each **column** has a **heading** so you know what's going to be recorded where.
3) The **units** should be in the **column** heading, not the table itself.

Farm	Length of hedgerows (km)	Number of species
1	49	21
2	90	28
3	155	30

Watch Out for Anomalous Results

Doing repeats makes it easier to spot anomalous results.

When you look at all the **data** in your **table**, you may notice that you have a result that **doesn't seem to fit in** with the rest at all. These results are called **anomalous results**. You should **investigate** anomalous results — if you can work out what happened (e.g. you measured something totally wrong) you can **ignore** them when **processing** your results.

If you **don't control** all the **variables** in an experiment, you **increase** the **possibility** of an **anomalous result**. In this case, you **won't** be able to draw **valid conclusions** from the results shown.

You Might be Asked to Devise an Investigation in Your Exams

If you have to **devise** an investigation in your **exam** you need to think about **everything** you have learnt about on pages 100-102. Here are some of the things that you should **make sure** you've mentioned:

- What the **dependent** and **independent variables** will be.
- What **variables** need to be **controlled** and **why** they need to be controlled (plus **how** it could be done).
- What should be used as a **negative control** or **placebo**.
- What should be done to make the results more **reliable**, e.g. use a **large sample size** if samples are needed (see p. 17).
- Which **apparatus** and **techniques** will be most appropriate, e.g. will a microscope be needed to observe the results?
- How the results should be **measured** and **recorded**, including any **units** that should be used.
- Any **safety** or **ethical issues** the investigation might raise, e.g. how any animals will be used and how to ensure they will be treated with respect.

A placebo is like a negative control for drug trials on humans. It's an inactive substance that looks exactly like the drug being tested. People aren't told if they are taking the placebo or the real drug in the trial.

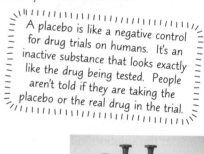

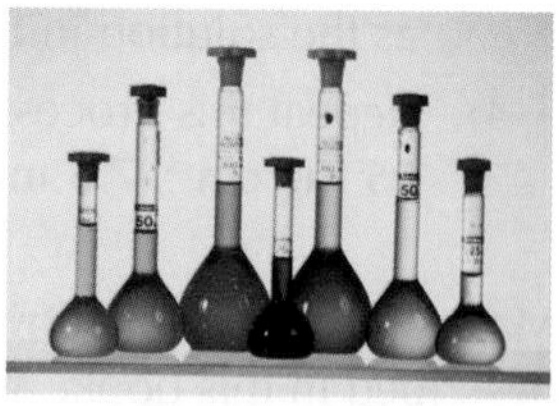

Simone felt that rainbow colours and symmetry were the most important features of a well designed experiment.

Examiners also love getting you to **comment** on **experimental design** or **suggest improvements** to **methods** — e.g. how a method could be improved to make the results more **reliable** (see page 100). You need to think about **everything** you've learnt about on the past few pages when criticising other people's experiments too.

Exam Question

*Q1 It has been suggested that fish oil can act as an anticoagulant in the blood, reducing its clotting ability.

Devise an investigation that would give valid results to show whether fish oil affects the clotting ability of the blood. [6 marks]

* You will be assessed on the quality of your written response in this question.

My best apparatus is the pommel horse...

It's not really, I just like the word pommel. Scientists are rightfully fussy about methods and equipment — I mean if you're going to bother doing an experiment, you should at least make sure it's going to give you results you can trust.

Processing and Presenting Data

Processing data means taking raw data and doing some calculations with it, to make it more useful.

***Processing** the Data Helps You to **Interpret** it*

*You Need to be Able to **Calculate Percentages** and **Percentage Change**...*

Calculating **percentages** helps you to **compare amounts** from **samples** of **different sizes**.
To give the amount **X** as a percentage of sample **Y**, you need to **divide X by Y**, then **multiply** by **100**.

E.g. a tissue sample containing **50** cells is viewed under the microscope. **22** are undergoing mitosis.
What percentage of the cells are undergoing mitosis? Answer: 22/50 × 100 = **44%**

Calculating **percentage change** helps to **quantify** how much something has changed, e.g. the percentage change in the growth rate of pea plants when a fertiliser is added. To **calculate** it you use this equation:

$$\text{Percentage change} = \frac{\text{final value} - \text{original value}}{\text{original value}} \times 100$$

A **positive** value shows an **increase** and a **negative** value shows a **decrease**.

E.g. a person's heart rate before drinking a cup of coffee was **80 bpm**.
Half an hour after drinking a cup of coffee it was **89 bpm**.
Calculate the percentage change.

$$\text{Percentage change} = \frac{89 - 80}{80} \times 100 = \mathbf{11\%} \text{ (2 s.f.)}$$

So the person's heart rate was **11% higher** after drinking the cup of coffee.

Percentage change in happiness upon arrival of balloons — an increase of 150%.

*...as Well as **Ratios***

1) Ratios can be used to **compare** lots of different types of quantities. E.g. an organism with a **surface area to volume ratio** of **2 : 1** would theoretically have a surface area **twice as large** as its volume.
2) Ratios are usually most useful in their **simplest** (smallest) **form**. To simplify a ratio, **divide each side** by the **same number**. It's in its simplest form when there's nothing left you can divide by. E.g. to get a ratio of 75 : 35 in its simplest form, divide both sides by 5. You get 15 : 7.
3) To get a ratio of **X : Y** in the form **X : 1**, **divide both sides by Y**. E.g. to get 28 : 34 into the ratio of X : 1, divide both sides by 34. You get 0.82 : 1.

Averages** and the **Range** Can be Used to **Summarise** Your **Data

1) When you've done **repeats** of an experiment you should always calculate a **mean** (a type of average). To do this **add together** all the data values and **divide** by the **total** number of values in the sample.

Test tube	Repeat (g)			Mean (g)	Range (g)
	1	2	3		
A	28	37	32	(28 + 37 + 32) ÷ 3 = 32.3	37 – 28 = 9
B	47	51	60	(47 + 51 + 60) ÷ 3 = 52.7	60 – 47 = 13

2) You might also need to calculate the **range** (how **spread out** the data is). To do this find the **largest** data value and **subtract** the **smallest** data value from it.

Like the mean, the **median** and **mode** are both types of average.
- To calculate the **median**, put all your data in **numerical order**. The median is the **middle value** in this list. If you have an **even number** of values, the median is **halfway** between the middle two values.
- To calculate the **mode**, count **how many times** each value comes up. The mode is the number that appears **most often**. A set of data might not have a mode — or it might have more than one.

Processing and Presenting Data

The **Standard Deviation** Tells You About **Variation Within a Sample**

1) The **standard deviation** tells you how much the **values** in a **single sample vary**. It's a measure of the **spread** of **values** about the **mean**.
2) Sometimes you'll see the mean written as, e.g. **9 ± 3**. This means that the **mean** is **9** and the **standard deviation** is **3**, so most of the **values** are spread between **6** to **12**.
3) A **large standard deviation** means the values in the sample **vary a lot**. A **small standard deviation** tells you that most of the sample data is around the mean value, so **varies little**.

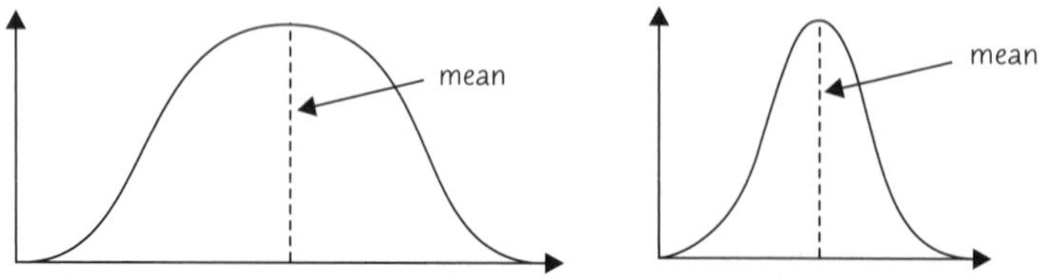

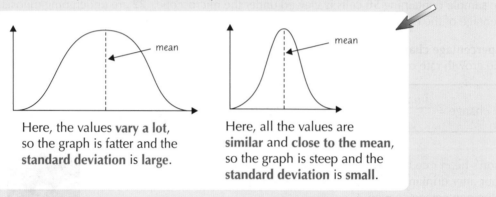

Here, the values **vary a lot**, so the graph is fatter and the **standard deviation** is **large**.

Here, all the values are **similar** and **close to the mean**, so the graph is steep and the **standard deviation** is **small**.

Standard deviation can be more useful than the **range** because it tells you how **values** are spread about the **mean** rather than just the **total spread** of data. A **small standard deviation** means the repeated results are all **similar** and **close** to the mean, i.e. **precise**.

You Need to be Able to Calculate the **Standard Deviation**

This is the **formula** for finding the standard deviation of a group of values:

$$s = \sqrt{\frac{\sum (x - \bar{x})^2}{n-1}}$$

'*s*' just stands for standard deviation.

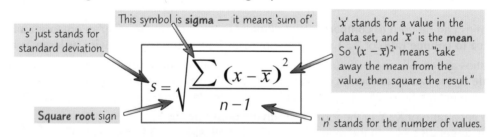

This symbol is **sigma** — it means 'sum of'.

'*x*' stands for a value in the data set, and '$\bar{x}$' is the **mean**. So '$(x - \bar{x})^2$' means "take away the mean from the value, then square the result."

Square root sign

'*n*' stands for the number of values.

Example:

The table shows the height of four different trees in a forest. To find the **standard deviation**:

Tree	Height (m)
A	22
B	27
C	26
D	29

1. Write out the **equation**. $s = \sqrt{\frac{\sum (x - \bar{x})^2}{n-1}}$
2. Work out the **mean** height of the trees, $\bar{x}$. $(22 + 27 + 26 + 29) \div 4 = \mathbf{26}$
3. Work out $(x - \bar{x})^2$ for each value of x. For each tree height in the table, you need to take away the mean, then square the answer.
   A: $(22 - 26)^2 = (-4)^2 = \mathbf{16}$ B: $(27 - 26)^2 = 1^2 = \mathbf{1}$
   C: $(26 - 26)^2 = 0^2 = \mathbf{0}$ D: $(29 - 26)^2 = 3^2 = \mathbf{9}$
4. **Add up** all these numbers to find $\sum(x - \bar{x})^2$. $16 + 1 + 0 + 9 = \mathbf{26}$
5. **Divide** this number by the number of values minus one, $(n - 1)$, then take the **square root** to get the answer.
   $26 \div 3 = 8.66...$
   $\sqrt{8.66...} = $ **2.9 to 2 s.f.**

Processing and Presenting Data

*You Can Use the **Standard Deviation** to Draw **Error Bars***

1) **Standard deviations** can be **plotted** on a graph or chart of **mean values** using **error bars**.
   For example:

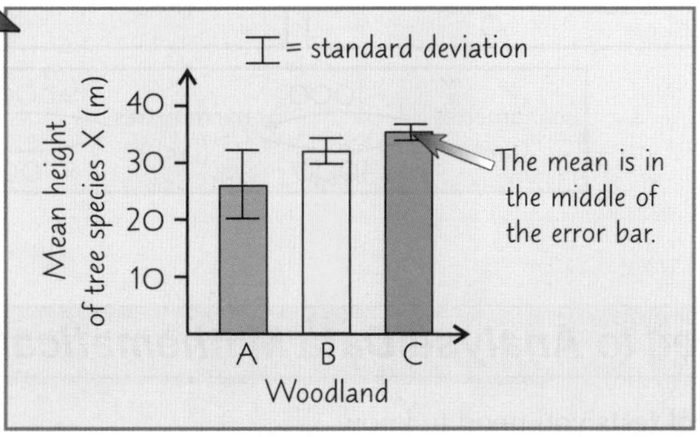

2) Error bars extend **one standard deviation above** and **one standard deviation below** the mean (so the total **length** of an error bar is **twice the standard deviation**).
3) The **longer** the **bar**, the **larger** the **standard deviation** and the **more spread out** the sample data is from the mean.

*Watch Out For **Significant Figures**...*

1) The **first significant figure** of a number is the **first digit** that **isn't a zero**. The second, third and fourth significant figures follow on immediately after the first (even if they're zeros).
2) When you're processing your data you may well want to round any **really long numbers** to a certain number of **significant figures**. E.g. **0.6878976** rounds to **0.69** to **2 s.f.**.
3) When you're doing **calculations** using measurements given to a certain number of significant figures, you should give your **answer** to the **lowest number** of significant figures that was used in the calculation.
   For example:

   $1.2 \div 1.85 = 0.648648648...$ $\quad$ $\mathbf{= 0.65}$

   2 s.f. (1.2) — 3 s.f. (1.85) — Answer should be rounded to 2 s.f. — Round the last digit up to 5.

   When rounding a number, if the next digit after the last significant figure you're using is less than five, you should round it down and if it's 5 or more you should round it up.

4) This is because the **fewer digits** a measurement has, the less **accurate** it is.
   Your answer can only be as accurate as the **least accurate measurement** in the calculation.

*...and **Standard Form***

1) When you're processing data you might also want to change **very big** or **very small numbers** that have **lots of zeros** into something more manageable — this is called **standard form**.

   E.g. 1 000 000 can be written 1×10^6 and 0.017 can be written 1.7×10^{-2}.

A rabbit playing the piano.
Definitely not standard form.

2) To do this you just need to **move the decimal point** left or right. The number of places the decimal point moves is then represented by a **power of 10** — this is positive for big numbers, and negative for numbers smaller than one.
   For example:

   $16\,500 = 1.65 \times 10^4$ — The decimal point has moved **four places** to the **left**, so the power of 10 is **+4**.

   $0.000362 = 3.62 \times 10^{-4}$ — The decimal point has moved **four places** to the **right**, so the power of 10 is **–4**.

Processing and Presenting Data

Make Sure You can **Convert Between Units**

When processing data, you'll quite often have to **convert** between **units**, e.g. seconds and minutes. Make sure you can convert between common units of time, volume and length.

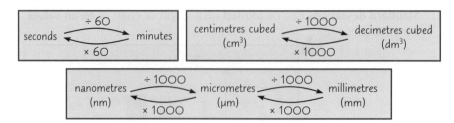

seconds → ÷ 60 → minutes; minutes → × 60 → seconds

centimetres cubed (cm^3) → ÷ 1000 → decimetres cubed (dm^3); decimetres cubed (dm^3) → × 1000 → centimetres cubed (cm^3)

nanometres (nm) → ÷ 1000 → micrometres (μm) → ÷ 1000 → millimetres (mm); millimetres (mm) → × 1000 → micrometres (μm) → × 1000 → nanometres (nm)

Statistical Tests Are Used to **Analyse Data Mathematically**

Here are some examples of **statistical tests** you need to know...

Student's t-test

1) You can use Student's t-test when you have two sets of **data** that you want to **compare**. It tests whether there is a **significant difference** in the **means** of the two data sets.
2) The value obtained is compared to a **critical value**, which helps you decide how likely it is that the results or 'differences in the means' were **due to chance.**
3) If the value obtained from the t-test is **greater than** the critical value at a **probability** (**P value**) of **5% or less** (≤ 0.05), then you can be 95% confident that the difference is significant and not due to chance. This is called a **95% confidence limit** — which is good enough for most biologists.
   If the result of your statistical test is greater than the critical value at a P value of less than 2% (or 1%) you can be even more confident that the difference is significant.

There's more information on critical values on page 53.

The Chi-squared test

1) You can use the Chi-squared test when you have **categorical** (grouped) **data** and you want to compare whether your **observed results** are **statistically different** from your **expected results.**
2) You compare your result to a **critical value** — if it's **larger** than or **equal** to the critical value at **P = 0.05**, you can be **95% certain** the difference is significant.
3) There's loads more on the Chi-squared test on pages 52-53.

John was stunned that the "chai test" involved more than just "add boiling water and brew for 4 minutes".

A correlation coefficient, e.g. Pearson's correlation coefficient (r).

1) Pearson's correlation coefficient allows you to work out the **degree** to which **two** sets of **continuous data** (see next page) are **correlated.**
2) The result is a value between 1 and –1.
   - A value of 1 indicates a **perfect positive correlation.**
   - 0 means there is **no correlation.**
   - –1 is a **perfect negative correlation.**
3) You can compare your result to a critical value to find out whether or not the correlation is **significant.**

See page 108 for more on correlation.

You can be more confident in your **conclusions** (see pages 108-109), if they're based on results that have been analysed using a statistical test.

Processing and Presenting Data

Use a Suitable **Graph** or **Chart** to **Present** Your **Data**

Graphs and charts are a great way of **presenting data** — they can make results much **easier to interpret**.

1) When you have **qualitative** data (non-numerical data, e.g. blood group) or **discrete** data (numerical data that can only take certain values in a range, e.g. shoe size) you can use **bar charts** or **pie charts**.
2) When you have **continuous** data (data that can take any value in a range, e.g. height or weight) you can use **histograms** or **line graphs**.
3) When you want to show how **two variables** are **related** (or **correlated**, see next page) you can use a **scatter graph**.

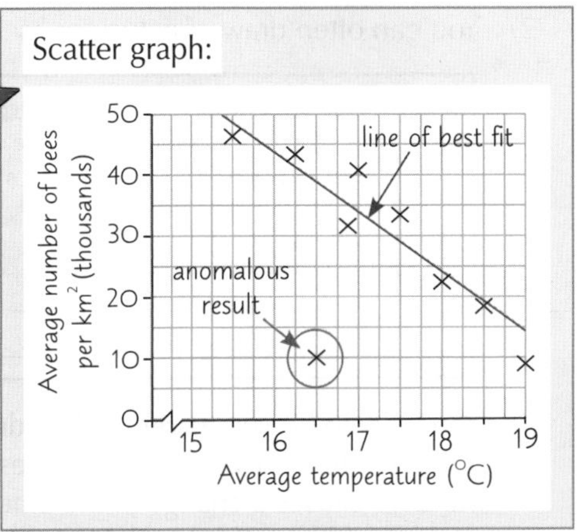

Whatever type of graph you use, you should make sure that:

- The **dependent variable** goes on the **y-axis** (the vertical axis) and the **independent** on the **x-axis** (the horizontal axis).
- You always **label** the **axes**, include the quantity and **units**, and choose a **sensible scale**.
- The graph covers **at least half** of the **graph paper**.

If you need to draw a **line** (or curve) **of best fit** on a **scatter graph**, draw the line through or as near to as many points as possible, **ignoring** any **anomalous** results.

Find the **Rate** By Finding the **Gradient**

Rate is a **measure** of how much something is **changing over time**. Calculating a rate can be useful when analysing your data, e.g. you might want to the find the **rate of a reaction**. Rates are easy to work out from a graph:

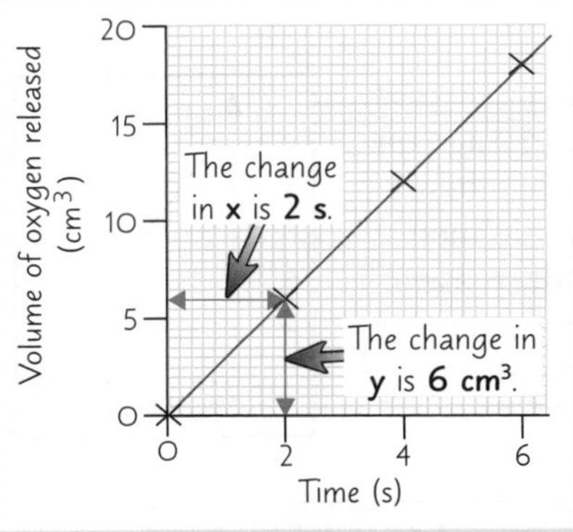

For a **linear** graph you can calculate the **rate** by finding the **gradient of the line**: ⟹ $\text{Gradient} = \frac{\text{Change in Y}}{\text{Change in X}}$

So in this **example**: $\text{rate} = \frac{6\ \text{cm}^3}{2\ \text{s}} = \mathbf{3\ cm^3\ s^{-1}}$ ← $\text{cm}^3\ \text{s}^{-1}$ means the same as cm^3/s (centimetres³ per second)

The **equation** of a **straight line** can always be written in the form **y = mx + c**, where **m** is the **gradient** and **c** is the **y-intercept** (this is the **value of y** when the line crosses the **y-axis**). In this example, the equation of the line is **y = 3x + 0** (or just **y = 3x**). Knowing the equation of the line allows you to estimate results not plotted on the graph. E.g. in this case, when x (the time) is **20 s**, y (the volume of oxygen released) will be 3x = 3 × 20 = **60 cm³**.

For a **curved** (non-linear) graph you can find the **rate** by drawing a **tangent**:

1) Position a ruler on the graph at the **point** where you want to know the **rate**.
2) **Angle** the **ruler** so there is **equal space** between the **ruler** and the **curve** on **either** side of the point.
3) **Draw** a **line** along the ruler to make the tangent.
   Extend the line right across the graph — it'll help to make your **gradient calculation easier** as you'll have **more points** to choose from.
4) **Calculate** the **gradient** of the **tangent** to find the **rate**.

Gradient = 55 m² ÷ 4.4 years = **12.5 m² year⁻¹**

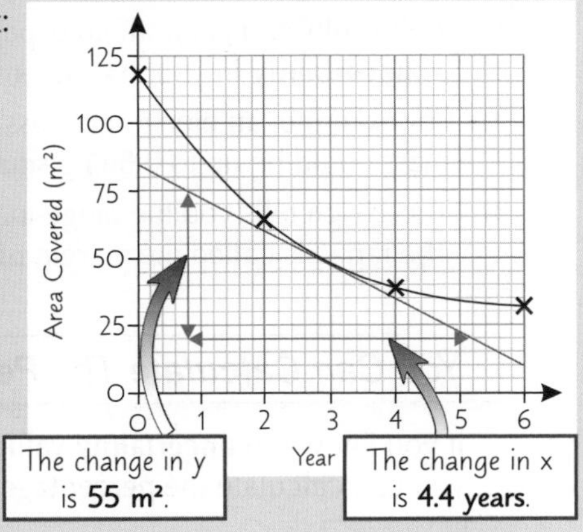

Significant figures — a result of far too many cream cakes...

Lots of maths to get your head around on these few pages, but stay calm and take your time with it all. You'll be fine.

Drawing Conclusions and Evaluating

There's no point in getting all those lovely results and just leaving it at that. You need to draw some conclusions...

You Need to be Able to **Draw Conclusions** From **Data**

1) Conclusions need to be **valid**. A conclusion can only be considered as valid if it answers the original question (see page 100).
2) You can often draw conclusions by looking at the relationship (**correlation**) between two variables:

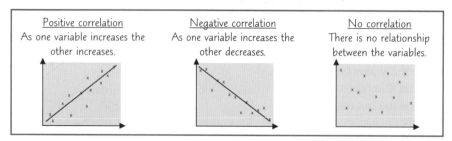

Positive correlation
As one variable increases the other increases.

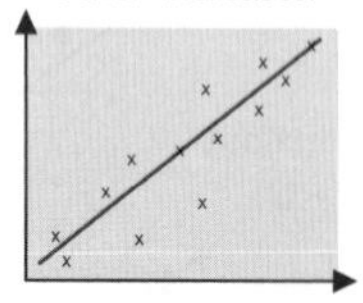

Negative correlation
As one variable increases the other decreases.

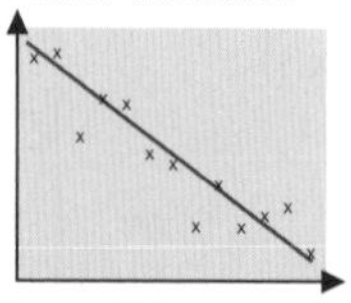

No correlation
There is no relationship between the variables.

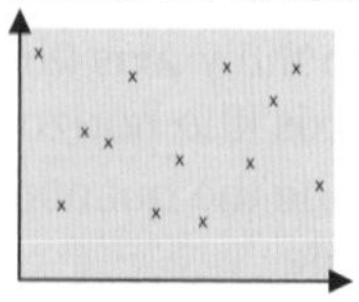

There is no correlation between the colour of your tights and the proportion of your life you spend upside down.

3) You have to be very **careful** when **drawing conclusions** from data like this because a **correlation** between two variables **doesn't** always mean that a **change** in one variable **causes** a **change** in the other (the correlation could be due to **chance** or there could be a **third variable** having an effect).
4) If there's a relationship between two variables and a change in one variable **does** cause a change in the other it's called a **causal relationship**.
5) It can be **concluded** that a **correlation** is a **causal relationship** if every other variable that could possibly affect the result is **controlled**.
6) When you're making a conclusion you **can't** make broad **generalisations** from data — you have to be very **specific**. You can only **conclude** what the results show and **no more**.

In reality this is very hard to do — correlations are generally accepted to be causal relationships if lots of studies have found the same thing, and scientists have figured out exactly how one factor causes the other.

Example

The graph shows the results from a study into the effect of penicillin dosage on the duration of fever in men. The only **conclusion** you can draw is that there's a **negative correlation** between penicillin dosage and duration of fever in men (as the **dosage** of **penicillin increases**, the **duration** of **fever** in **men decreases**). You **can't** conclude that this is true for any other antibiotic, any other symptom or even for female patients — the **results** could be **completely different**.

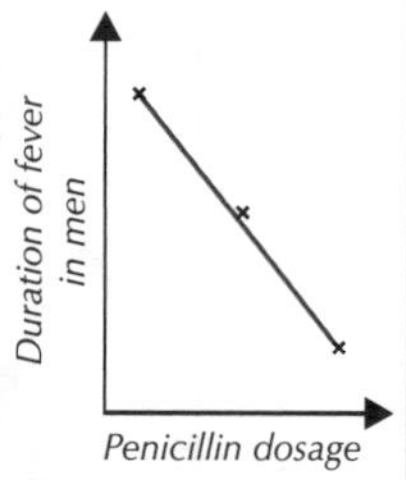

Uncertainty is the Amount of **Error** Your **Measurements** Might Have

1) The results you get from an experiment won't be completely perfect — there'll always be a **degree of uncertainty** in your measurements due to limits in the **sensitivity** of the apparatus you're using.
2) For example, an electronic mass balance might measure to the **nearest 0.01 g**, but the real mass could be up to **0.005 g smaller or larger**. It has an **uncertainty value** of **± 0.005 g**.
3) The ± sign tells you the **range** in which the **true value** lies (to within a certain probability). The range is called the **margin of error**.

You Can **Calculate** The **Percentage Error** of Your **Measurements**

If you know the **uncertainty value** of your measurements, you can calculate the **percentage error** using this formula:

$$\text{percentage error} = \frac{\text{uncertainty}}{\text{reading}} \times 100$$

Example

50 cm³ of HCl is measured with an uncertainty value of ± 0.05 cm³.

$$\text{percentage error} = \frac{0.05}{50} \times 100 = \mathbf{0.1\%}$$

Drawing Conclusions and Evaluating

You Can *Minimise* the *Errors* in Your *Measurements*

1) One obvious way to **reduce errors** in your measurements is to buy the most **sensitive equipment** available. In real life there's not much you can do about this one — you're stuck with whatever your school or college has got. But there are other ways to **lower the uncertainty** in experiments.
2) For example, you can plan your experiment so you **measure** a **greater amount** of something:

If you use a **500 cm³** cylinder that goes up in **5 cm³** increments, each reading has an uncertainty of **± 2.5 cm³**.

So using a 500 cm³ cylinder to measure **100 cm³** of liquid will give you a percentage error of:

$$\frac{2.5}{100} \times 100 = \mathbf{2.5\%}$$

But if you measure **200 cm³** in the same cylinder, the percentage error is:

$$\frac{2.5}{200} \times 100 = \mathbf{1.25\%}$$

Hey presto — you've just **halved** the uncertainty.

You Also Need to Be Able to *Evaluate Methods* and *Results*

1) In the exams, you might get asked to **evaluate** experimental results or methods. Here are some things to think about:

- **Repeatability**: Did you take enough repeat readings of the measurements? Would you do more repeats if you were to do the experiment again? Do you think you'd get similar data if you did the experiment again?
- **Reproducibility**: Have you compared your results with other people's results? Were your results similar? Could other scientists gain data showing the same relationships that are shown in your data?
- **Validity**: Does your data answer the question you set out to investigate? Were all the variables controlled?

2) Make sure you **evaluate** your **method**. Is there anything you could have done to make your results more **precise** or **accurate**? Were there any **limitations** in your method, e.g. should you have taken measurements more **frequently**? Were there any **sources** of **error** in your experiment? Could you have used more sensitive **apparatus** or **equipment**? Think about how you could **refine** and **improve** your experiment if you did it again.
3) Once you've thought about these points you can decide how much **confidence** you have in your **conclusion**. For example, if your results are **repeatable**, **reproducible** (i.e. reliable) and **valid** and they back up your conclusion then you can have a **high degree** of **confidence** in your conclusion.

Solving Problems in a *Practical Context*

In the exams, you'll get plenty of questions set in a 'practical context'. As well as answering questions about the methods used or the conclusions drawn, you'll need to be able to **apply** your **scientific knowledge** to **solve problems** set in these contexts. For example:

Q1 A scientist is investigating how the rate of an enzyme-controlled reaction is affected by substrate concentration. The results are shown in the graph.

a) Suggest why the graph levels off at substrate concentrations higher than 0.08 M. [2 marks]

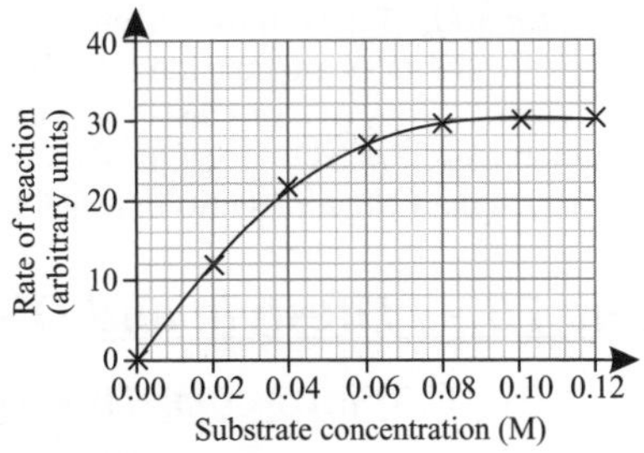

You should remember from page 39 that once all the enzymes' **active sites** are **full** (the saturation point has been reached) adding more substrate won't increase the rate of reaction any further — which is why the rate levels off.

Correlation Street — my favourite programme...

Don't ever, ever assume that correlation means cause. There, I've told you again. No excuses now. A good evaluation is a sign that you really understand what makes a good experiment, so make sure your evaluation-writing-skills are top notch.

Answers

Topic 1A — The Circulatory System

Page 5 — Water and Transport

1 In a water molecule, the shared electrons are pulled closer to the oxygen atom than the hydrogen atoms, making the molecule dipolar ***[1 mark]***. This makes water a good solvent for other ionic substances, which allows it to transport them ***[1 mark]***. Water is also cohesive due to its dipolar nature, which helps water to flow, allowing it to transport substances ***[1 mark]***.

Page 7 — The Heart and Blood Vessels

1 C ***[1 mark]***

2 The valves only open one way and whether they open or close depends on the relative pressure of the heart chambers ***[1 mark]***. If the pressure is greater behind a valve (i.e. there's lots of blood in the chamber behind it), it's forced open, to let the blood travel in the right direction ***[1 mark]***. Once the blood's gone through the valve, the pressure is greater in front of the valve, which forces it shut, preventing blood from flowing back into the chamber ***[1 mark]***.
Here you need to explain how valves function in relation to blood flow, rather than just in relation to relative pressures.

3 Their walls are only one cell thick to allow efficient diffusion of substances (e.g. glucose and oxygen) ***[1 mark]***. Capillaries form networks called capillary beds, which provide a large surface area for exchange ***[1 mark]***.

Page 9 — Cardiac Cycle

1 a) 0.2 - 0.4 seconds ***[1 mark]***
The AV valves are shut when the pressure is higher in the ventricles than in the atria.

b) 0.3 - 0.4 seconds ***[1 mark]***
When the ventricles relax the volume of the chamber increases and the pressure falls. The pressure in the left ventricle was 16.5 kPa at 0.3 seconds and it decreased to 7.0 kPa at 0.4 seconds, so it must have started to relax somewhere between these two times.

c) $16.5 - 0.5 = 16$ ***[1 mark]***
$(16 \div 0.5) \times 100$ ***[1 mark]*** = **3200%** ***[1 mark]***
In this question you need to calculate the percentage increase from 0.5 kPa (blood pressure at 0.0 s) to 16.5 kPa (blood pressure at 0.3 s). To do this you find the difference between the two blood pressures (16 kPa), divide this by the starting blood pressure (0.5 kPa), and multiply the whole thing by 100.

Page 11 — Investigating Heart Rate

1 a) The graph shows a positive correlation between caffeine concentration and *Daphnia* heart rate/as caffeine concentration increases, *Daphnia* heart rate increases ***[1 mark]***.

b) Any two from: e.g. the temperature of the caffeine solutions/ *Daphnia* ***[1 mark]***. / The amount of light the *Daphnia* are exposed to ***[1 mark]***. / The volume of caffeine solution used ***[1 mark]***.

c) E.g. invertebrates are considered to be simpler than vertebrates ***[1 mark]***. / They're more distantly related to humans than other vertebrates ***[1 mark]***. / They have less sophisticated nervous systems than vertebrates, so may feel less/no pain ***[1 mark]***.

Topic 1B — Lifestyle and Disease

Page 15 — Cardiovascular Disease

1 E.g. people may overestimate the risk because they may have known someone who smoked and died from CVD, and therefore think that if you smoke you will die of CVD ***[1 mark]***. Also, there are often articles in the media that highlight the link between smoking and CVD and constant exposure to information like this can make people worry that they'll get CVD ***[1 mark]***.

2 a) thrombin ***[1 mark]***

b) Fibrin, red blood cells and platelets ***[1 mark]***.

c) calcium ions ***[1 mark]***

d) Their blood clotting mechanism will be impaired/their blood won't clot as fast as the blood of people without the disorder because less prothrombin is available to be converted to thrombin ***[1 mark]***. This means that less fibrinogen will be converted to fibrin, which in turn reduces blood clot formation ***[1 mark]***.

3 An atheroma plaque may break through the endothelium (inner lining) of the artery, leaving a rough surface ***[1 mark]***. This damage could cause a blood clot (thrombus) to form over the area ***[1 mark]***. If the blood clot completely blocks a coronary artery, it will restrict blood flow to part of the heart muscle ***[1 mark]***, cutting off its oxygen supply and causing a heart attack ***[1 mark]***.

4 ***5-6 marks:***
The answer explains fully at least three ways in which smoking increases the risk of developing CVD.
The answer has a clear and logical structure and ideas are well-linked. The information given is relevant and detailed.
3-4 marks:
The answer attempts to explain more than one way in which smoking increases the risk of CVD.
The answer has some structure and attempts to link ideas. Most of the information given is relevant and there is some detail involved.
1-2 marks:
The answer mentions at least one factor involved in smoking that increase the risk of developing CVD, but there is little or no attempt made to explain them.
The answer has very little clear structure and ideas are not well-linked. The information given is basic and lacking in detail. It may not all be relevant.
0 marks:
No relevant information is given.
Here are some points your answer may include:
Carbon monoxide in cigarette smoke combines with haemoglobin, which reduces the amount of oxygen transported in the blood. This reduces the amount of oxygen available to body tissues. If the heart muscle/brain doesn't receive enough oxygen it can cause a heart attack/stroke. Nicotine in cigarette smoke makes platelets sticky. This increases the chance of blood clots forming, which increases the risk of CVD. Smoking also decreases the amount of antioxidants in the blood. Fewer antioxidants means cell damage in the artery walls is more likely, and this can lead to atheroma formation, which increases the risk of CVD.

Page 17 — Interpreting Data on Risk Factors

1 a) A large sample size was used ***[1 mark]***.
The sample included many countries ***[1 mark]***.

b) E.g. the study could take into account other variables, such as diet, smoking and physical activity which could have affected the results ***[1 mark]***. The study could be repeated by other scientists to see if they produce the same results ***[1 mark]***.

Page 19 — Treatment of CVD

1 a) E.g. the number of prescriptions of each type of treatment have increased ***[1 mark]***. The numbers of prescriptions of platelet inhibitory drugs have increased gradually, whereas the number of prescriptions of antihypertensive drugs and statins have increased more rapidly ***[1 mark]***.

b) Platelet inhibitory drugs. A benefit of this treatment is that they can be used to treat people who already have blood clots or CVD ***[1 mark]***. However, there is a risk of side effects occurring, such as rashes/diarrhoea/nausea/liver function problems/excessive bleeding ***[1 mark]***.

Answers

c) Prescriptions in 2006: 42 000
Prescriptions in 2011: 62 000
Increase of 62 000 – 42 000 = 20 000
Percentage increase = (20 000 ÷ 42 000) × 100 = **48%** ***[1 mark]***

d) Statins work by reducing the amount of LDL cholesterol produced inside the liver, which reduces blood cholesterol ***[1 mark]***. This reduces atheroma formation, which reduces the risk of CVD ***[1 mark]***.

2 a) The GP could prescribe antihypertensive drugs to reduce his patient's blood pressure ***[1 mark]***. Lower blood pressure would reduce the risk of damage occurring to the artery walls, reducing the risk of atheroma/clot formation and CHD ***[1 mark]***.

b) Antihypertensive drugs can cause side effects, e.g. palpitations/ abnormal heart rhythms/fainting/headaches/drowsiness/allergic reactions/depression ***[1 mark]***.

Topic 1C — Diet and Health

Page 21 — Diet and Energy

1 a) 0.2 mg cm^{-3} ***[1 mark]***

b) Any three from: e.g. volume of DCPIP ***[1 mark]*** / concentration of DCPIP ***[1 mark]*** / time taken to shake the vitamin C and DCPIP solution ***[1 mark]*** / temperature ***[1 mark]***.

2 a) i) Energy input – energy output = energy budget,
2000 – (1200 + (2 x 513) + (2 x 328)) = **–882** ***[1 mark]***.

ii) The woman's energy output is greater than her energy input, so she will lose weight ***[1 mark]***.

b) The woman would become (severely) underweight ***[1 mark]***.

Page 23 — Carbohydrates

1 a)

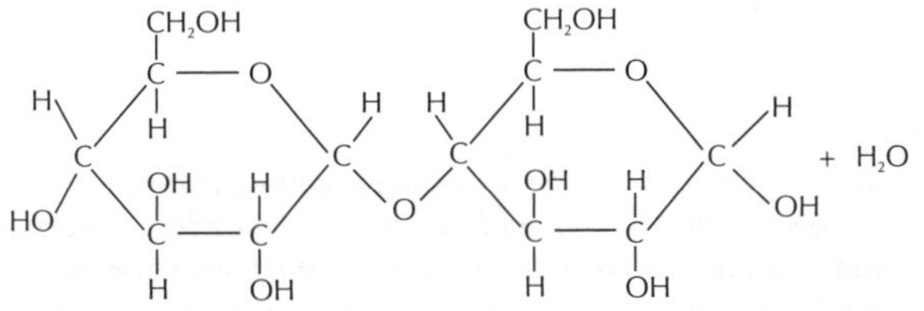

[1 mark for correct structure of maltose, 1 mark for showing water molecule.]

b) A molecule of water reacts with the glycosidic bond to split the glucose molecules apart / a hydrolysis reaction splits the glucose molecules apart ***[1 mark]***.

2 Amylose is a long, unbranched chain, which forms a coiled shape making it compact so good for storage ***[1 mark]***. Amylopectin is a long, branched chain, which allows stored energy to be released quickly, as the enzymes that break it down can reach the glycosidic bonds easily ***[1 mark]***. Starch is insoluble in water, which makes it good for storage, as water doesn't enter cells by osmosis ***[1 mark]***.

Page 26 — Lipids and Cardiovascular Disease

1 a) E.g.

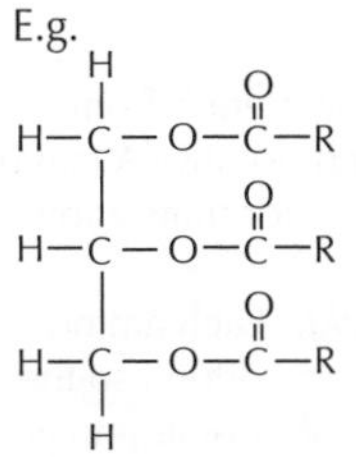

[1 mark]

b) ester bonds ***[1 mark]***

2 Saturated lipids don't have any double bonds between their carbon atoms ***[1 mark]***. Unsaturated lipids have one or more double bonds between their carbon atoms ***[1 mark]***.

3 a) High density lipoproteins/HDLs are mainly protein, whereas low density lipoproteins/LDLs are mainly lipid ***[1 mark]***. High density lipoproteins/HDLs transport cholesterol from body tissues to the liver, whereas low density lipoproteins/LDLs transport cholesterol from the liver to the blood ***[1 mark]***. High density lipoproteins/ HDLs reduce the total blood cholesterol level when it's too high, while low density lipoproteins/LDLs increase the total blood cholesterol level when it's too low ***[1 mark]***.

b) Having a high low density lipoprotein/LDL level has been linked to an increased risk of CVD (cardiovascular disease) ***[1 mark]***.

Page 27 — Reducing Risk Factors of CVD

1 a) waist-to-hip ratio = waist (cm) ÷ hips (cm)
= 76 cm ÷ 95 cm
= **0.8** ***[1 mark]***

b) BMI = body mass (kg) ÷ height^2 (m^2)
body mass (kg) = BMI × height^2 (m^2)
= 18.9 × 1.68^2
= 18.9 × 2.82
= **53.3 kg**

[2 marks for correct answer, otherwise 1 mark for correct working.]

You need to rearrange the BMI formula to be able to find out the person's body mass.

Topic 2A — Gas Exchange, Cell Membranes and Transport

Page 29 — Gas Exchange

1 E.g. lungs contain many alveoli giving a large surface area ***[1 mark]***. The alveolar epithelium and capillary endothelium are each only one cell thick, so there is a short diffusion pathway ***[1 mark]***. Each alveolus has a good blood supply, which constantly removes oxygen and delivers carbon dioxide, maintaining a high concentration gradient of each gas ***[1 mark]***. Concentration gradients are also maintained by breathing in and out, which refreshes the oxygen supply and removes carbon dioxide ***[1 mark]***.

2 The patient would have a reduced number of alveoli in their lungs, so the surface area available for gas exchange would be decreased ***[1 mark]***. This would decrease the rate of diffusion of oxygen and carbon dioxide ***[1 mark]***.

Page 31 — Cell Membranes and Osmosis

1 B ***[1 mark]***

2 a) The concentration of water molecules in the sucrose solution was higher than the concentration of water molecules in the potato ***[1 mark]***. Water moves by osmosis from a higher concentration of water molecules to a lower concentration of water molecules ***[1 mark]***. So water moved into the potato, increasing its mass ***[1 mark]***.

b) The concentration of water molecules in the potato and the concentration of water molecules in the sucrose solution were the same ***[1 mark]***.

c) – 0.4 g ***[1 mark]***. The difference in concentration of water molecules between the solution and the potato is the same as with the 1% solution, so the mass difference should be about the same, but negative / mass should be lost not gained ***[1 mark]***.

A 5% sucrose solution has a lower concentration of water molecules than the potato. This means that water will move out of the potato into the sucrose solution, decreasing the mass of the potato.

Answers

Page 33 — Transport Across the Cell Membrane

1 Facilitated diffusion involves channel proteins, which transport charged molecules across the membrane ***[1 mark]*** and carrier proteins, which transport large molecules across the membrane ***[1 mark]***. Both types of protein transport molecules down a concentration gradient ***[1 mark]***.

2 Endocytosis takes in substances from outside the cell ***[1 mark]*** via vesicles formed from the cell membrane ***[1 mark]***. Exocytosis secretes substances from the cell ***[1 mark]*** via vesicles made from the Golgi apparatus ***[1 mark]***.

Make sure you don't get these two processes mixed up — try to remember endo for 'in' and exo for 'out'.

Page 35 — Investigating Cell Membrane Structure

1 a) Cut five equal-sized pieces of beetroot and rinse them to remove any pigment released during cutting ***[1 mark]***. Make up five test tubes with alcohol concentrations 0, 25, 50, 75 and 100% ***[1 mark]***. Place a piece of beetroot in each test tube for the same length of time ***[1 mark]***. Remove the piece of beetroot from each tube and use a colorimeter to measure how much light is absorbed by each of the remaining solutions ***[1 mark]***.

b) As the concentration of alcohol increased the absorbance also increased ***[1 mark]***. This means that more pigment was released by the beetroot as the alcohol concentration increased, which suggests that the cell membrane became more permeable ***[1 mark]***.

c) E.g. alcohol dissolves the lipids in the cell membranes, so the membrane loses its structure ***[1 mark]***.

Topic 2B — Proteins and Genetics

Page 37 — Protein Structure

1 More than two amino acids ***[1 mark]*** join together in a chain via condensation reactions ***[1 mark]***. Each reaction forms a peptide bond and releases a molecule of water ***[1 mark]***.

Page 41 — Enzymes

1 a) Gradient = 40 cm^3 ÷ 3 s ***[1 mark]*** = **13.3 cm^3 s^{-1}** ***[1 mark]***
[Accept between 10 cm^3 s^{-1} and 20 cm^3 s^{-1}.]

b) Increasing the enzyme concentration leads to a higher initial rate of reaction ***[1 mark]*** because more enzyme active sites are available to collide with the substrate and form enzyme-substrate complexes ***[1 mark]***.

c) The experiment should have also been carried out with a tube where no enzyme was added ***[1 mark]***. This ensures that only the independent variable (enzyme concentration) is affecting the dependent variable (volume of product released) ***[1 mark]***.

d) The enzyme and substrate could be mixed together in a cuvette and then placed in a colorimeter, which measures the absorbance of the solution ***[1 mark]***. The absorbance could be recorded every 10 seconds for 1 minute and plotted on an absorbance against time graph ***[1 mark]***.

Page 43 — DNA and RNA Basics

1 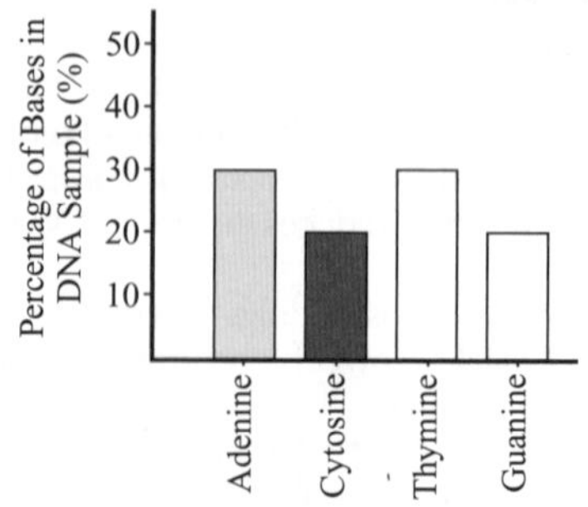

***[1 mark for a bar drawn for thymine at 30%.
1 mark for a bar drawn for guanine at 20%]***

Remember, thanks to complementary base pairing, there are always equal amounts of adenine and thymine in a DNA sample and equal amounts of cytosine and guanine. Double-check your answer by making sure the percentages of all four bases add up to 100%.

2 a) Mononucleotides are joined between the phosphate group of one mononucleotide and the deoxyribose sugar of the next ***[1 mark]*** in a condensation reaction ***[1 mark]***.

b) Two polynucleotide strands join through hydrogen bonding between the base pairs ***[1 mark]***. Base pairing is complementary (e.g. A always pairs with T and C always pairs with G) ***[1 mark]***. The two antiparallel polynucleotide strands twist to form a DNA double helix ***[1 mark]***.

Page 45 — The Genetic Code and Protein Synthesis

1 C ***[1 mark]***

2 a) 4 ***[1 mark]***

b) GUG = valine
UGU = cysteine
CGC = arginine
GCA = alanine
Correct sequence = **valine, cysteine, arginine, alanine**.
[2 marks for all 4 amino acids in the correct order. 1 mark for a minimum of 3 correct amino acids in the correct order.]

3 a) The mRNA sequence is 18 mononucleotides long and the protein produced is 6 amino acids long ***[1 mark]***. 18 ÷ 6 = 3, suggesting three mononucleotides code for a single amino acid ***[1 mark]***.

b) E.g. The sequence produced began leucine-cysteine-glycine. This would only be produced if the code is non-overlapping, e.g. UUGUGUGGG = UUG-UGU-GGG = leucine-cysteine-glycine ***[1 mark]***.
If the code was overlapping, the triplets would be, e.g. UUG-UGU-GUG-UGU, which would give a sequence starting leucine-cysteine-valine-cysteine.
Also, this part of the DNA sequence produces 6 amino acids. This is only correct if the code is non-overlapping — the sequence of amino acids would be longer if the code overlapped ***[1 mark]***.

Page 47 — Transcription and Translation

1 a) CGCUUCAGGUAC ***[1 mark]***

b) GCGAAGUCCAUG ***[1 mark]***

2 The drug binds to DNA, preventing RNA polymerase from binding, so transcription can't take place and no mRNA can be made ***[1 mark]***. This means there's no mRNA for translation and so protein synthesis is inhibited ***[1 mark]***.

3 (10 × 3 =) 30 mononucleotides long ***[1 mark]***. Each amino acid is coded for by three mononucleotides (a codon), so the mRNA length in mononucleotides is the number of amino acids multiplied by three ***[1 mark]***.

Answers

Topic 2C — Inheritance

Page 49 — Replication of DNA

1 a) Any five from: e.g. DNA helicase breaks the hydrogen bonds between the two DNA strands and the DNA helix unwinds ***[1 mark]***. / Each strand acts as a template for a new strand ***[1 mark]***. / Individual free DNA nucleotides join up along the template strand by complementary base pairing ***[1 mark]***. / DNA polymerase joins the individual nucleotides together, so that the sugar-phosphate backbone forms ***[1 mark]***. / Hydrogen bonds then form between the bases on each strand ***[1 mark]***. / Two identical DNA molecules are produced ***[1 mark]***. / Each of the new molecules contains a single strand from the original DNA molecule and a single new strand ***[1 mark]***.
[Maximum of 5 marks available.]

b) Two samples of bacteria were grown — one in a nutrient broth containing light nitrogen, and one in a broth with heavy nitrogen ***[1 mark]***. As the bacteria reproduced, they took up nitrogen to help make nucleotides for new DNA ***[1 mark]***. A sample of DNA was taken from each batch of bacteria, and spun in a centrifuge. The DNA from the heavy nitrogen bacteria settled lower down the centrifuge tube than the DNA from the light nitrogen bacteria ***[1 mark]***. Then the bacteria grown in the heavy nitrogen broth were taken out and put in a broth containing only light nitrogen. The bacteria were left for one round of DNA replication, and then another DNA sample was taken out and spun in the centrifuge ***[1 mark]***.

c) The DNA spun in the centrifuge after one round of DNA replication in a light nitrogen broth, settled out in the middle, showing that the DNA molecules contained a mixture of heavy and light nitrogen. This showed that the bacterial DNA had replicated semi-conservatively in the light nitrogen ***[1 mark]***. If the bacterial DNA had replicated conservatively, the DNA would have settled into two bands with the light new strands at the top and the heavy original strands at the bottom ***[1 mark]***.

Page 51 — Genes and Inheritance

1 a) genotype — Yy ***[1 mark]***, phenotype — yellow ***[1 mark]***.

b) E.g.

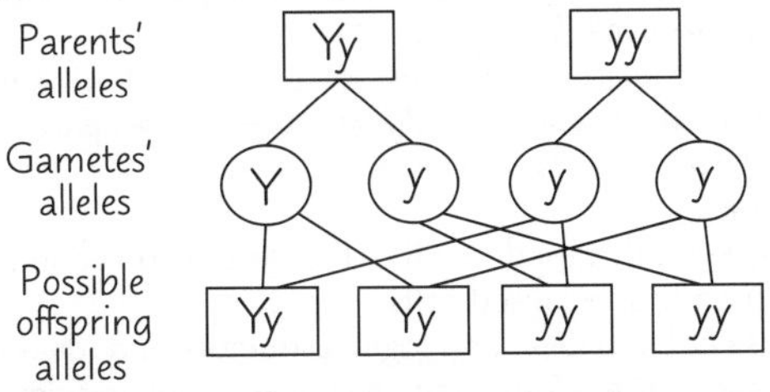

[1 mark for parents' alleles correct, 1 mark for gametes' alleles correct, 1 mark for possible offspring alleles correct.]

c) 1:1 ***[1 mark]***

Page 53 — The Chi-Squared Test

1 a) That there is no significant difference between the observed and expected results ***[1 mark]***.

b)

Phenotype	Ratio	Expected result (E)	Observed result (O)	O – E	$(O-E)^2$	$\frac{(O-E)^2}{E}$
Tall	3	39	43	4	16	0.41
Dwarf	1	13	9	–4	16	1.23

$$\chi^2 = \Sigma \frac{(O-E)^2}{E} = 1.64$$

The chi-squared value is smaller than the critical value (1.64 < 3.84) so the difference between the observed and expected results is not significant. This means that the null hypothesis can't be rejected, so the results from this experiment support the scientist's theory.
[1 mark for correct calculation of expected results, 1 mark for correct calculation of $(O-E)^2 \div E$, 1 mark for correct calculation of χ^2, 1 mark for correct conclusion.]

Page 55 — Cystic Fibrosis

1 a) Emma is homozygous for the CF allele ***[1 mark]***. Martha/James is a carrier ***[1 mark]***.

b) E.g.

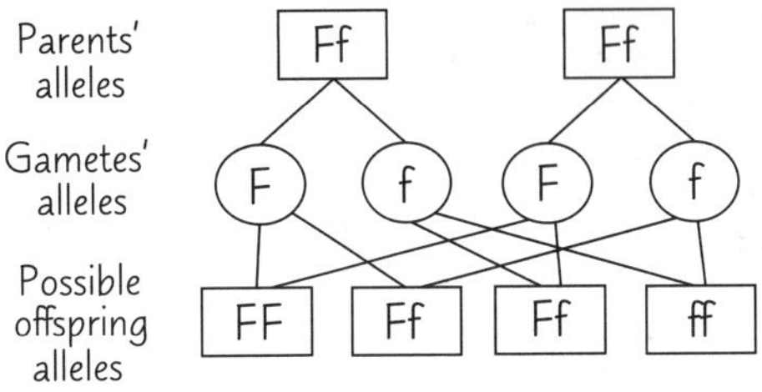

1 in 4/25%
[1 mark for parents' and gametes' alleles correct, 1 mark for possible offspring alleles correct, 1 mark for correct final answer.]

c) ***5-6 marks:***
The answer provides a detailed explanation of the ways in which the digestive system is affected by cystic fibrosis.
The answer has a clear and logical structure and ideas are well-linked. The information given is relevant and detailed.
3-4 marks:
The answer explains some ways in which the digestive system is affected by cystic fibrosis.
The answer has some structure and attempts to link ideas. Most of the information given is relevant and there is some detail involved.
1-2 marks:
One or two points are given relating to how the digestive system is affected, but there is little or no explanation.
The answer has very little clear structure and ideas are not well-linked. The information given is basic and lacking in detail. It may not all be relevant.
0 marks:
No relevant information is given.
Here are some points your answer may include:
Cystic fibrosis leads to the production of abnormally thick and sticky mucus. The thick mucus can block the tubes connecting the pancreas to the small intestine, preventing digestive enzymes from reaching the small intestine. The mucus can also cause cysts/growths to form in the pancreas, which inhibits the production of digestive enzymes. These both reduce the ability of someone with cystic fibrosis to digest food and so fewer nutrients can be absorbed. The mucus lining the small intestine is very thick, which inhibits the absorption of nutrients.

Page 57 — Genetic Screening

1 C ***[1 mark]***

2 a) To see if they're a carrier, because if they are, it will affect the chance of any of their children having the disorder ***[1 mark]***. Testing means that they can make informed decisions on whether to have children ***[1 mark]*** or whether to have prenatal testing if the mother is already pregnant ***[1 mark]***.

b) i) Screening embryos produced by IVF for genetic disorders before they're implanted into the uterus ***[1 mark]***.

ii) E.g. it reduces the chance of having a baby with a genetic disorder as only 'healthy' embryos will be implanted ***[1 mark]***. / Because it's performed before implantation, it avoids any issues about abortion raised by prenatal testing ***[1 mark]***.

iii) E.g. it can be used to find out about other characteristics, leading to concerns about designer babies ***[1 mark]***. Decisions could be made based on incorrect information (false positives and false negatives) ***[1 mark]***.

Answers

Topic 3A — Cells

Page 60 — Eukaryotic Cells and Organelles

1 C *[1 mark]*

2 a) i) mitochondrion *[1 mark]*

ii) Golgi apparatus *[1 mark]*

b) Mitochondria are the site of aerobic respiration / are where ATP is produced *[1 mark]*. The Golgi apparatus processes and packages new lipids and proteins / makes lysosomes *[1 mark]*.

Page 61 — Prokaryotic Cells

1 C *[1 mark]*

2 Prokaryotic cells have a long coiled-up strand of circular DNA *[1 mark]*. They can also have small loops of DNA called plasmids *[1 mark]*.

Page 63 — Looking at Cells and Organelles

1 Magnification = image size ÷ object size

= 80 mm ÷ 0.5 mm *[1 mark]*

= **× 160** *[1 mark]*

Always remember to convert everything to the same units first — the insect is 0.5 mm long, so the length of the image needs to be changed from 8 cm to 80 mm.

2 Image size = magnification × object size

= 100 × 0.059 mm *[1 mark]*

= **5.9 mm** *[1 mark]*

Hint: To convert 59 μm into mm, divide by 1000.

3 a) mitochondrion and nucleus *[1 mark]*

b) All of the organelles in the table would be visible *[1 mark]*.

4 a) 10 ÷ 6.5 = **1.5 μm** ***[2 marks for the correct answer or 1 mark for the correct calculation.]***

b) 14 × 1.5 = **21 μm** ***[1 mark for multiplying 14 by answer to part a), 1 mark for an answer of 21 or 22 μm.]***

Page 65 — Cell Organisation

1 It's best described as an organ *[1 mark]* as it is made of many tissues working together to perform a particular function *[1 mark]*.

2 A *[1 mark]*

3 Similar cells are organised into tissues to carry out a particular function (e.g. squamous epithelium in the alveoli is made up of a single layer of flat cells) *[1 mark]*. Different tissues that work together to perform a particular function are organised into organs (e.g. the lungs are made of squamous epithelium tissue, fibrous connective tissue and endothelium tissue) *[1 mark]*. Organs work together to form organ systems with a particular function (e.g. the lungs are part of the respiratory system) *[1 mark]*.

Page 67 — The Cell Cycle and Mitosis

1 a) A — Metaphase *[1 mark]*, B — Telophase *[1 mark]*, C — Anaphase *[1 mark]*.

b) X — Chromosome/Chromatid *[1 mark]*, Y — Centromere *[1 mark]*, Z — Spindle fibre *[1 mark]*.

2 32 ÷ 42 = **0.76** ***[2 marks for the correct answer or 1 mark for the correct calculation.]***

Topic 3B — Reproduction and Inheritance

Page 69 — Gametes and Fertilisation

1 Sperm have flagella/tails, which allow them to swim/move towards the egg cell *[1 mark]*. They contain lots of mitochondria to provide the energy needed for swimming/movement *[1 mark]*. The acrosome in the sperm head contains digestive enzymes that break down the egg cell's zona pellucida, enabling the sperm to penetrate the egg *[1 mark]*.

2 Following the acrosome reaction, the sperm head fuses with the cell membrane of the egg cell *[1 mark]*. This triggers the cortical reaction, where the contents of the cortical granules are released from the egg cell *[1 mark]*. The chemicals from the cortical granules make the zona pellucida thick and impenetrable to other sperm *[1 mark]*. The sperm nucleus enters the egg cell and fuses with the egg cell nucleus — this is fertilisation *[1 mark]*.

This question asks you to describe the events that occur after the acrosome reaction, so you won't get any marks for describing the acrosome reaction or anything before it, e.g. the sperm swimming towards the egg cell in the oviduct.

Page 71 — Meiosis and Inheritance

1 a) It means the genes are both on the same chromosome *[1 mark]*.

b) The closer together the loci of two genes, the more likely it is that they will stay linked *[1 mark]*. This is because crossing over is less likely to split them up *[1 mark]*.

2 a) Before the first division of meiosis, homologous pairs of chromosomes come together and pair up *[1 mark]*.
The chromatids twist around each other and bits of the chromatids break off and rejoin onto the other chromatid *[1 mark]*.
The chromatids now contain different combinations of alleles, so each of the four daughter cells will contain chromatids with different combinations of alleles *[1 mark]*.

b) Independent assortment means the chromosome pairs can split up in any way *[1 mark]*. So, the cells produced can contain any combination of maternal and paternal chromosomes with different alleles *[1 mark]*.

Topic 3C — Differentiation and Variation

Page 73 — Cell Differentiation and Gene Expression

1 a) Totipotent stem cells can produce all cell types, including all the specialised cells in an organism and extraembryonic cells *[1 mark]*. Pluripotent stem cells have the ability to produce all the specialised cells in an organism, but not extraembryonic cells *[1 mark]*. This is because the genes for extraembryonic cells have become inactivated *[1 mark]*.

Be careful not to get totipotent and pluripotent mixed up. It might help you to think of <u>toti</u>potent as <u>tot</u>ally potent — they can produce absolutely every cell type needed for an organism to develop.

b) ***5-6 marks:***
The answer fully describes all of the steps involved in the production of specialised cells.
The answer has a clear and logical structure and ideas are well-linked. The information given is relevant and detailed.
3-4 marks:
The answer describes most of the steps involved in the production of specialised cells.
The answer has some structure and attempts to link ideas. Most of the information given is relevant and there is some detail involved.
1-2 marks:
The answer outlines one or two of the steps involved in the production of specialised cells.
The answer has very little clear structure and ideas are not well-linked. The information given is basic and lacking in detail. It may not all be relevant.
0 marks:
No relevant information is given.
Here are some points your answer may include:
All stem cells contain the same genes, but not all of them are expressed/active. Under the right conditions, some genes are activated and others are inactivated. mRNA is only transcribed from the active genes. mRNA from the active genes is translated into proteins. These proteins modify the cell by changing the cell structure and controlling the cell's processes. The changes cause the cell to become specialised, and they're hard to reverse.

Answers

Page 75 — Stem Cells in Medicine

1 a) Any one from: e.g. stem cells could be used to save lives ***[1 mark]***. / Stem cells could be used to improve a person's quality of life ***[1 mark]***. / Accept a description of stem cells being used to cure a specific disease ***[1 mark]***.

b) i) E.g. embryonic stem cells can develop into all types of specialised cells ***[1 mark]***, whereas adult stem cells can only develop into a limited range of cells ***[1 mark]***.

ii) Some people believe that fertilised embryos have a right to life from the moment of fertilisation ***[1 mark]***. Some people believe it is wrong to destroy (viable) embryos ***[1 mark]***.

Page 77 — Variation

1 a) Histones are proteins that DNA wraps around to form chromatin, which makes up chromosomes ***[1 mark]***.

b) Histone modifications can affect how condensed the chromatin associated with the histones is/ how accessible the DNA is ***[1 mark]***. This affects whether the proteins/enzymes needed for transcription are able to bind to the DNA and transcribe the genes ***[1 mark]***.

Topic 4A — Biodiversity

Page 80 — Biodiversity and Endemism

1 a) The number of different species ***[1 mark]*** and the number of individuals/population size of each species ***[1 mark]***.

b) N = 35 + 25 + 34 + 12 + 26 = 132
N (N – 1) = 132 (132 – 1) = 17292
Σ n (n – 1) = 35 (35 – 1) + 25 (25 – 1) + 34 (34 – 1) + 12 (12 – 1) + 26 (26 – 1) = 3694
Use of N (N – 1) ÷ Σ n (n – 1) to calculate diversity index of 17292 ÷ 3694 = **4.68**
[3 marks for correct answer, otherwise 1 mark for N (N – 1) = 17292 and 1 mark for Σ n (n – 1) = 3694.]
It's always best if you put your working — even if the answer isn't quite right you could get marks for correct working.

c) The diversity of bumblebee species is greater at site 2 ***[1 mark]***. This suggests there's a link between enhanced field margins and an increased diversity of bumblebee species ***[1 mark]***.

Page 83 — Adaptation and Evolution

1 a) E.g. the new species could not breed with each other ***[1 mark]***.

b) Different populations of flies were physically/geographically isolated and experienced different selection pressures (different food) ***[1 mark]***. This led to changes in allele frequencies between the populations ***[1 mark]***, which made them reproductively isolated/unable to interbreed and produce fertile offspring, and eventually resulted in speciation ***[1 mark]***.

2 The brown owls may be better camouflaged/blend in with the landscape better than the grey owls when there's no snow cover, making them less likely to be eaten by predators ***[1 mark]***. The decrease in the amount of snowfall puts a selection pressure on the grey owls ***[1 mark]*** making them less likely to survive ***[1 mark]***. This leads to fewer owls in the population and reduces the competition for resources ***[1 mark]***. The brown owls are more likely to survive, reproduce and pass on the allele for darker/ brown colouring to their offspring, increasing the frequency of the allele for darker/brown colouring in the population ***[1 mark]***.
Snow makes everything white, so lighter coloured owls blend in better when there's snow around. They stick out more when there's no snow though.

Page 85 — The Hardy-Weinberg Principle

1 q = 0.23
p + q = 1
so p = 1 – 0.23 = 0.77
The frequency of the heterozygous genotype = 2pq
= 2(0.77 × 0.23) = **0.35** ***[1 mark]***

2 a) Frequency of genotype TT = p^2 = 0.14
So the frequency of the dominant allele = p = √0.14 = 0.37
The frequency of the recessive allele = q
q = 1 – p
q = 1 – 0.37 = **0.63** ***[1 mark]***

b) Frequency of homozygous recessive genotype tt = $q^2 = 0.63^2$
= **0.40** ***[1 mark. Allow 1 mark for evidence of correct calculation using incorrect answer to part a).]***

c) Those that don't have a cleft chin are homozygous recessive tt = 40%, so the percentage that do have a cleft chin, Tt or TT, is 100% – 40% = **60%** ***[1 mark]***.
There are other ways of calculating this answer, e.g. working out the value of 2pq and adding it to p^2. It doesn't matter which way you do it as long as you get the right answer.

Page 87 — Classification

1 a)

Domain	**Kingdom**	Phylum	**Class**	**Order**	**Family**	Genus	Species
Eukaryota	Animalia	Chordata	Actinopterygii	Salmoniformes	**Salmonidae**	**Salmo**	**trutta**

[1 mark for 4 or more answers correct. 2 marks for all 7 answers correct.]

b) They are unable to reproduce to give fertile offspring ***[1 mark]***.
Although brook trout and brown trout do sometimes mate to produce offspring, those offspring are infertile.

Page 89 — Conservation of Biodiversity

1 E.g. it might be difficult to recreate the exact conditions of the lizard's environment in captivity, so they may have problems breeding ***[1 mark]***. Some people think it's cruel to keep animals in captivity, even if it's done to prevent them becoming extinct ***[1 mark]***. The reintroduced lizards could bring new diseases to the habitat, harming any organisms that are already there ***[1 mark]***. Because they were born in captivity, any reintroduced lizards may not exhibit all their natural behaviours in the wild (e.g. they may have problems finding food or communicating with other members of their species) ***[1 mark]***.

Topic 4B — Resources from Plants

Page 91 — Plant Cell Structure

1 D ***[1 mark]***

2 a) chloroplast ***[1 mark]***

b) It is the site where photosynthesis takes place ***[1 mark]***.

Page 93 — Plant Stems

1 a) X — sclerenchyma fibres ***[1 mark]***, Y — xylem vessels ***[1 mark]***

b) The function of sclerenchyma fibres (X) is to provide support ***[1 mark]***. The function of xylem vessels (Y) is to transport water and mineral ions up the plant, and provide support ***[1 mark]***. ***[Accept correct function of phloem tissue if identified incorrectly in part a).]***

Page 95 — Starch, Cellulose and Plant Fibres

1 a) The cell wall contains cellulose microfibrils in a net-like arrangement ***[1 mark]***. The strength of the microfibrils and their arrangement in the cell wall makes plant fibres strong ***[1 mark]***.

b) Secondary thickening is the production of another cell wall between the normal cell wall and the cell membrane ***[1 mark]***. The secondary cell wall is thicker and usually has more lignin than the normal cell wall, which gives plant fibres lots of strength ***[1 mark]***.

Answers

2 a) E.g. for each of the four different types of plant fibre the students could have attached the fibre to a clamp stand at one end and hung a weight from the other end ***[1 mark]***. Weights could then have been added one at a time to each of the fibres until they broke and the mass taken to break each fibre recorded ***[1 mark]***. In order to reduce the effect of random error and make their results more precise they could have repeated the experiment at least three times and calculated the mean for each type of fibre ***[1 mark]***.

b) Any two from: e.g. they should have ensured that all the fibres tested were of the same length ***[1 mark]***. / They should have kept the temperature the same ***[1 mark]***. / They should have kept the humidity of the environment constant ***[1 mark]***.

c) Fibre B would be most suitable because it has the highest tensile strength/can hold the most weight without breaking ***[1 mark]***.

Page 97 — Sustainability and Plant Minerals

1 1 — Nutrient broth containing all essential nutrients except magnesium ions.
2 — Nutrient broth containing all essential nutrients except nitrate ions.
[1 mark for both specific mineral deficient broths.]
3 — Nutrient broth containing all essential nutrients.
4 — Broth lacking all essential nutrients.
[1 mark for both control broths.]

Page 99 — Drugs from Plants and Drug Testing

1 ***5-6 marks:***
The answer gives a full description of a valid investigation, which is fully supported by scientific knowledge.
The answer has a clear and logical structure and ideas are well-linked. The information given is relevant and detailed.
3-4 marks:
The answer gives some description of a valid investigation, which is sometimes supported by scientific knowledge.
The answer has some structure and attempts to link ideas. Most of the information given is relevant and there is some detail involved.
1-2 marks:
The answer attempts to describe an investigation.
The answer has very little clear structure and ideas are not well-linked. The information given is basic and lacking in detail. It may not all be relevant.
0 marks:
No relevant information is given.
Here are some points your answer may include:
A sample of bacterial species X should be spread onto an agar plate. A disc of absorbent paper should be dipped into an extract of the plant, an equally-sized disc should be dipped in mouthwash Y and another equally-sized disc should be dipped in ethanol (to act as a control). The control is used to show that it's the plant extract or mouthwash (independent variables) inhibiting the growth of bacteria (the dependent variable). The discs should then be placed on the plate, widely spaced apart. The plate should then have a lid taped on, be inverted and incubated at about 25 °C for 24-48 hours to allow the bacteria to grow.
The clear zones around each disc should then be measured by measuring the diameter/calculating the area. The procedure should be repeated another two times and a mean of the results calculated to increase the reliability of the results. Throughout the experiment, variables such as the incubation temperature, the composition of the agar etc. should all be kept the same to ensure that the results are valid. Aseptic techniques should be used throughout the experiment to prevent contamination of microbial cultures.

Practical Skills

Page 102 — Planning an Experiment

1 ***5-6 marks:***
The answer gives a full description of a valid investigation, which is fully supported by scientific knowledge.
The answer has a clear and logical structure and ideas are well-linked. The information given is relevant and detailed.
3-4 marks:
The answer gives some description of a valid investigation, which is sometimes supported by scientific knowledge.
The answer has some structure and attempts to link ideas. Most of the information given is relevant and there is some detail involved.
1-2 marks:
The answer attempts to describe an investigation.
The answer has very little clear structure and ideas are not well-linked. The information given is basic and lacking in detail. It may not all be relevant.
0 marks:
No relevant information is given.
Here are some points your answer may include:
A study should be carried out using two groups of participants. Give one group of participants the same daily dosage of fish oil (the independent variable) and give another group a placebo, to ensure that only the fish oil is having an effect on the clotting ability of the blood (the dependent variable). Control other variables by selecting participants who eat a similar diet/are not on any medication, as these could affect the validity of the results. The groups should have a similar mix of ages/genders as these could also affect the validity of the results. Use a large sample size to increase the reliability of the results. Before the test begins, take a small blood sample from each participant and time how long it takes for the blood to clot, recording the result in seconds. The same volume of blood should be taken from each participant as this could affect clotting time (affecting the validity of the results). After a set period of time on the trial, test the participants' blood clotting time again.

Index

index